About the book

Some years after the murder of Dian Fossey, a horribly mutilated male corpse is found on the shores of Lake Kivu in Rwanda. Chief Inspector Jean-Bosco Kabeera and his team, including the visiting German criminal investigator from the Federal Criminal Police Office (BKA), Ariane Manstein, face intense pressure to solve the murder. First, it stands to reason the crime is connected to the trade of Rare Earths Elements, a thriving business in the border region around Goma/Gisenyi. Nevertheless, it is possible it was a ritual murder. The dead man's face was covered with a wooden mask. However, while their investigation bears noticeably strange similarities to Dian Fossey's murder in 1985, it is rather difficult to connect it to their current case. The investigation eventually leads them to the eastern part of the Congo where the investigators encounter extreme danger. The investigation continues with the help of the Goma headquarters commander Joseph Likongo until Kabeera and his team identify the main perpetrator ultimately responsible for the murder of Dian Fossey as well as for other crimes committed in eastern Congo. Bosco Kabeera has to convince the prosecutor general to let him look at Dian Fossey's case file because only her notes, which had been classified top secret, can provide final proof.

Obviously, the criminal plot of this book is fictitious. I took the liberty of integrating certain unexplained circumstantial evidence to the plot. The *clarification* of the title question will spark dissent; however, it does provide one possible scenario that was explored after Dian Fossey's murder.

In one way or another, all characters are based on actual persons, some who I remember vividly from my work and travels abroad. Geographical and geological conditions largely correspond to reality. The flashbacks into Rwanda's and the Congo's history, are generally accessible historical facts.

Karl H. Cron, Hamburg, December 27 2015

The author

Karl H. Cron is a graduate geologist and worked for many years as a hydrogeologist and consultant in water supply projects at home and abroad. Numerous missions abroad have taken him to Yemen, Afghanstan, Syria, Jordan and several countries in Africa, most recently Rwanda. After retiring, Karl H. Cron worked as a freelance consultant and was a lecturer at the University of Hamburg, his hometown. In 2015, his first novel "Who Killed Dian Fossey?"

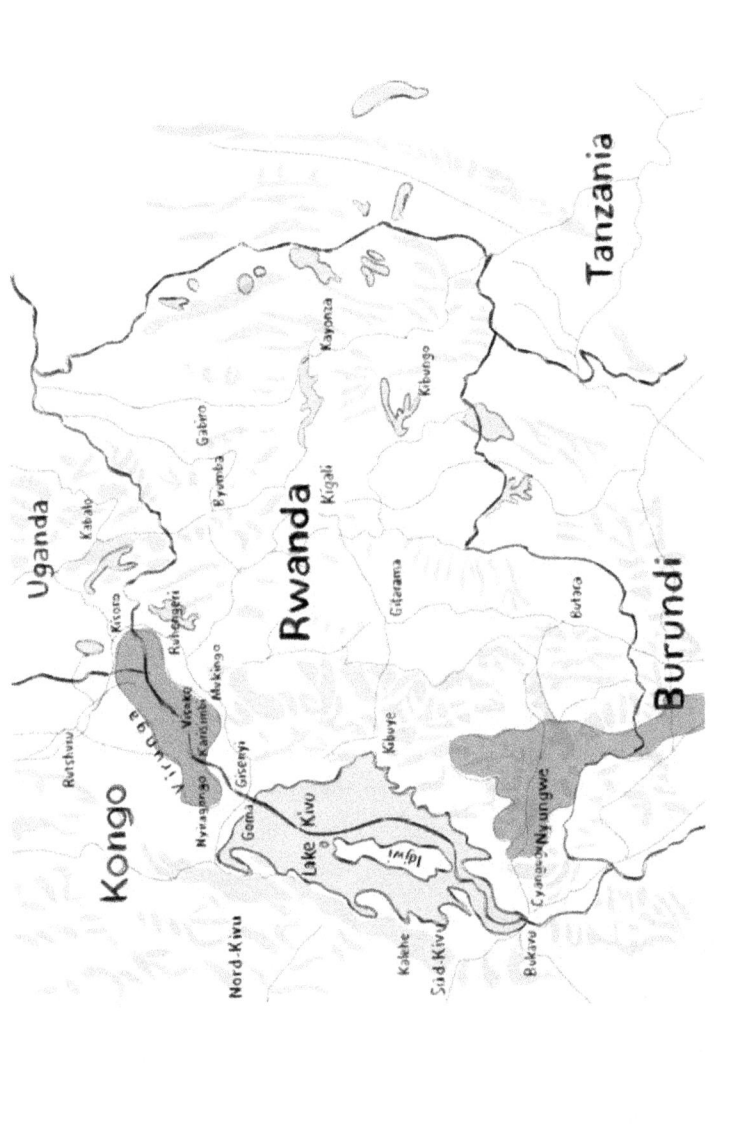

Legal Notice

Who killed Dian Fossey?
Amazon KDP publishing
1. Edition 2015 (paperback)

Karl H. Cron
c/o AutorenServices.de
Birkenallee 24 36037 Fulda

Mail: kcautor.kontakt@gmail.com
Info Google Foto:
English : google.com/view/rwandaquest
German : google.com/view/ruandaquest

Map: Maren Amini
Proofreading: ebokks, Hildesheim
Translated from German by: buchuebersetzer.webs.com

Copyright: Karl H. Cron
All rights reserved. All parts of the novel are protected by copyright. Total or partial reproduction, printing, or copying of any kind is prohibited. Permission to make copies is granted solely by © Karl H. Cron.   V202411

Karl H. Cron

Who killed Dian Fossey?

Novel

Fictional characters

Jean-Bosco Kabeera:
Chief Inspector of the Criminal Investigation
Department (CID) of Rwanda

Chantal (wife), Grégoire, Nadège (children):
Family of Bosco Kabeera

Ariane Manstein:
German Chief Detective in the team of the CID of
Bosco Kabeera

Fabien Kagire and Alphonse Butera:
Inspectors of the CID in the team of Bosco
Kabeera

Jean-Baptiste Makolo:
Constable of the CID in the team of Bosco Kabeera

John Mugambage:
Prosecutor General of Rwanda, called *General* or *PG*

Théonèste Mugisha (Théo):
Inspector of the CID in Gisenyi

Vana (wife), Julie and Raymond (children):
Théo's family

Joseph Likongo:
Commander in charge of North Kivu in Goma
(Eastern Congo)

Nathalie Baranyanca:
Doctor of the Kigali Forensic Laboratory (KFL)

Prince:
Chauffeur and courier driver with own vehicle

Tom Darcy (Belgian):
Owner and CEO of TD Nature Film Production

André Piquard , Festus Woodrow Dallaway , Ernst Krauskopf :
Team of TD Nature Film Production

Antoine Marchal:
Head of a Belgian NGO with office in Kigali to support agriculture

Isaam Kabiya:
Employee of the Belgian NGO in support of agriculture

Thomas Mayeye:
Warlord in eastern Congo. Owner of militarily organized security company SÉCOMA

Captain Samuel Matengo:
Head of the operational business of SÉCOMA

Marie Kamanda:
Congolese from Bukavu (Eastern Congo)

Gahiji:
Hunter, Indigenous Batwa - Pygmy

Eugene Muhoza:
Doctor in Gisenyi

Dr. Le Roux:
Scientist of the Musee Royal de l'Afrique Central in Tervuren near Brussels

Historical figures

Dian Fossey:
American primatologist, murdered in 1985. Researched the behaviour of mountain gorillas in the Virunga National Park of Rwanda.

Nyiramacyibili: →Kinyarwanda word for *the woman who lives alone in the forest*. The Rwandan population used the name for Dian Fossey. The word's spelling differs greatly. In this book, I used the same spelling as the Rwandan memorial plaque on her grave.

Paul Kagame:
President of Rwanda

Juvénal Habyarimana:
Former President of Rwanda. Crashed with the plane shot by unknown

Agathe Uwilingiyimana: short-term prime minister of the Hutu government under Habyarimana. Murdered by Hutu militias

Valérie Bemeriki:
Radio presenter who incited the militias during the genocide. Sentenced to life imprisonment

Rosamond Halsey Carr:
Close friend, but also critic of Dian Fossey. Founder of the orphanage Imbabazi in Gisenyi

Laurent Nkunda:
Warlord in eastern Congo

Laurent-Désiré Kabila (Kabila Senior):
From 1997 to 2001 President of the Democratic Republic of the Congo

Joseph Kabila Kabange:
Son of Laurent Désiré Kabila. Since January 26, 2001 President of the Democratic Republic of the Congo

Ché Guevara:
Cuban revolutionary. Guevara and a handful of advisers supported Kabila's revolutionary army against Mobutu in 1964. The undertaking failed miserably.

Note:
A addendum about the story of Dian Fossey and a list of terms, abbreviations and names can be found at the end of the book.

Prolog

Nothing unusual had happened the previous night, yet the next morning major worldwide media networks all devoted headlines to one small country in East Africa.

Almost noiselessly, the man crept through the light scrub. Skillfully, he navigated the barely visible paths known only to locals. Despite the prevailing darkness, he managed the climb to his destination unhindered. All was quiet as he approached the clearing in the tropical rainforest, even though light still flickered through the simply constructed walls of a few huts. It was midnight and patches of fog drifted through the giant trees and lush vegetation, surrounding them like fluffy clouds of cotton candy. By the time all lights were extinguished, the man waited patiently, hidden in the lush vegetation. He had to be sure all inhabitants were asleep.

In northern Rwanda on the southern slope of the dormant volcano Mount Bisoke, the research station *Karisoke* sat at an altitude close to ten thousand feet. It was where the way of life and behavior of the last wild mountain gorillas were observed and studied.

The hour was imminent for dawn was slowly approaching, promising a beautiful day. The first gentle penetrating rays of the sun would burn away the fog, transforming the dew on the moss and orchids growing around and the trees of the species *hagenia abyssinica* into a dazzling kaleidoscope.

No one noticed the figure purposefully approaching one of the huts. The man refrained from stepping onto any of the paths covered with pebbles and lava stones. Only a pair of grazing bushbuck lifted their heads briefly and not sensing any danger, immediately continued searching for their beloved shoot tips. The nocturnal visitor ignored his surroundings. Time was of the essence. He had to be out of the area before sunrise. He knew the way. Still unnoticed, he reached the left corner of the hut's rear exit. Carefully, he slid one of the green painted corrugated sheets of tin aside and entered. To his surprise, not eight feet in front of him, the formidable woman just shy of six feet lay on a makeshift bed constructed from two cots. He had not expected her to be there. On a small coffee table next to an empty glass stood a half-empty bottle of scotch—her companion in solitude—and a kerosene lamp. On the wall next to the bed hung a *panga*—the traditional tool of sugar cane plantation workers—that she had taken from a poacher. In the background, a decorated Christmas tree stood, under which lay wrapped presents for the research station's employees. Due to a surprising announced visit, this year's Christmas party had been postponed until New Year's Day.

A sound startled the woman awake. She sat up and looked directly at the dark shadow in front of her crude bed. Quickly, she grabbed the unloaded gun lying on the ground next to her and attempted to insert a clip. The man took two steps toward the woman, smacked the weapon from her hand and it fell to the ground out of her reach. However, it wouldn't have made a difference anyway. Later, it would be discovered that the clip was loaded with the wrong ammunition. The researcher known as very resolute, would not be intimidated. The man hadn't expected such fierce resistance from the tall woman. A struggle ensued and the table was knocked over, causing the bottle and glass to break, scattering shards across the floor. After a short and violent confrontation, the unarmed stranger grabbed the *panga* hanging on the wall and placed three well-aimed blows to the woman's head. Although the researcher was injured, she was still strong enough to fend off the intruder. The distressed man prepared for one final blow, then viciously brought the *panga* down over the woman's head. She cried out briefly one last time before the blade split her skull in half. The world-renowned primatologist Dian Fossey was already dead when she fell backward onto the ground next to the makeshift bed with a frozen expression of utter horror.

The killer carefully looked around. He paid no attention to the money, traveler checks of more than three thousand dollars, jewelry, cameras, or other valuable equipment lying around. Feverishly, he searched the hut. He was interested in only two specific items. One of the items was found while ransacking the closets and dressers then quickly stowed in his pocket. Anxious now, he looked around for the second object, but it remained hidden. It was time to leave. Without another look, he opened the locked front door and left the *mausoleum*, as the former occupant had jokingly referred to her simple hut. A moment later, the man disappeared into the jungle of Mount Bisoke.

For years, the American Dian Fossey had fought a fierce and successful uphill battle so gorillas would have a habitat. The fight of her life, led to her death during the early morning hours on December 27, 1985.

1

Some years later. The Toyota SUV battled the evening traffic in Kigali, the capital of Rwanda. Although Chinese and German companies had already made great progress in expanding the road network in the country, cities still had a difficult time coping with the increased volume of traffic. Even though Rwanda is one of the world's poorest countries, the established well-paid middle-class relish their status symbols, such as new vehicles, and are only too happy to show them off. Somewhat rare, but conspicuous on the roads are the Japanese and European luxury-class SUVs whose occupants discreetly hide behind dark tinted windows. Generally, Jean-Bosco Kabeera drove his service vehicle the shortest route home after working at the National Police Headquarters, taking Avenue du Lac Kivu to the Kinyinya district. Today, he took Place du 5. Juillet to pick up his wife Chantal and two of his three children at the market in Remera. Bosco, as friends and associates called him, knew his loved ones expected this from him once a week. Occasionally, when he was needed at the Criminal Investigation Department, the CID, which happened quite often, his wife would later present the receipt for the taxi wearing a mock expression of displeasure. And, every time she made sure to point out how having her own car would greatly improve her mobility in the widely populated capital of Rwanda.

Using accumulated savings from his meager government income as well as the help of government grants, they had purchased a five-room house and were currently paying off the mortgage. Therefore, he was reluctant to buy a car and instead, used the government vehicle occasionally for private trips, which he was permitted according to his rank. Nevertheless, he tried not to abuse this privilege. Like he, many of his colleagues were in full support of the government's campaign against corruption and made sure their families remained honest. Success was inevitable. Transparency International ranked Rwanda as the least corrupt country in Africa.

A guard opened the gate and helped his employers unload their purchases. He wasn't available for any other tasks even though his workload wasn't too difficult to manage.

Owners or tenants of houses in Kigali needed a guard, whether they wanted one or not. Those who didn't or couldn't afford expensive security service could hire young men whose education didn't qualify them for a job in the primary labor market. This easy and unwritten rule applied to all countries in Africa, akin to a continentally established organization of guards. Many guards had previously been petty criminals, looting houses without security before gaining employment. Residents who employed one weren't harassed. The task of protecting a residence didn't necessarily require a guard's nonstop presence. As long as the neighborhood watchmen agreed to keep an eye on the gated community and took turns opening the gate, a guard could step away from his post without the house under his protection being left defenseless. It was obvious burglars especially targeted houses occupied by foreigners, but even the locals and police officers couldn't be sure their residences would be spared. Considering a security guard's wage was rather modest, house owners and tenants universally agreed that it was best to hire social outsiders for those positions. Johnson, a Congolese, as the man had introduced himself, came to Rwanda and married a Rwandan when there was unrest in the eastern part of his country. His wife gained employment in a household, but when needed, she also helped Bosco's family.

Bosco knew he eventually had to give in and buy a car. He knew how tenaciously his wife pursued her goals. She belonged to the Tutsi ethnic group and until the year 2000, six years after the genocide took place, she had worked as a lawyer bringing those involved in the genocide to justice.

Chantal and Bosco had known each other since 1981. At that time, he had been a ranger employed by the administration of the Virunga National Park and in charge of endangered mountain gorillas. The skills and experience he acquired during confrontations with armed poachers came in quite handy later on. Despite his muscular body, which almost seemed too much for his six-foot frame, he was extremely agile. Behind his back, his colleagues called him *Uncle Bert*. The name was borrowed from the gorilla that was part of primatologist Dian Fossey's behavioral research. Naturally, Bosco knew all along but got a chuckle out of it. Later, the gorilla, as well as many others, was killed by poachers.

As the poachers' activities increased, Dian Fossey

established her own security force whose purpose was to destroy traps and arrest poachers. She absolutely refused to cooperate with the park authority since they were pushing for the animal sanctuary to be opened to tourism, which she vehemently opposed. As confrontations with poachers escalated, Dian Fossey became convinced the government and her backers had abandoned her and started acting increasingly paranoid. Bosco was not the only one who thought she crossed the line in her fierce struggle to protect the mountain gorilla sanctuary. Fed-up with the never-ending conflicts between the researcher and the staff of the park administration, he resigned and took a new position as deputy director of the Nyungwe Forest National Park administration in southern Rwanda.

According to her meticulously kept records, Dian Fossey founded the research station on September 24, 1967, at four-thirty in the afternoon. The inhabitants of the Virunga volcano chain, of which only the shrouded-in-myth Mount Nyiragongo on Congolese side is active, called her *Nyiramacyibili* (the woman who lives alone in the woods). However, many residents of the villages surrounding Virunga National Park simply referred to her as the *Witch*. The research station Dian Fossey founded and dubbed *Karisoke* - derived from the names of the neighboring volcanoes Karisimbi and Visoke - was her purpose in life until she was murdered. The researcher was the architect and driving force behind the gorilla sanctuary and at times struggled with exceedingly strange methods. After her murder, one of her former trackers,

Emmanuel Rwelekana, and an American student, Wayne McGuire, were accused of committing the crime and arrested. Rwelekana died in prison under mysterious circumstances. McGuire, however, was allowed to leave the country after the American Embassy intervened and, presumably, through some support of the Rwandan authorities. The student was later sentenced to death in absentia. Nevertheless, speculations about the murder of *Nyiramacyibili* continued. Further research revealed the initial investigation into the murder had definitely lacked professionalism, resulting in all parties concluding that the convicted men could hardly have been the perpetrators.

After Grégoire was born, Bosco married Chantal. Nadège followed two years later. Jean-Bosco Kabeera belonged to the Hutu ethnic group and enjoyed a fairly straightforward rise in his career until he became Chief Inspector of the CID. After the genocide and the overthrow of the Hutu regime in 1994, the administration of President Kagame tried to end the colonial legacy of ethnic division in the country. An official statutory new law was established, making all native-born and naturalized people Rwandans. Aligning with an ethnic group was prohibited.

Following an obligatory examination, it was verified that Bosco belonged to the Hutu ethnic group. He was assigned three employees after his promotion to Chief Inspector, two with the rank of Inspector, Fabien Kagire and Alphonse Butera, and one Constable, Jean-Baptiste Makolo. As part of an exchange program with the Federal Criminal Police

Office in Wiesbaden, Germany, Chief Detective, Ariane Manstein, joined the team. Alphonse and Jean-Baptiste shared an office. Both men were married and often took on routine office work.

Jean-Baptiste revealed repeatedly his penchant for wearing unusual clothes combinations when he was not obliged to appear in uniform. His wife owned a small clothing store that primarily sold *mitumba*. *Mitumba*, (Swahili for bundle), are garments sold from clothing donations by well-meaning citizens of western industrial countries and then shipped to Africa via charitable organizations. The central hub is located in the port city of Dar es Salaam in Tanzania on the eastern coast of Africa. The lucrative business is almost entirely run by Lebanese and Indian wholesalers. There, retailers buy the goods by the kilo and resell them to consumers throughout the region. An unfortunate side effect of the globalized trade in used clothes was the decline of the formerly well-functioning textile industry of Tanzania.

Ariane found working space in Fabien's big office. Both were single. After a few failed relationships in Germany, Ariane was currently unsure how she wanted her life to progress. Her decision to switch after her first state law exam to the police force was met with little enthusiasm. So, spontaneously, she accepted the offer to spend two years in Rwanda. The separation from her familiar surroundings also offered the opportunity to escape the repeatedly needling questions about her single status by her conservative parents as well as her friends. Ariane and Fabien were both into martial arts and met on a weekly basis in the police station's gym to practice.

Even after twenty years, Rwanda still hadn't yet recovered from the trauma of the genocide. Newspapers featured daily reports on new revelations and witnesses' testimonies. Oftentimes, the press depicted the conflict between the Hutu and Tutsi in a superficial light and at other times, they entirely misrepresented it. Hints that it was an age-old conflict between farmers and herdsmen, just as they existed in one form or another in other parts of the world, were insufficient. Both groups lived and mingled together peacefully in Rwanda for a long time. An ethnically based definition was uncommon. However, what was important was status. The Tutsi and their kings, the *mwami*, were the ruling group, and then there were the Hutu who had to pay tribute. However, when a Hutu acquired enough cattle and thus, more social recognition, he was then allowed to join the group of Tutsi. But, the Batwa, an indigenous group of pygmies who probably represent the native population, were soon the minority and even nowadays, for the most part, still socially marginalized. Social advancement was not forbidden, but real living conditions rarely allowed this.

Such flexible handling of social order was too much for the bureaucratic-oriented Belgian protectorate that had taken over the German colonial run administration after the First World War. It was hardly surprising the racism some Europeans still had, could thrive again and be used as a suitable instrument of domination. A racially oriented categorization of the population helped stabilize the understaffed colonial administration. They ensured the support of the Tutsi and their kings, the *mwami*, by making them a racially more significant ethnic group – a profound turning point in the Rwandans' social life. Pressured by the Belgians, the Tutsi were quick to play the part. Formerly representing the generally accepted ruling minority, they turned into the oppressors of the Hutu majority. From then on, a person's ethnicity was shown on his ID-card. After the Hutu' revolt in 1959 and the subsequent flight of many Tutsi, Rwanda finally gained independence in 1962. After the overthrow of the initial republic regime in 1973, the Hutu established a government under Juvénal Habyarimana. The method of categorizing and recording the population through ID-cards was later used by the Hutu government in order to prepare for the genocide.

The slaughter began on April 6, 1994. Unknown perpetrators used a ground-to-air missile to shoot down President Habyarimana's plane as it approached Kigali. The Tutsi population was immediately accused even though evidence pointed to Hutu extremists as responsible for the assassination. The broadcasting station, Radio Television Libre des Mille Collines, RTLM, called to hunt for *inyenzi*—cockroaches, as the Tutsi were hatefully referred to. Since Chantal was Tutsi, it placed her, as well as Bosco and their children, Grégoire and Nadège, in extreme danger. During the genocide, they hid in an empty space underneath a tank at the water utility in Ruhengeri until the invasion of general Kagame's army, the Rwandan Patriotic Front, the RPF. Murdering gangs of Hutu, the *interahamwe* paramilitary organization, canvassed residential areas using lists to look for Tutsi members.

The one hundred-day-long slaughtering spree resulted in an estimated eight hundred thousand to one million Tutsi being killed, among them Hutu who refused to join the bloodthirsty gangs. Many victims were slaughtered with machetes. Women, however, were first raped and brutally abused. If a woman was allowed to live as a sex slave, her Achilles tendon was cut to prevent escape. Even children weren't spared. Anyone requesting to be shot rather than hacked to death by a machete had to pay thirty dollars for that act of mercy.

Thankfully, a cousin of Bosco's, a member of the regular Hutu army, the Force Armées Ruandaise, the FAR, helped his family survive the nightmare while placing his own life in danger.

The perpetual fear of being discovered, especially during Bosco's nightly excursions to procure food along with the uncertainty of whether he would return, shaped their existence. After leaving the hiding place to search for food, Bosco once heard on his return the hate speech of RTLM moderator Valérie Bemeriki:

> "Death, death! The mass graves are only filled halfway with Tutsi corpses. Hurry up, fill them completely. Save your ammo and hack them to death with your machetes."

That was followed by the song "Rape Me", by the rock band Nirvana and Bosco immediately knew their hiding place had been discovered. Two roaming young men of the *interahamwe* tried to rape Chantal. One man held her while the other ripped the clothes from her body. She put up a good fight and received several blows to the face, leaving her looking battered. The children huddled together in a corner, their eyes opened wide in horror. Bosco often remembered that incident and continued to try to come to terms with what he had felt. He, who until that moment had been a rather peaceful-minded man, as well as a good husband and father, turned immediately into a deadly fighting machine. As if in a trance, he unsheathed his hunting knife instead of drawing his gun so as not to attract attention, and then charged into the hiding place and unleashed his fury. The man in the process of raping Chantal had his back turned to him. Before the rapist had a chance to turn around, Bosco stabbed him in the neck and withdrew his knife as he pushed the dying man aside. With his cervical spine severed, the man fell paralyzed and gurgling to the ground on his face. The other man released Chantal and tried to grab his gun as Bosco's knife pierced his heart. Dying, he watched through frightened eyes as Bosco disarmed him. Under the cover of darkness, Bosco, with the help of his cousin, made the two marauders disappear. This experience weighed heavily on him for years. He never believed he was capable of killing someone in such a cold-blooded manner. As far as Bosco was concerned, he never wanted to talk about the incident again. He knew Chantal was resilient enough to cope with what had happened and he was also sure she would help Grégoire and Nadège to come to terms with it.

Once general Kagame seized power, Bosco was offered a position with the police in Kigali. His diligence and sharp instinct soon attracted attention. Benevolent sponsors recommended him for further legal and forensic courses, some of which he completed at the BKA in Wiesbaden, Germany. Ever since then, he considered Germans to be friends and thought he'd discovered a somewhat historically spiritual kinship. It filled him with hope seeing that the Germans had overcome their past and were presenting themselves confidently in the international community fifty-nine years after the disaster of World War II. In Rwanda, the wounds of the one-hundred-day-long slaughter healed sluggishly. After the genocide and with the help of foreign lawyers, the administration installed a judiciary system and at the same time launched a campaign to reconcile the nation. When those who had been mainly responsibility for the brutal regime were handed over to a UN-tribunal in Arusha, Tanzania, the Rwandan justice department relentlessly continued hunting down the marauders, even to this day. Those not sentenced to death lived a miserable existence for many years in prison as a *flamingo*, so named because the prison uniform for political prisoners was pink. The lowest level of the judiciary, the *gacacas*, was established according to the model of the old village courts and gained worldwide recognition. His children, Bosco hoped, would no longer suffer the burden of the past.

Like many Rwandans, Bosco didn't understand the worldwide criticism of the persistent, at times, even across borders, hunt for the hundred-day butchers. This rang especially true for German critics. After World War II, they did not prevent active members of the NSDAP from acquiring influential positions, but, naturally, no one wanted to be reminded of it.

Soon, English became the third official language. Officially, this was justified by the desire to strengthen the relationship with their Anglophone neighbors in Tanzania and Uganda. Undoubtedly, the Tutsi lack of language skills, who primarily grew up in neighboring countries, played a role in this decision. Many returning Tutsi neither had sufficient French language skills nor the local language, Kinyarwanda. The desire to distance themselves from the French was obvious. France had supported and supplied weapons to the Hutu terror regime until the end. Bosco learned of it by studying English trade publications as well as the Kigali newspaper, The New Times, with Chantal's excellent knowledge of English at times. His colleagues and superiors greatly appreciated his language skills since many colleagues were part of the group of English-speaking exiles. Others belonged to the local unencumbered Hutu. They had, like him and his family, somehow managed to elude capture by the marauding militias. Thus, they were lucky to escape the alternative of roaming the land with the murdering mob only to eventually be hunted down.

By the time the newly born Agathe was five years old and starting school, Bosco thought it appropriate to have a serious conversation with Chantal about birth control, which she acknowledged with an indulgent smile.

At the moment, the CID was engaged in the case of a missing employee of a non-governmental organization (NGO). The investigation was still in its infancy.

After the horrific events of 1994, the international community tried to monitor the refugee problems in the Kivu provinces of the Congo and Rwanda, which required enormous financial resources. Many NGO advisors, as well as governmental aid agencies and, naturally, the United Nations, subjugated the still existing state institutions in the region to on-going assessments. The objective was to improve infrastructure, expand energy and water supply, political training, optimizing agricultural technology, and advances in many other areas. Even though success did not come quickly, over time it eventually paid off because most financial backers of reconstruction programs had allocated funds for training of local skilled labor, who in turn gained employment in project regions and provided valuable work.

Some clues were pursued after the Kigali office manager reported the NGO employee's disappearance, yet nothing panned out. Since the man was Congolese and working on projects in the Kivu region in the eastern Congo, they tried to get help from the Congolese administration in Kinshasa, but they could only wait and see whether their request would be granted.

2

Saturday, August 13, 2005. Bosco's cell phone sounded the first notes of the unofficial anthem, *Inzinzi*. The display showed the private phone number of his colleague in Gisenyi, Théoneste Mugisha. Since their time together as rangers in the Virunga National Park, they had been close friends and all colleagues called him Théo. Yet, unlike Bosco, who now looked slightly out of shape, Théo still participated in numerous sports. In competitions between police departments, he always finished in the top tier. Since his wife Vana was Congolese, Théo was related to a large family in North Kivu province, a fact that was extremely helpful in the border town of Gisenyi. Even Théo and Vana's children had become good friends with Bosco's kids.

He and Théo's family shared many memories together. Time and again, usually on the weekends, they met for joint activities in the country's national parks, Lake Kivu, or even in Kigali when they visited. But, the best weekends were in Gisenyi where they swam untroubled in Lake Kivu.

Lake Kivu is the only lake in the region where you could go into the water and feel safe. The lake is located in the rift of the East African tectonic plate and the water is enriched with carbon dioxide and methane through the volcanic activity on the lake bottom. This condition and the relatively high salinity make the lakeshore uninhabitable for a wide range of flora and fauna. The constant supply of gasses also makes the lake one of the most dangerous in East Africa. The methane concentration has increased dramatically over the last twenty years. Oversaturating the water with the never-ending inflowing gasses could eventually change the equilibrium pressure and ultimately cause an eruption, wiping out all life around the lake. The recent exploitation of gas from Lake Kivu, to counter the chronic shortage of energy in the country, was met with skepticism among scientists. The horrific gas eruption in 1986 at Lake Nyos in Cameroon that caused more than seventeen hundred deaths was still fresh in everyone's mind.

Visitors to the area never thought twice about such incidents. The reason for the decline of the formerly thriving tourism to Lake Kivu was merely due to the political situation. Obviously, this had dire consequences, in particularly, for Gisenyi, but the Congolese city of Bukavu at the southern end of Lake Kivu also suffered greatly. Sometime in the past, both cities had managed to acquire certain prosperity. The few colonial mansions still standing were a testament to that fact.

Meanwhile, at least on some weekends, more and more tourists frolicked on the beach. Even hotels of lesser standards were booked in advance because they had charm and provided a rustic atmosphere.

Bosco and Chantal sat at the table after lunch enjoying a cup of coffee when Théo called. Bosco assumed the call was to remind them it had been quite some time since they had last gotten together. However, his friend was all business.

"Bosco, we found a horribly mutilated male corpse. I'd appreciate it if you stop by."

"When did you find him?"

"Border control called us. They were notified by a

fisherman who saw the body this morning at a quarter past eight when he was out with his boat. They recorded his name and address and let him go. The dead man is lying right on shore near the border to Goma at Grande Barrière."

"Have you informed the *PG* ?"

"He's left for the weekend, but I did send word."

"Do you have any possible suspects yet?"

"No! Um, Bosco, there's something else."

"What?"

"The dead man is a *mzungu*." Bosco remained quiet, breathing deeply. Théo added, "un blanc", in case he hadn't grasped the meaning. But, Bosco had understood. A white man, probably a foreigner.

He, like many other Rwandans in the northern part of the country, oftentimes used the Swahili word *mzungu*, plural *wazungu*, for whites instead of the Kinyarwanda word *umuzungu*.

It wasn't good news at all, but it explained the request for assistance. Théo, who he regarded as a particularly capable colleague, usually never required assistance. Both men immediately knew this case would attract the attention of the Kigali Public Prosecutor's Office, the NPPA. Thus, it wouldn't be long before Bosco would find the case file on his desk. The CID called the prosecutor general *General* or *PG* . John Mugambage, Chief Prosecutor, performed his job meticulously and ruthlessly but was also quite pragmatic. He was an old comrade of the president and a member of the Tutsi elite. Nevertheless, no one would ever entertain the idea that Mugambage received his post only because of his network. He was intelligent yet a little vain. Whenever he had a decision to make, wisdom always prevailed. It was unlikely he would not get involved with the case. The word was out that he had his eye on a ministerial position. The mention of his office in the press and on Rwanda's national TV station would certainly be beneficial.

Théo continued before Bosco could reply. "His face was covered with a mask."

"Say what? A mask? What type of mask?"

"A wooden mask, like Congolese villagers wear during various celebrations and rituals. Nowadays, many of them are sold to tourists. We haven't yet removed the mask. This certainly is something new, but it probably indicates plenty of trouble."

Bosco was silent for a moment. So far, like many Africans in postcolonial times, he had little contact with the tribal rites and customs of his ancestors. The educated elite urged Rwanda towards modern times.

"Is that someone's idea of a bad joke, Théo?"

"A rather macabre joke, the man's legs were cut off."

Bosco, who was about to take a sip of coffee, put the cup down again and remained silent. Like many times, he had trouble suppressing the horrible images of the past that threatened to occupy his mind again.

"Are the legs with the corpse?"

"No, and we couldn't find them in the immediate vicinity either."

Bosco regarded his watch. It was noon. He could be there in three and a half to four hours. Considering the case hadn't been assigned to him yet, he decided against recording the drive to Gisenyi as official business. He could always come up with an excuse for his unexpected presence if it became necessary. Théo had indeed privately called him.

"All right, Théo, I'm on my way. Secure the crime scene and make sure the mask isn't removed. I would like to see it for myself. Another thing, I believe it is better to keep it from the public for the time being. I'm leaving right away."

"Okay, the site is already cordoned off. See you soon, thank you."

Chantal, like many times before, showed great understanding when he had to go on the road over the weekend and quickly wrapped a bottle of Bordeaux for Vana and Théo. The politically motivated movement away from Francophonie didn't mean not enjoying certain things. Both friends, as well as Chantal, loved French wine, which they always had a few bottles in stock and gladly brought along when visiting. Bosco wondered if he should stop by Chantal's mother on the way to Gisenyi.

Like he, Chantal and her family also came from Ruhengeri, the capital in the northern province with the same name. Her father was no longer alive. He had been an employee of Agathe Uwilingiyimana, the former short-term Prime Minister of the Hutu government of Habyarimana. He, along with others, had become victims of genocide. He and ten soldiers were murdered by a mob of *interahamwe,* despite the UN peacekeepers.

He quickly dismissed the idea. Time was of the essence and Chantal didn't mention it either. Nevertheless, he would stop briefly at his chicken coop in Ruhengeri and grab a bird for Théo and his family.

Apart from some distant relatives, Bosco only had his family. His father had separated from his mother a long time ago, his current whereabouts unknown. Bosco tried not to think about it, but he was afraid one day he might learn his father had been involved in the genocide. His mother had died a few years earlier. His parents' old house in Ruhengeri sustained considerable damage during the riots by marauding militias. They had suspected his mother of hiding her daughter-in-law. While his mother was still alive, Bosco and a few neighbors had fixed up the house so it was habitable again. However, there was still extensive damage and had now fallen into an irreparable ruin. Bosco had only been able to save one barn, which he used to raise chickens. During his absence, a boy from a family of peasants took care of the birds for a small fee. The family was in charge of working a few fields at the foot of Mount Karisimbi. Since its summit lies at more than four thousand five hundred meters, it was the highest mountain in the Virunga National Park, Bosco's former place of employment.

At the front door, he gave his wife a kiss on the cheek and briefly hugged little Agathe. Automatically, he waved to his two older kids who already were fighting over their mother's cell phone in order to contact their friends. Taking the shortest route via Avenue du Lac Kivu, he drove passed the bus station toward the Kigali-Ruhengeri Road.

After ten minutes on the road, he groaned in exasperation. Up ahead in the distance he saw traffic had come to a standstill.

Merde, I should have thought of that.

Despite his Catholic upbringing, at times, he couldn't help but swear, even though he found it more civilized sounding in French than in any other languages, including Kinyarwanda. Awkwardly, he fumbled in his pocket and pull out his official ID while simultaneously slowing down. He always forgot that it was *umuganda* day, the traditional coming together of Rwandans to clean up the land. Just before the bridge crossing the small river Nyabugogo, several cars were stopped in front of a roadblock. The drivers were in a heated discussion and gesticulating violently with one of the guards. Bosco recognized one of the men, the short one in a suit, white shirt, and tie sweating profusely. Despite being annoyed, Bosco had to chuckle. The man was an employee of the mortgage house, who had given him a hard time back when they were inquiring about a loan on the house. Gleefully, he watched as the still protesting man was given a poker and a garbage bag so he could pick up trash by the roadside.

Like everywhere else, when it came to an individual's sacrifice for the good of the community, citizens were exceedingly creative when it came to avoiding their tasks. It wasn't easy for a Rwandan to escape *umuganda*, unless, of course, a person was exempt, like police officers. Anyone who didn't want to be involved had better stay home that day. However, the ultimate success of that campaign eventually led to its general acceptance. In many African countries, discarded garbage and plastic bags were an ever-present testament of the *wazungu* - culture. Now, importing plastic bags was prohibited and thanks to *umuganda,* Rwanda was probably the cleanest country in Africa.

After presenting his service badge, he was allowed

to cross the bridge, but not without first receiving a few dirty looks. After another three hours of driving without any further interruption, he finally reached his chicken coop at the outskirts of Ruhengeri. Bosco selected an exceptionally plump chicken, tied its feet together with a piece of hemp, and placed the fluttering, cackling in protest bird in the back of his SUV.

"Don't make a fuss my beauty; I'm sure Vana will gently roast you to perfection."

After another hour, he greeted Théo outside his house in Gisenyi.

"Hello, my friend. It's nice to see you. How are your family and colleagues?"

"The family is doing well, thanks. The CID was busy with a missing person case, but other than that, it was business as usual. However, considering the new development, that might change pretty soon. I can't help feeling we'll soon find ourselves under pressure."

Théo got in the car and gave Bosco direction to Avenue de la Révolution towards the Congolese border.

"I guess it will improve Ariane's mood," Bosco said. "Lately, she definitely shows signs of not being challenged."

Théo smiled sympathetically. He once worked a case with the German female officer and was familiar with her overzealousness.

"Well, have you found any viable clues?"

"Not really. I doubt the few we did find will help us in our investigation. I'm hoping forensics will uncover something useful."

Bosco's expression darkened.

"Robbery as a motive seems rather unlikely with this type murder," Théo surmised.

"Have you canvassed the area surrounding the crime scene?"

"We certainly did, but only on our side of the border. Nothing was discovered."

While driving, Bosco noticed a sign that said

Kivu Shores, Paradise Awaits.

Considering the situation in the Kivu region, it was a somewhat pathetic attempt to put things in a better light. Granted, many visitors marveled at the beautiful sight of Lake Kivu, but those who came knew it to be the same limbo as the Congolese side of the demarcation line.

After Bosco parked the car in the parking lot at the Grande Barrière border installation, the two men walked over to the red and white tape cordoned off area. The two Constables to the Gendarmerie guarding the crime scene came to attention and saluted. Meanwhile, crowds had assembled on both sides of the border, excitedly discussing and commenting on the incident. Discovering victims of violence was unremarkable in the region, but a murdered *mzungu* was not an everyday occurrence. The corpse was lying on black sand near the lakeshore at the foot of a steep embankment where the surf had carved out a small inlet. A tarp had been fastened to tree branches so that the little cove, the crime scene, was shielded from onlookers on the street above. The low-hanging tree branches almost reached all the way to the water's surface. The couple of meters of coastline to the Congolese border were made up of porous boulders with sharp edges, the typical lava rock formation of the Virunga volcano chain. As recently as 2002, magma had flowed down Mount Nyiragongo and caused major devastation before it ended up in Lake Kivu close to the border to Rwanda. The areas most affected had been the center of Goma and the nearby airfield. At the time, only the upper floors of multi-story houses were visible. Undeterred, they diligently restored Goma to its former glory.

Bosco had a difficult time following Théo, who had already climbed halfway down the embankment. Using his hands for support, he injured himself on the sharp edges of the rocks while descending to the shore.

There are more convenient places one can die.

The dead man lay on his back, his gaze directed in a southwesterly direction as if his dying wish was to witness one last sunset as it descended over the distant towering Nile-Congo watershed. Out of a pair of shorts were two bloodless stumps where his legs were severed. Several men in protective suits were packing up forensic equipment. Two of Théo's employees waited for the corpse to be released for transport. The forensic team had outlined the man's dead body as it was found and placed several markers in the sand surrounding it. On his face, a wooden mask was held in place by a hank of hemp tied around the head. A few tufts of blond hair stuck out from behind. Bosco took a few minutes to inspect the crime scene and then took a closer look at the deceased. It was obvious the wooden mask was supposed to instill fear. Its distorted facial features and protruding teeth conveyed its meaning.

After receiving the signal from Théo, one of his officers removed the mask from the victim's face.

It seemed the deceased had an arduous journey into paradise. Then again, someone sent to the afterlife in such a fashion might have problems being admitted to begin with, was Bosco's first thought. After solving several violent crimes, which he was instrumental in, he wasn't easily shaken. However, this dead man affected him. The legs had been cut off above the knees and the skull was split by a diagonal slash across the face. The latter fact made him think of the past and sent a shiver surging through his body. The injury to the skull was literally identical to a case that had attracted worldwide attention some twenty years ago, namely, the murder of Dian Fossey. Granted, Bosco had not seen the murdered researcher, but the description in the news was detailed and discussed throughout the country. He stopped reminiscing and instead, memorized a few details of the new crime scene. Théo was dictating his preliminary findings into his Smartphone with professional detachment.

"Male victim, Caucasian, approximately fifty-eight to sixty-two years of age. Face covered with wooden mask, fastened with hemp hank. Both legs separated at thighs, not with body or in immediate vicinity. Estimated height around six feet, muscular build, presumably strong. Blond, two-inch crew cut with a one-inch hairless furrow, angled from the left ear to the forehead, no visible scar. Dressed in shirt and shorts made by the Swedish company Fjällräven. Scar on inside right humerus, presumably from a bite. Left arm bears a tattoo of a red rooster. One wound on forehead, two additional wounds on back of head."

"One thing is obvious," he said to Bosco after recording a few more details on his device, "we can assume the victim wasn't killed here. The body is almost exsanguinated and there are only a few traces of blood."

"Perhaps the lake's surf washed all traces away?"

"No, that's unlikely. For more than a week now, this area has been experiencing extreme heat without the slightest breeze or waves. Look at that disturbed spot of sand on the waterline. Looks like someone obscured their footprints. The surf would have washed over it and smoothed it out."

"It stands to reason the corpse arrived by boat and was placed here. There was no evidence someone came down the embankment."

"Yes, that's a likely scenario. Coming from the road would've certainly attracted attention. This is quite a busy route."

The still present doctor joined them and shook hands with Bosco. Eugène Muhoza was an old acquaintance from Kigali that Bosco had worked with before on cases involving violent crimes. He had transferred to Gisenyi for family reasons.

"Hi Bosco"

»Ho Eugène. Nasty business. Do you have a time of death yet?"

"*Rigor mortis* hasn't set in yet. So, I guess the time of death occurred no more than two days before the corpse was discovered. The body is presently starting to show signs of livor mortis. The body bled out quickly with this injury."

They regarded the corpse in silence.

"Clean cuts, as if his legs were severed with a single blow. Incredible, considering the thickness of the thighs," he further noted.

"Any idea which weapon was used?" Théo asked.

The doctor merely shrugged.

"Well, the skull may have been split by a *panga*, but it certainly wasn't used on the thighs. It's impossible. Anyway, that's all I can say at the moment."

"Were the legs severed before or after the man died?" Bosco asked.

"Definitely after, the stumps aren't bloody."

"Does the murder have to do with smugglers or was it a ritual murder? Damn, who would do such a thing, not to mention why?" Théo muttered aloud.

"Maybe he was one of the *wazungu* who couldn't get enough of Africa. He ventured out to the tribal areas to listen and learn how to play the drums and to meet the Chieftain's daughters, the whole shebang, for cash of course. Perhaps he overstepped the boundaries," Bosco mocked and, considering the gruesome situation, immediately regretted his remarks. He didn't mention how similar it was to Dian Fossey's murder. Théo ignored Bosco's sarcastic comments. It was his way of staying emotionally detached. Many colleagues shared the same method in order to deal with such horrible situations better and remain objective.

"Well, that's not so far-fetched. Granted, the Chiefs in the villages have abandoned most of their original ways of life, but when certain taboos are violated they like to make use of their ancestors' animistic rituals, which can go as far as cannibalism," Théo stated. "However, I've never heard of a ritual that involved cutting off someone's legs."

"Neither have I. Then again, perhaps many rituals are kept secret. I know back in 1959, my dear Hutu relatives used this method during one uprising when they exerted their revenge on the Tutsi. That was a traumatic experience for the family of our president, who, at the time, had been forced to flee to Uganda. If we don't find some tangible clues here, we won't stand a chance of nabbing the perpetrator, at least not in our neck of the jungle and certainly not in the Congo. And given the fact we're already investigating a case where we needed the cooperation of Kinshasa, I presume they won't be too enthusiastic when we ask for their cooperation again."

Bosco looked at the dead man again.

"Okay, so we agree, it's a possibility. But, he doesn't look like a freaky hippie in search of adventure in the rain forest. Perhaps someone is attempting to steer our investigation in this direction."

"You're right, the well-trained body stature, the haircut, he looks more like a businessman, perhaps someone who routinely exercises in the mornings," Théo commented.

"Or, he was a legionnaire guarding the mines."

"I thought the mining companies only recruit young people? Our victim is at least in his late fifties."

"True, but some of the commanding officers are old-timers."

They fell silent again for a moment and studied the crime scene until Bosco addressed the doctor.

"Are there any signs of torture or other marks such as defensive wounds that would point to a struggle?"

"No, I only see some bruising and marks on the

wrists from restraints. The scar on the inside of the right humerus is quite old. There are a few abrasions on the back, presumably caused during transport. One of the wounds on the back of the head indicates a blow rendered him defenseless. That scenario would fit with the wound on the forehead, which he sustained when he was unconscious and fell forward. That's quite a common pattern."

"The tat of a red rooster may tell us he was a Frenchman. The *Coq Gaulois*, isn't that a French national symbol, or am I mistaken?" Bosco's gaze wandered back and forth between the doctor and Théo.

"I'm not quite sure, but I think the French *Coq Gaulois* looks somewhat different," Théo said.

"We should contact the Congolese and see if we can find any clues on their side of the border. I believe you know the commander in Goma."

"Yes I do. Also, we cannot rule out that the man might've lived in a community of foreigners in Goma. I guess we cannot avoid talking with our dear colleague Joseph Likongo. I'm sure he won't be thrilled."

"That makes two of us," Bosco said dryly.

The slight irony in Théo's voice was hard to miss. He had already mentioned Likongo several times in previous conversations regarding events in the Congo.

Joseph Likongo was a true blue Congolese who earned the rank of Inspector Divisionnaire of the Police Nationale Congolaise, presently the commander in charge of North Kivu province, based in Goma. He had one hundred eighty men and women of various ranks under his command. Likongo was a descendant of the Tetela tribe in Kasai province. His family was distantly related to a famous son of that tribe, Prime Minister Patrice Lumumba, who was assassinated in 1961. It was due to this circumstance that he enjoyed certain prestige, which benefitted him often. He'd been living alone ever since his long-time girlfriend, who had worked at the UN, had a fatal accident. The position of headquarters commander in Goma required a high degree of diplomacy and organizational skills. Likongo had both, but he could also claim he was assigned the position because his opponents had underestimated his relaxed manner. However, a few colleagues seriously thought about challenging him for his position. Opportunities to supplement a salary with extra cash were everywhere, but in Kinshasa, it was simply more convenient, more profitable, and less dangerous. They repeatedly tried to discredit him because of his pragmatic way of dealing with less than desirable characters, like the warlords who had their residences in Goma. Regardless, he wouldn't be influenced because the situation in the eastern Congo left no room for alternative compromises. Nevertheless, the warlords were never able to buy or exploit him. And, even though they went about their business in front of the entire retinue of MONUC and numerous NGO's without a care in the world, Likongo made it a habit to keep an eye on them. For some time now, considering the desperate situation of the country, he had to focus more on robberies and violent crimes. He was powerless to do anything about the activities of various groups outside Goma, petty crimes, smuggling, and prostitution. His informal network that reached all the way to the capital worked quite well. He wasn't pleased with the activities of bandits and profiteers, but with few resources, there was little he could do about it. Since he couldn't trust some of his employees, he was practically on his own. Naturally, Likongo also watched over the international community providing they followed the guidelines or to be more precise, as long as they obeyed his rules. For a fee, he was also willing to lend bureaucratic support. It was quite common for him and his men not to receive their wages, so they had no choice but to be creative to make up for it. The failed state paid its employees according to a lottery. So, he thought it was better to ensure his team received some kind of salary before they ran off and joined a group of rebels, as was known to happen quite often. Nevertheless, he considered himself a righteous man who earned his living the hard way. Every once in a while, he also visited church on Sundays and made a small donation to the abbé.

After the genocide in 1994, numerous aid organizations from the international community were sent to the Congo. At the time, all Hutu who were still able to walk and were somehow affiliated with the system or couldn't prove otherwise, fled across the border into Goma. Later on, in 2002, after the Nyiragongo Vulcano that menacingly loomed over Goma had effused its extremely low viscous lava over the city, more and more aid workers and UN soldiers arrived in the region. The MONUC soldiers were recruited mainly from armies of some developing countries. In contrast to the relatively low wages soldiers received, the UN's expenditure to respective nations was considerable. Within a short time, the peacekeepers behavior ruined the entire UN's reputation. Although MONUC and NGO personnel undeniably devoted themselves to their tasks and provided limited assistance, they, of course, were unable to find lasting solutions for the problems. However, local merchants, as well as house, hotel, and brothel owners took great delight in all the money they spent in their establishments. From the consumers' perspective, MONUC and NGO forces had firm control of Goma, yet looking at it from a profiteer's point of view the general consensus was that some behind the scenes businessmen were in control, respectively, organized warlords. Providing you could afford it, everything was available in the tri-country cross-border black market of the Congo, Rwanda, and Uganda. Whenever they talked about the old days, Théo always concluded that it had been a typical win-win situation if you disregarded how the majority of the population had fared.

"Théo, if at all possible, I think we should try to determine his identity first and for the time being, postpone asking the commandant for help. If the victim was associated with MONUC or an NGO, it should be child's play."

"I'll check on that. However, our chances are slim if he was one of those adventurers who like to hang around the border. I'll get in touch with our border officials and see if they have visa data on file corresponding to his profile. If that is unsuccessful, I can always try the Congolese border guards. But, if that happens, we must involve Likongo."

Bosco's mood bottomed out. "And if that doesn't help, we'll have to turn to Kinshasa."

"Yes, and then it will become political. That's when you and *PG* will be in charge of the investigation."

"Right, but it could also end up solely in our hands."

Both fell silent for a moment, each man picturing what kind of consequences this would have for them if the case turned political. Bosco didn't want to leave this possibility to chance so he again thought about the motive. Granted, prospects were plentiful and, unfortunately, in this region of the world murders were committed without motive, providing pure bloodlust was ignored. It was rather unlikely it was a common day murder, like it sometimes happens during a dispute. Did the severed legs point to a ritual murder or were they supposed to steer the investigation in the wrong direction? Was the murder connected to the business of smuggling Rare Earths Elements such as coltan? Warlords didn't take kindly to business disruptions. The victim could've been a wholesaler who attempted to cheat his suppliers.

The flourishing Rare Earths Elements trade was nothing new. The last war in the Congo and the genocide in Rwanda had reshuffled the deck. Under Mobutu, the government of the Congo retained control of assigning licenses to foreign mining companies. The autocrat did everything to consolidate his authority in the country and thereby demonstrated a certain flair for the mentality of his citizens. Before taking command, he went by the name Joseph Désiré Mobutu, but then he forced

Africanization, where every Congolese should adopt additional African names. From then on he went by the name "Mobutu Sese Seko Kuku Ngbendu wa za Banga" (Mobutu the mighty cock that leaves no hen unmolested). In doing so, he ensured that his name would never be forgotten. Internationally it was thought at first to be a joke until it turned out it was the correct translation of his name. Naturally, it didn't pose a problem in the Congo because the man knew his people.

Considering the explosive political situation and the fact that the murder could be related to the trade of Rare Earths Elements or even blood diamonds, Bosco knew he could end up between a rock and hard place. It was always good to have contacts in high places when investigating a crime of this type. Many influential citizens of Kigali had contacts and were quite blatant when trading resources. Conducting an investigation of such a crime always led to a balancing act, which so far was something he had been spared. Therefore, Bosco was unsure if he should try to avoid the case and not get further involved, but immediately rejected the idea. Besides, Théo had asked for his assistance. If the case became politically sensitive, there was a chance the Chief Prosecutor in Kigali would assign it to Crime Intelligence.

"Okay, go ahead and finish gathering all the information and write your report while I drive back to Kigali to see how *PG* is going to react."

He dropped Théo off at his house, but before departing, he sent his regards to Vana and the kids and handed him the chicken and bottle of wine. With the motor running, Bosco rolled down the driver's window.

"You know Mugambage's ambitions. There'll be lots of pressure on us if he's involved. Don't take too long sending your case file over."

After agreeing to talk every day, Bosco finally headed home. He arrived around midnight and fell exhausted into bed next to the already sleeping Chantal. Remembering it was Sunday, sleep came easier.

3

Since Thomas Mayeye, a former supporter of the warlord known as Laurent Nkunda, started doing business in the Congolese border town of Goma, the political situation had become exceedingly more hostile.

With the invasion of future President Kabila's ADFL liberation movement in the Congo, a new shift in power was not only regional but also international. During that time, the support was welcomed by Rwanda's military. The masterfully planned and carried out final campaign to overthrow Mobutu was led by them. This was publicly justified to protect the group of Banyamulenge in the Congo, who were ethnically related to the Tutsi and whom Mobutu had denied citizenship. The invasion of Kinshasa left a bloody trail of retaliation. All Hutu captured were massacred. The campaign was logistically supported by the Americans, who, in contrast to the French, were then able to consolidate their influence for a second time. The latter supported the Hutu army through arms sales during the genocide. Even the son of former French President Mitterand was involved in the despicable affair. They felt obliged to ensure the *Système France-Afrique*, which was meant to guarantee the continued existence of power through economic relations after the withdrawal from the colonies. The French clung too long to Mobutu after this sustained, to date, rift between Rwanda and France.

At the end, a power vacuum arose in large parts of the eastern Congo and the warlords stepped in, to the extent that mining companies without security, usually mercenaries, provided protection. As if the situation wasn't bad enough, former soldiers of the standard troops that had been abandoned by the government in Kinshasa started roaming the country more or less leaderless in order to terrorize the rural population as compensation for not receiving wages.

This condition didn't change when Mobutu's successor, Laurent Kabila, was assassinated in 2001. The assumption that his sudden change of heart and declaring contracts with foreign mining companies null and void had something to do with his death sentence wasn't far-fetched. Bearing a resemblance to a hereditary succession, his son Joseph Kabila assumed the mantle. His efforts to gain democratic legitimacy were limited. One of his first acts after assuming command was to exile not only the former ally, the Rwandan Tutsi, but he also tried to get rid of their Congolese relatives, the Banyamulenge.

In 2002, Joseph Kabila made certain Nkunda's rebel movement was integrated into the national army as part of the Pretoria Accord and he promoted himself to general. However, he resigned shortly later, arguing that the central government would do little to oppose Hutu extremists. Along with Nkunda, Mayeye, a former major in the Rassemblement Congolais pour la Démocratie, (RCD), as well as a Sergeant named Samuel Matengo, resigned their posts. They united and established a new rebel movement. A little later they joined the Congrès national pour la défense du peuple), (CNDP), at which time Nkunda assumed leadership. Subsequently, the government in Kinshasa decided to get rid of the former workers in the struggle for power. With the approval of the population, Kabila showed the infamous Tutsi the door. Even in Kinshasa, they were already establishing political contacts.

Meanwhile, their Congolese brothers tried to get the eastern regions under their control by pillaging. In 2004, they occupied the town of Bukavu. Certain of their security, they foolishly assumed their Tutsi relatives in Rwanda and President Paul Kagame would support them. After the image-damaging news reports about mass rape, child soldiers, and illegal exploitation of resources, the Rwandans worried about their reputation. Tired of being accused of supporting their actions they distanced themselves from their relatives. President Kagame, the Prussian of Africa, as he was often called, did not intend to let a bunch of criminals ruin his undeniable success at stabilizing the country.

In Kinshasa, the capital of the Democratic Republic of Congo, the DRC, the first free elections were imminent. The UN, under the mandate to protect the population and to assist the government with democratization, continued to enlist more and more MONUC soldiers in order to stop the excessive activities of the unrestrained rebels. Nkunda was unable to maintain his position in Bukavu and eventually withdrew. After receiving Nkunda's consent, Mayeye and his sergeant, who had previously laid the foundation for their operations, settled in Goma for good.

In this tense situation, additional problems that could disrupt Mayeye's activities were extremely undesirable. He tried to get rid of his image as a warlord collaborator and establish himself as a reputable businessman, although, he had his own definition of what constituted reputable. By then he had ceased most of his prostitution business and instead, focused more and more on commodities trading. He also ran the military uniformed security agency SÉCOMA. Their services ranged from building security to private escorts, to guarding transports as well as mining operations. Mayeye entrusted the operational management to his former *sergeant*, Matengo, consequently promoting him to *captain*. Matengo had served under Mobutu, but soon left the army. During the turmoil that followed the advancing disempowerment of Mobutu, he recruited a few people with whom he had terrorized the population. By the time he and Mayeye rejoined the military, he was once again a henchman.

It was well known that Mayeye's protection force wasn't subtle in their methods when it came to dealing with problems. Scoffers alleged the agency offered protection from them—the *gardien* principle. Business flourished.

Once Joseph Likongo received a call by the border guards and learned about the discovery of the body, he immediately ordered one of his men to mingle with the spectators to see if he could determine the name of the dead man. The man managed to identify the victim despite precautions the Rwandan police had taken. the Police Nationale Congolaise, (PNC), in Goma knew the man. As the observer relayed the information to his superior, the commander immediately knew this case would land in his lap. The victim had the approval of influential patrons in Kinshasa for his activities in the eastern Congo, so it only seemed prudent to deal with this at once. Sooner or later the Rwandans would learn about the deceased's business dealings in Goma. Wanting to find out more, the commander reached for his cell phone and dialed a number he reluctantly contacted.

Thomas Mayeye recognized the caller by the number on his screen and guessed the reason for the call because he had already been informed. This gangster knew perfectly well he was presently facing a problem he couldn't solve in his usual way since the cause of the problem was already dead and making the body disappear without anyone being the wiser was no longer possible.

Thomas Mayeye and Joseph Likongo had been acquainted for a long time and they addressed each other by first names. Their relationship, however, could not be categorized as friendly. But, the desolate location of the Congolese border town and the real balance of power made collaborations necessary that wouldn't exist under normal circumstances. And, the situation in Goma was anything but normal. The Chief of police knew better than to get too involved with Mayeye. It was difficult to keep his gang in check, but Mayeye was sometimes helpful in obtaining information. Once again, it was clear to the gangster that it was best to allow Likongo do his job while trying to control him. It wasn't in his best interest to risk Kinshasa assigning the post to a stranger.

The call wasn't unexpected, but Mayeye hadn't devised a strategy as to how he should act. Before he could flaunt his self-assuredness, Likongo came straight to the point.

"Darcy has been found murdered. Thomas, it's imperative I talk to you."

Unintentionally, the receiver's tone betrayed his irritation.

"What for? Do you suspect me?"

"Of course not, I just want to know where I stand. Your dealings with him are well known and eventually you will be confronted. I'll be at your place in an hour."

Likongo ended the call without waiting for an answer. Mayeye's emotions ran wild, but ultimately he concluded it was better to play along.

The sun was approaching the horizon when Likongo reached his destination after a short drive— *La Résidence*, as Mayeye liked to call the unadorned mud brick structure and adjacent outbuildings. The property lay just outside town and reflected itself in a reddish tinge on Lake Kivu. Visitors to the area could hardly help but feel they were standing in front of a medieval fortress. The entire place was surrounded by a ten-foot-high wall topped with embedded shards of glass. The narrow windows in the main building permitted only a little light and resembled embrasures. Although the commander had only set foot in the living room, which Mayeye also used as a receiving room, he knew the layout of the entire property because he had procured the plans a long time ago. The living room was approximately sixteen by twenty feet. On the opposite side of its entrance, the ground floor continued through an arched passage into another room approximately twelve by sixteen feet. A billiard table occupied the middle of that room. A nook featured a bar with a selection of high-proof liquors, above it a photo of Rwandan President Kagame. Concealed behind a door in the living room was a washroom. A door on the other side of the second room led to a kitchen and another bathroom. Next to a storage chamber were three additional small rooms for the staff. Upstairs, Mayeye's private quarters were two furnished rooms and a bathroom. The staircase led from the corridor in the receiving area all the way up to the roof terrace where watchmen surveyed the surrounding environment twenty-four-seven. The building had a basement. A few rooms could also be accessed by the stairway in the receiving area. One basement room was easily accessible from the outside and used as a laundry room. The basement also possessed a tunnel that ended at the lake close to a deserted small cove where two concealed motorboats were tied up to a pier. The other building on the approximately two and a half acre property served as accommodations for the guards.

Normally, everyone was frisked before being allowed to enter the premises, but the guards had received prior instructions to give the police officer free access. Mayeye, a tall Banyamulenge, greeted him in the living room of the spacious ground floor. He sat on a zebra skin couch with his legs spread far apart. Despite the dim lighting, Mayeye wore imitation, Chinese made Ray-Ban sunglasses, a popular item in the Congo. The wide-open, roaring lion print shirt drew attention to the heavy gold necklace adorning his bronze skin. Unlike the warlord Nkunda, who only appeared in uniform, Mayeye preferred civilian clothes.

Mayeye deliberately looked at his Rolex, a gift from Nkunda, and stood up. With a disarming smile, he approached his visitor. The thick carpet muffled his footsteps. Likongo saw no reason to return the smile.

His gaze instills as much confidence as a pregnant crocodile - he's just way more dangerous.

"Commander Joseph, why so glum? It's nice you came to visit me in my humble abode," he said to the policeman.

"Well, you know I have nothing better to do," he said, trying his hand at irony without making a face.

His host roared with laughter. With feigned enthusiasm, he first clapped his hands together and gave his visitor a jovial pat on one shoulder, before turning serious again. In front of the couch was a longitudinally cut, highly polished lacquered table made from a seven-foot slab of mahogany and a huge chair. Mayeye pointed to a spot on the couch. He sat down in the large chair. His bent knees towered over the table's edge.

The massive pieces of furniture were also a gift. It was the way the director of a foreign timber company, who had placed himself under the protection of SÉCOMA, cultivated contacts. Mayeye was a partner in the company and both men not only shared the profit, they also shared the same opinion that a lush, vast, and unchecked rainforest was impeding the development of the country. The profit was seen as fair compensation for their efforts to change the situation.

On the wall, behind and above the couch, hung the famous portrait of Che Guevara by Alberto Korda, his somewhat captivating version of *Guerillero Heroico*. Mayeye was proud of his father's involvement with the revolutionary and saw it as his duty to preserve the heritage. He never missed an opportunity to praise the heroic struggle of the Congolese revolution against the government at the time. Che Guevara had his own thoughts on his Congolese associates.

Back in the '60s, Kabila senior was already a leader of the Congolese opposition troops. First, young Kabila fought Moise Tsombé and after his defeat, against Mobutu. He, however, preferred to use his combat skills in the nightclubs of Dar es Salaam in Tanzania, his place of exile, instead of at the front with his revolutionary army. Soon, he needed help. His reputation dwindled. In 1965, in order to impart higher military professionalism in the Congolese revolution, Fidel Castro sent Cuban military advisers into the Congo under the leadership of Che Guevara. Kabila's fighters and Cuban advisers failed miserably. Later on, Che Guevara made a note on Kabila in his diary "The African Dream" that Kabila enjoyed too much alcohol and women.

Another entry, at the end of the mission when pressure was mounting and frustration had set in, he accused the Congolese revolutionary soldier of being the most pathetic fighter he had ever encountered.

The assessment of the fighting skills was certainly due to the anger he felt over the revolution's slow progress. His records indicated that the Congolese couldn't quite grasp the notion of revolutionary thought. Che Guevara had a difficult time explaining what should be fought for.

From the backroom, a door opened and a pretty, young woman appeared carrying a tray from which she served Mützig Beer from the Bralirwa Brewery in the neighboring Rwandan city of Gisenyi with a cheerful smile.

Joseph Likongo was still relatively young compared to his position. In keeping with his character, he wasn't reserved toward young women. His charm was public knowledge and he was well liked and respected. Since his female companion, an African employee of MONUC, lost her life, he never again became romantically involved. In spite of his position, which could open doors for him to all kinds of worldly pleasures available in the numerous establishments of Goma, he was strictly conservative in this regard and didn't tolerate his men stepping over the line either. This attribute made him stand apart from most men in this country, where you had the feeling that even orchids reeked of testosterone. A report from the UN stated that the northern and southern areas around Lake Kivu were the world's most dangerous places for women to live. That was probably before it became public that men were also rape victims. Joseph was familiar with the report and knew most of it spoke the truth. Knowing this, he had even more appreciation and respect for the incredible exuberance of the women of the Congo, who represented the still existing normality. A constant dance on the volcano, wherein on several occasions, the erupted Nyiragongo has demanded the least amount of sacrifices.

Joseph thanked the young woman, returned an unpretentious smile, and leaned back.

Mayeye opened the conversation by coming right to the point. "I don't want any problems with the government, we already have enough. He needed guards and hired a couple of my men, which he paid for. Other than that, I have no business dealings with him. I know he and three employees produced nature films. That's all I know. I never had any interest in learning about his other dealings."

"So, am I to understand he had other business dealings? Hm, you are usually so inquisitive about everything going on around here. You really have no idea? Are you sure?"

Likongo had doubt written on his face, which didn't escape Mayeye. At least now, his initial somewhat defensive attitude had lessened. The *crocodile*, as he referred to him in his head, leaned forward, took off his glasses, and looked his visitor straight in the eyes. His right index finger pointed at the commander.

"I hope you don't get the wrong impression. His death is unfortunate, but I cannot help you."

Unperturbed, Likongo held his gaze.

"Okay, calm down, I'm only trying to shed some light on the matter, that's all."

"I just want to reiterate: I'm not responsible for every murder committed here. What about his two associates in Goma? I take it you already interviewed them? They should know about Darcy's business dealings."

Joseph refrained from commenting on his *every murder* gaffe.

"According to the statements of the two employees in Goma, they only know about the film production company. It is being investigated. As for the two employees, at the moment they are under guard and cannot leave the city."

"Are they aware Darcy was murdered?"

"No yet, but that will soon change. So far they only seem surprised they haven't heard from their boss yet."

"Okay, so what's your plan?"

"To sit back and watch. Before long I reckon the Rwandans will drop the case and file it under unsolved. That's when my superiors will decide whether the case requires my attention."

"I heard he had a mask on his face. Everyone will believe it was a ritual murder and perhaps it was one. Actually, that would be to our advantage. The investigation would come to a standstill. Given the current situation, I doubt anyone is willing to investigate all the villages."

"The villagers are only too happy there is a lull in the constant raids by certain bandits. I don't think they would ask for more trouble by killing a white man and then presenting the corpse with such an adornment."

Likongo knew the speaker had once been involved with Nkunda and his men in such raids. Being reminded of it was met with anger and he hissed at the policeman.

"What is this? Enough with the innuendos, that's not the issue here."

The commander nodded and rose at once. "It's not, but your past doesn't exactly exclude you from the list of suspects."

Mayeye's eyes narrowed. He rose and escorted the police officer to the door.

"Joseph, I'm warning you. Keep me out of this

affair."

"Why should I? Apparently, you have nothing to hide; therefore, you'll have no trouble. Besides, I'm afraid that decision is out of my hands. Sooner or later, the Rwandans will come across your name. Your ties to Darcy automatically make you a suspect."

As he was leaving the building, he remembered Mayeye only inquired about two of the dead man's employees even though he knew Darcy had three. The whereabouts of the third employee, a German, apparently didn't concern him.

I'd bet my uniform he knows more than he admitted. Likongo got in his car and drove off. Mayeye glared angrily at the vehicle until it disappeared in a cloud of dust. He was a control freak and the Rwandans involvement presented him with situation he had no control over. Somehow, he knew he could not avoid this problem, so he decided to change it. Instinctively, he turned his head toward Mount Nyiragongo. A few gray clouds swelled announcing the next rainy season. This year it would start much earlier. Without paying any attention to the saluting sentry at the door, he walked straight back into his house.

Sunday. After breakfast, Chantal tried to persuade her husband to attend mass with her at the Catholic Church of St. Michael, however, Bosco turned her down. She called a taxi and left with the two youngest children. Clad in athletic clothes, Grégoire disappeared to play basketball with friends. Normally, Bosco took every opportunity to spend time with his family, yet there were days where he simply felt the need to be alone. His mind was occupied with the deceased. Who or what would bring them results in this case?

He sat down at his desk and summarized:

Facts:
- White male, blond hair
- Tall, athletic
- Head injuries
- Severed legs
- Split skull (like Dian Fossey)
- Face covered with wooden mask
- Old scar on right upper arm
- Tattoo of a red rooster on the left upper arm
- Little evidence at the scene

Questions:
- Motive?
- Nationality?
- Mask?
- Ritual? Commodity trading?
- Murder instrument(s)?
- Legionnaire, businessman, NGO, tourist?

Before he could gather his thoughts, his cell phone played *Inzinzi*, telling him Théo wanted to speak with him. For a brief second, he ruminated on all the advances in telecommunications technology.

The main focus in Rwanda, together with American help, had been the mobile radio network while the landline network had been neglected. However, this didn't only apply to Rwanda, the entire continent's telecommunications development technology had made a one hundred and fifty-year leap.

"Théo, anything new?"

"No, actually we're stuck at the moment. Kigali has instructed us to transfer the corpse to pathology. We don't have the equipment to perform a proper autopsy. I'm optimistic and feel it will present us with a few more clues. The doctor even mentioned he wouldn't have wanted to find himself in a quarrel with the deceased when he was still alive. The man was in incredible shape. This case is mysterious. I haven't mentioned your name, but I presume you'll be notified soon by the authorities."

"I admit, at the moment, I'm also at odds," Bosco replied. "We really should talk about how we're going to approach our Congolese colleagues. I'm not sure the *PG* wants to officially pursue it."

"Nonetheless, I have a way to unofficially gather preliminary information in Goma. The man's name is Prince; he's a Congolese from South Kivu and 25 years old. At the age of twelve, Madame Carr from the *imbabazi* orphanage took him in. He stayed until he turned eighteen. That's when he found a job in Cyangugu as a car mechanic. He must have made good use of that time and developed his skills."

Once again, Bosco scribbled a mask on a piece of paper.

"How do you know the young man?"

"I met him through Vana. She found him injured on the ground, extremely disheveled, and his body emaciated, so she brought him to Ross Carr."

"Is he Congolese?"

"He comes from the eastern Congo; I believe he's Banyarwanda."

"And, is he reliable?"

"Yes, I believe he is. From time to time, he gets involved in somewhat questionable activities, providing he can execute them without placing himself in danger, but other than that, his references check out. And, he's always well-informed."

"What's he doing at the moment?"

"He's a chauffeur for *wazungu* and wealthy Africans. If required he even uses his own vehicle. He is considered an extremely skilled driver and has never been involved in an accident. He's also acquainted with Joseph and receives jobs from him."

Rosamond Carr was an American who had immigrated to Rwanda when she was a young woman. After her separation from her husband, she founded Farm Mugongo to grow chrysanthemums for pyrethrum extraction, a natural insecticide. During that time, she was also an important friend to primatologist Dian Fossey, with whom she maintained an intense correspondence. In 1994, once the riots started, she was forced to leave the country, but eventually returned and established the *imbabazi* orphanage. She had a house in Gisenyi, where the orphanage was originally located. However, it wasn't long before she relocated the orphanage to her former farm in Mugongo at the foot of Mount Karisimbi.

Bosco couldn't decide. He knew there were a few informants in the border region who worked for his colleagues at Crime Intelligence. Yet, getting them to collaborate would be problematic. They were obsessed with, and almost exclusively devoted to, hunting down the scattered members and supporters of the *interahamwe*. Ever since Kabila had sent the Rwandan military home, relations with the government in Kinshasa were extremely tense. Most colleagues kept their distance from Crime Intelligence because they were already paranoid enough as it was.

"I think it's better to inform the procecutor beforehand and see if he agrees to let Prince obtain information. The entire affair is just too risky and if it becomes public, it might cause diplomatic problems," Bosco suggested.

Théo had no objections, so they decided to wait until Bosco had talked to the *General*.

"Mugambage! Listen, Jean-Bosco. A murder case in Gisenyi needs to be solved. The matter is quite delicate and top priority. Please come see me at once, we need to discuss something," the prosecutor general told Bosco when he answered the telephone early Monday morning just as he arrived at his office.

He had expected the call and refrained from asking the *PG* for an explanation, something that was even under normal circumstances not advisable. It wasn't until after a certain period of cooperation, Bosco realized, quite to his surprise, that he enjoyed certain privileges without having been aware of them.

"I'll be right over, Sir."

Bosco made his way to the nearby NPPA on Boulevard de l'Umuganda. After a brief welcome nod from the office manager, he immediately entered Mugambage's spacious office.

Summons to see the *General* were often fateful. He was feared as a merciless interrogation strategist who was unrivaled. It never took long to determine if someone had something to hide. He literally could take suspects apart until they confessed. This rang especially true for uncooperative visitors who were personally interrogated in connection to political crimes. In his defense, it was necessary to acknowledge that *PG* was impartial and he ignored a suspect's reputation, rank, or social standing. At times, he had to interrogate ministers who had been accused of, for example, corruption, and even they didn't receive preferential treatment. The nationwide campaign against corruption, which he led, was one of the most remarkable features of the Kagame administration. This was also well received abroad. Many donor countries had a problem justifying financial assistance to the mainly corrupt elite of Africa. Thankfully, Rwanda, in this respect, was an exception. It had already ratified the UN Convention against Corruption. Corruption, although not entirely preventable, was rigorously pursued. The political path of Rwanda was occasionally the subject of discussions between Bosco and Ariane, where she often voiced stark criticism. To Ariane's annoyance, Bosco usually countered by mentioning the UN Convention. Germany presumptuously took it upon itself to make use of the German Agency for International Cooperation (GIZ), in order to teach other countries Good Governance, yet it had no intention of ratifying the agreement. That placed the Germans on par with countries such as Syria and North Korea, both of which also refused to ratify it.

Today, *PG* immediately showed his visitor to the conference table surrounded by six of the finest upholstered leather chairs. His kitchen staff had already prepared a tray with two cups and a pot of Rwandan Arabica coffee. The *General*, still standing, personally filled the cups himself, an honor that at least deserved an acknowledgment with a remark about the excellent flavor. Mugambage owned a plantation and served his own brand – naturally, export quality.

"Like I said, the murder of the foreigner in Gisenyi is delicate and requires immediate action."

Sitting down now, Bosco took a sip from his cup but refrained from commenting. *What murder isn't a delicate?*

"Therefore," Mugambage continued, pushing a file across the table, "I have decided that not only will you be in charge of the investigation of this case but, in accordance with Article 52 of the Organic Law No. 15, you will also assume the function of investigating prosecutor. In plain English, I'm making you my deputy. All involved have already been informed: your supervisor, the commissioner, as well as the inspector general. You report directly to me. The forensic report isn't in yet."

Bosco nearly made the mistake of asking for preliminary details, which he already knew, when the *General* continued, "I can save myself from explaining the particulars since you already know," he said with a cryptic smile.

Bosco was sure Théo hadn't said anything about his presence in Gisenyi, but considering the crowd of spectators at the scene of the crime it was not surprising his appearance had become known. He smiled sheepishly.

"I would like your permission to use an informant in Goma. He comes highly recommended by Inspector Mugisha. He might come in handy at the beginning of the investigation. Otherwise, it's likely we'll become stuck," Bosco replied. After a brief pause he added, "We believe it's still too early to involve our colleagues in Goma. But, if we involve an informant we might run the risk of creating political turmoil."

Once again, the *General* proved to be decisive and pragmatic.

"Don't you worry about that, we know of a few Congolese informants in Kigali who can take the blame if there are problems. But, your colleague in Goma, Commander Likongo, is not really known to toe the line of bureaucracy. Anyway, use your informant if you think it's prudent."

4

"The dead man was found here."

The conference room of the CID featured a large wall map of Rwanda and the Kivu region in the scale of 1:50,000. Bosco used the antenna of a discarded portable radio as a pointer to indicate the location of the murder victim.

Every CID colleague was present. Bosco had already gone over the previous findings with them. Everyone had their own file with all summarized facts from the prosecutor's office. It didn't matter that each colleague had made his own notes on the case, the prosecutor demanded everyone have the same official written version.

"That's all for the time being. Everyone study all the clues we have so far." Bosco concluded his briefing. "I think it wouldn't hurt for us to drive to the forensic laboratory in Kigali and have Natalia Baranyanca tell us her findings in person. She's already expecting us."

After a short ride in Bosco's official car, during which each was in deep thought, they reached the Kigali Forensic Laboratory in the Nyarugenge district, the city center.

The corpse lay on a mobile, height-adjustable, stainless steel autopsy table. Florescent light lit the scene. The Y-incision necessary to perform an autopsy was already sutured. The lower torso was covered with a cloth, the stumps of the severed legs sticking out. None of the visitors were immune to the morbid atmosphere of the room.

Natalia Baranyanca came from an old aristocratic Tutsi family in Burundi. Her family members had been persecuted and some even murdered during the ethnically motivated unrest between Hutu and Tutsi. Part of her relatives fled abroad and their descendants grew up in exile all over the world.

"How nice to see you all here together for a change," she said, welcoming her colleagues from the CID. Bosco introduced her to Ariane, who was still a stranger to her. While the women briefly chatted about Natalie's stay in Germany, the others examined the corpse. Once the women joined them, Natalia briefly consulted her notes.

"I ... cannot hide the fact that this corpse gives us a glimpse into some past dark times. I haven't heard of a case recently that equals such frenzied violence, at least not here in Rwanda. We, as is apparent in the Gisenyi police report, also believe the site where the body was found isn't the actual crime scene. We should know more once the findings of the forensic examination and lab analysis, as well as certain clues from the crime scene reconstruction come in."

After a brief pause she continued.

"The dead man is around sixty, male, white, overall height – approximately six feet, give or take an inch. The eyes are blue, the body is muscular and toned. Considering rigor mortis hadn't set in yet when the body was discovered, we can narrow down the time of death. Under normal conditions, rigor mortis sets in sometime between six and ten hours. Taking into account the current prevailing night temperatures we're experiencing, that narrows down the time. And the norm, for rigor mortis to subside would be after twenty-four hours. So, assuming rigor mortis had already set in at six hours that would place the time of death within in a time frame of around thirty hours before the corpse was found." She took another brief pause. "Any questions so far?"

"Can the time of death be further reduced by taking the body's rectal temperature?" Ariane inquired.

"Yes, to some extent. This method can be used within the first twenty-four hours after death, but it requires consistent ambient temperature, which wasn't the case. A doctor in Gisenyi took the rectal temperature, which registered at eighty-two point four degrees Fahrenheit. The normal temperature of a living body is ninety-eight point six degrees. Moreover, the body temperature didn't drop below the ambient temperature of sixty-eight degrees at the scene. So, at an average temperature loss of one point eight degrees per hour, it would make the time of death at least nine hours prior to determining the body temperature."

Everyone had their eyes glued to the question mark next to the highlighted temperature in the KFL report.

"Okay, what does all the other evidence tell us?"

"Well, *livor mortis* wasn't all that pronounced due to substantial blood loss. When a body is turned over, *livor mortis* is subject to gravity. This process only takes place within a period of up to a maximum of twelve hours after death. And, moving livor mortis by pushing it with a finger was also no longer possible. This can be done up to twenty hours after the time of death. At least nothing contradicts the regular temperature method."

Natalia paused again to give her audience a chance to collect their thoughts.

Bosco cleared his throat and recapped. "In essence, the man was murdered sometime between August twelfth and thirteenth, most likely during the night."

"That's what I would conclude from the findings."

The medical examiner consulted her notes again.

"The man is probably Belgian, perhaps a Walloon nationalist."

She looked at the group and saw expressions of puzzlement, so she quickly added, "I'm referring to the tattoo. It is not the Gallic rooster as previously suspected but the heraldic animal of Wallonia, the *Coq Hardi*, the bold rooster."

Most former colonies continued cultivating good relations with their previous colonial masters. As strange as it might seem, this was nothing more than pure pragmatism. All colonialists where white people, at least that was the general consensus, so they might as well deal with someone they already knew, if need be. They knew each other and dealing with each other was familiar. Like the Portuguese in Angola and Guinea Bissau or the French in Senegal, many Belgians were once again active in the Congo, in Rwanda, and in Burundi, some even moved back for good.

No one commented.

"In the wounds of the severed legs, the impurities found were identified as sand. We had a few samples examined by the Geochemistry and Mineralogy Laboratory of the Rwanda Natural Resources Authority. The sample analysis also found traces of so-called heavy minerals, mainly tin ore cassiterite, but also traces of coltan. As we all know, these raw materials are industrially extracted here in the Congo, but oftentimes without any oversight. And, both types of ore do not exist in the vicinity of the crime scene since that ground is exclusively made up of volcanic deposits. I added a detailed report of the mineralogical analysis."

The investigators leafed through their files. Everyone was thinking the same thing. *The murder is connected to the coltan black marketers.*

Since no one present wanted to comment she simply continued.

"The separation of the legs right above the knee required great strength and a razor sharp instrument."

Natalia pointed to the cross sections. Inconspicuously, Jean-Baptiste stepped out of the room. The medical examiner briefly glanced at her audience before she continued.

"Considering the victim's extremely strong thighs, it is difficult to imagine the legs were severed in one clean cut, but, nevertheless, it's irrefutable. What murder weapon was used is a mystery to us. The legs were severed *post mortem*, as the doctor in Gisenyi correctly noted. In addition, the cross sections also showed traces of steel as well as minute traces of lead. That makes things even more complicated because it appears we are not dealing with a conventional weapon of forged steel."

Once again, Natalia regarded the faces of the assembled investigators. Bosco came back to the mineral analysis.

"I understand a murder weapon leaves traces of steel. However, why is lead not seen as an impurity like cassiterite and coltan and instead, is believed to have come from the murder weapon?"

"That's a good question, Bosco. Even I had to get expert advice to make sense of it. Lead does not co-exist in nature together with cassiterite and coltan and neither we nor the surrounding mines in the Congo excavate it."

Natalia's eyes met Bosco's expression of disbelief.

"You aren't convinced, are you?"

"Not really, but I cannot come up with a good explanation either. There's no indication lead bullets were involved."

"Yes, we can rule that out." Natalia took another brief look at her audience before she consulted her notes again. "He has bruises and abrasions on both wrists from restraints. The back of the skull shows a bending fracture caused by a blow with a heavy item. The resulting fall caused a laceration on the forehead. Both injuries caused trauma to the brain."

"Is that the actual cause of death?" Fabien interrupted her.

"No, the blow to the head only incapacitated him for a brief moment. The slash to the head is unequivocally the cause of death. No one here is a psychologist, but I'm sure you're aware facial wounds are oftentimes the result of profound hatred. The perpetrator's intention is to depersonalize the victim. I presume the blow was carried out with a *panga*."

"Just like Dian Fossey," Ariane whispered softly without addressing anyone in specific.

Bosco, who was standing next to her, shot her a sideways look of surprise. Nobody except Bosco seemed to have heard her remark or put it into perspective for that matter.

"The object in question, does it have sharp edges or

is it rather blunt?" Bosco spoke up again, ignoring Ariane's remark.

"Everything points to a blunt instrument, for example, a rock with round edges," the medical examiner clarified. "The massive loss of blood, as I've already mentioned, caused only a weak postmortem phenomena of the corpse, such as the formation of *livor mortis*. The pale internal organs confirm this. As I've said, *rigor mortis* had not yet dissolved and putrefaction had not set in yet. We refer to this as a fresh corpse."

"Have you found any fiber traces?" Fabien asked.

"Yes, of course. The technicians in Gisenyi used scotch tape to take samples from the entire body. You can find it in my report under preserved evidence. We also found coarse fibers of cotton. However, the deceased wore clothes made out of synthetic material. This leads us to believe that the cotton fibers came from the perpetrator or perpetrators. Hair and blood samples were also taken and have been preserved as evidence. Also, we could only identify the fingerprints of the dead man. However, blood samples taken indicate a second blood group, presumably from the perpetrator. Needless to say, we cannot do anything with the DNA analysis unless we have comparative samples."

Natalia again consulted her notes briefly.

"The bite marks on the arm look rather interesting, even though they are already healed."

She turned towards the corpse and lifted its left arm for all to see. The bite marks clearly match those of a human set of teeth.

"We often see this in rape cases," Ariane

commented.

"Correct," the medical examiner replied, "but the wound has long since healed and we didn't find any evidence suggesting the man had sexual contact shortly before his death."

"But, we should check on that," Fabien said. "He could be a rapist and when he attempted to rape another woman, she knocked him unconscious with a rock before sexual contact occurred."

"That is a possibility, but I find it difficult to imagine a woman went ahead and split his skull as well as severed his legs instead of immediately concentrating on getting away," Ariane pointed out.

"What reason could anyone have for cutting off the legs of an already dead body? As far as I know, a sadist would have done it differently," Alphonse stated.

"Okay, that brings us back to a ritual murder," Bosco remarked, yet his voice lacked proper conviction.

"Well, my dear colleagues, I leave it in your capable hands to make that determination. The perpetrator or perpetrators didn't care if the body could be identified, otherwise, they would have cut off his hands and his head as well. One more thing, the corpse is missing a small tuft of hair at the back of his scalp, like it became stuck on something during transport and then was ripped off when the corpse was moved. I sent you the fingerprints and DNA analysis via e-mail. Okay, that's all I got. You know how to reach me if any other questions arise. Let me know when you're planning to have another nice evening at *La Galette*. You know, even I enjoy the company of the living every now and then."

They said their goodbyes and headed back to the

CID where they gathered in Bosco's office.

"Okay, we need to investigate three possible leads. I have to admit, the fact that traces of coltan were found clearly suggests only one lead, which we'll give priority. Nevertheless, considering the peculiar circumstances of the murder, I also want to follow up on the bite marks. We cannot exclude a retaliatory act of revenge. Plus, we have to establish the origin and significance of the mask. Okay, let's split up the tasks." When no one spoke up Bosco continued, "Ariane and Fabien, would you please look into the bite mark. I think we might get better results if a woman conducts the interviews. I know it's a long shot, but as long as the coltan lead isn't confirmed I'd like to pursue all possible leads."

Ariane sighed. "Acts of rapes are quite common in the northern and southern regions surrounding Lake Kivu and they have been going on for ages. Where do you suggest we start?"

"Well, since it involves a *mzungu* I think you have a good chance of making headway. You should drive to Bukavu and make inquiries at the shelter for abused women. Wait until we have contacted the police in Goma and Bukavu. Regardless, we also have to ask around in our neck of the jungle. For the time being, start making inquiries here. Let's presume the deceased had dealings here or in Goma, which means he crossed the border on a regular basis, as do many foreigners."

Ariane and Fabien showed little enthusiasm as they got up. They knew perfectly well what their investigation had in store for them. It would mean conducting endless tedious interviews of women who were extremely introverted and in the end, most of their statements wouldn't amount to anything.

"Alphonse, Jean-Baptiste...," Bosco addressed his other two teammates, "...I want you to follow up on the mask. Go ask the people at Le petit village de l'artisanat and make sure to talk to the Congolese. Also, send a picture of the mask to the National Museum Rwanda in Butare und Nyanza. Also, contact all eligible experts in Europe and in the US and ask for their assistance. Oh yeah, and ask the Rwanda Natural Resources Authority for a list of all the places that store coltan deposits, here and in the Kivu region. Tell them we are looking for a place that stores coltan as well as cassiterite."

As his team left the office he asked Ariane as she was about to depart to stay behind and close the door.

"What do you know about Dian Fossey's murder?"

"I only know the facts available to the general public. There are two authors, Farley Mowat, a Canadian, and Harold Hayes, an American. Both have written an extensive biography on her. Also, her former colleagues, the research couple Bill Weber and Amy Vedder, have published their account of her story in their book "In the Kingdom of Gorillas." In Mowat's book "Woman in the Mists: The Story of Dian Fossey and the Mountain Gorillas of Africa", he closely detailed her last days and her murder. Hayes placed more focus on her affairs in his book "The Dark Romance of Dian Fossey." Before I left for Rwanda, I read everything on her, including her book "Gorillas in the Mist", as well as everything on the genocide and Rosamond Carr's biography "Land of a Thousand Hills: My Life in Rwanda." In addition, I also read various news reports and watched documentaries on the Internet."

Bosco had listened to all the local reports on the internationally sensationalized case, however, other than that, he didn't pursue the case. If memory served him correctly, the murdered of *Nyiramacyibili* was the inevitable result of her inappropriate dealings with the population of the Virunga National Park. Afterwards, the controversial accusations and imprisonment of her Rwandan staff and the conviction of the fleeing American student Wayne McGuire were accepted without objection. It seemed as if no one had any interest in getting to the bottom of things. Even her co-workers and closest friends, who had mourned her loss and felt devastated, for whatever reasons seemed glad the case was finally closed.

"And have those books shed light on something we are not aware of?"

"They pretty much say the same things as the official investigation records. Apparently, it is not widely known that prior to her death, she had been warned by a *sumu*, a wooden puff adder, telling her she was in possession of a list of names of people who were dealing in the prohibited trade of protected species. She kept that list in an orange folder. I noticed nothing was noted about the whereabouts of the wooden puff adder or her list. As a police officer, I immediately recognized two important pieces of evidence. Both, Mowat and Hayes, as well as Weber and Vedder, did not elaborate further on it. It's possible her file was confiscated by the former authorities so they could quickly close the case. Do you think there might be a connection to our deceased in Gisenyi? I'm intrigued by the facial injury. Nevertheless, I can't really see a connection."

"No, me either. Let's simply ignore any far-fetched circumstantial evidence until we have a little bit more to go on."

The call came in the early morning hours and Bosco sensed who the caller was by the sound of the ring. His intuition was right on the money — it was the *General*.

"Jean-Bosco, I have urgent matters to discuss with you. Please come and see me."

"I'm on my way, Sir," Bosco replied brusquely.

A short time later, he entered the public prosecutor's office where he was met and immediately shown to a seat. While the *General* adjusted his chair, he came straight to the point.

"Kinshasa has gotten wind of the incident, although they reacted rather unexpectedly. My colleague there has contacted the Goma headquarters commander, Division Inspector Joseph Likongo, who agreed you could conduct investigations in the provinces of North and South Kivu, of course, at your own risk."

Bosco was bewildered.

"Excuse me, Sir, how would that work?"

"Likongo will guarantee your protection. Granted, usually he's only in charge of North Kivu province, but for this case, he was given authority for all Kivu provinces. The only condition is that we e-mail our results to Kinshasa on a regular basis and that you and your team don't carry any weapons. I personally will liaise with Kinshasa."

"Well then, I guess we limit our activity exclusively to investigating. The Congolese police can take care of any arrests."

"Exactly, Jean-Bosco, and one more thing, the commander has assigned you a driver, a man named Prince. Isn't he the contact man Inspector Mugisha suggested?"

"That's correct, Bosco," replied somewhat hesitantly, for once again he was amazed at the prosecutor general's informal network. He had never mentioned Prince's name.

The *PG* knew his often-demonstrated informal superiority caused mixed feelings among his employees and gracefully ignored Bosco's brief expression of surprise. "Either it is coincidence or Likongo has been informed about Prince's involvement and he's telling us he's also being vigilant. That's how he can control him from the start and Prince is no longer a secret informant. This Joseph Likongo seems to be quite an eminent character. By the way, I held a press conference. The interview will run in tomorrow's papers. Sorry, but I simply couldn't put it off any longer."

"I understand, hopefully Likongo will cooperate. All in all, this is good news and it will benefit the investigation. So, how come he's so forthcoming without an official request for assistance?"

"I've been asking myself the same question. Perhaps they already have more information than we do and decided it was better for them not to run the investigation."

"So, that would mean the answers to this case are on the Congolese side, Sir."

"You're right, Jean-Bosco. However, there are more peculiarities. The involvement of MONUC has been expressly forbidden even if they usually participate in any and all criminal investigations."

"Hm, I wonder why?"

"I have no idea, but that doesn't necessarily mean there is a deeper meaning behind it. Maybe our colleagues in Kinshasa simply want to prove they can manage without the help of UN forces. Anyway, it's not like the central government and MONUC get along all that well."

"It actually seems they really do know more. At least we can rule out that the deceased wasn't associated with the MONUC team. If that was the case, I'm sure they wouldn't have been excluded so easily."

"Presumably, yes. However, if you do require their help I can still arrange it. Officially, the international community occasionally insults us because we all don't admire their model of law enforcement. They just don't understand yet that we have many other problems. But, behind closed doors, they are happy we are the only stable factor in the region."

"For the time being we'll try to manage on our own. When I think of the red tape and decision-making processes of the United Nations..."

The *General* grimaced and nodded in agreement.

"Given our experience with the UN, I'm not all too eager to ask for their cooperation. They already left us hanging back in 1994 during the massacre."

"What happens when we step on someone's toes in Kinshasa?"

The question elicited a smile from the Procecutor General. "Oh, Jean-Bosco, you know perfectly well what will happen. If the results of the investigation benefit the administration in Kinshasa, they will take credit and the official story will be that it was a joint operation. But, if that's not the case, they will question the investigation's results and regard it as a politically motivated accusation. We will pull through. Furthermore, I can only submit the request for assistance at a later date."

"It almost seems as if the case provides the ideal means to offend the Congolese on a political level."

"Oh come on, Jean-Bosco, we are doing that constantly, both sides do," the *General* replied calmly. "I understand your reserved enthusiasm for this case, but don't worry so much. I have your back as far as my reach goes."

Both men rose and the prosecutor offered Bosco his hand. The message was clear: mistakes could happen, as long they didn't compromise the *PG* personally.

"Good luck, Jean-Bosco, and tread lightly."

When formalities arose, Bosco liked to slip into French and he almost replied, *Merci monsieur,* but remembered that even though the *General* tolerated French, he maintained a certain distance from Francophonie as much as possible and preferred to converse in English. Therefore, Bosco ended the conversation with a simple, "Thank you, Sir."

At the same time, Prince was already visiting Joseph Likongo for instructions.

Bathed in sweat, the man got up several times during the night and restlessly paced back and forth in his bedroom. Eventually, he entered another room and grabbed a book from a series of well-used volumes on ancient manufacturing methods. He sat down in an armchair and started reading. Insatiably, like a drowning man gasping for breath, he read line after line until, exhausted, he drifted off to sleep.

5

This was the second time they had met. Joseph Likongo deemed it necessary to send a message to the 'crocodile'. However, the message wasn't good and he didn't feel all that comfortable in his skin. Even his people feared Mayeye's angry outbursts, which had already claimed victims. It was precisely because of that, his unpredictability, why he had to warn him. As usual, he was driven by his driver to the mud brick stronghold.

"What is it, Joseph?" Lying in wait, Mayeye surprised him. "Are you going to arrest me? You should have brought a couple of your people along."

Joseph decided to ignore the brazen threat. Despite their peaceful yet fragile coexistence, he had taken precautions and had already worked out a plan on how to arrest people of Mayeye's caliber. However, that time hadn't yet arrived.

"I just stopped by to warn you. We didn't anticipate that Kinshasa and Kigali would agree to the Rwandan police conducting the investigation in our area. I have been ordered to give assistance to Chief Inspector Kabeera and his team from Kigali, as well as to Inspector Mugisha from Gisenyi. Both will be assigned a driver and vehicle. If the need arises, I must accompany him wherever he wants to go. In case we end up here, you might want to be accommodating."

Mayeye held his breath for a moment before he burst out cursing. "Those damn bureaucrats, I would love to kick their asses!" As soon as he had vented, he calmed down again. "Okay, so what could they discover? That I had a business relationship with him?

So what? That doesn't mean anything."

"In principle you are right, but it wouldn't hurt if you had an alibi proving you had nothing to do with the murder. Think about it, Thomas. You and your people's reputations in Kinshasa aren't good. I wouldn't dismiss the idea that this unexpected cooperation will be used to pin something on you."

Mayeye didn't flinch, but his insides were in turmoil. The murder of the *mzungu* could actually become a problem for him. He knew Darcy had good contacts in the capital and through generous contributions, he had kept those people happy. Likongo was pleased to see that Mayeye had turned rather pensive.

"I haven't found anything in his home or office that could tie him to you except for a message on his cellphone. Regardless, the Rwandans will continue to search once they find out about your former relationship with the Belgian."

As will I.

"You did delete the message, I hope?"

"What makes you think that? I certainly did not. There's no way to cover up the fact that you knew the deceased. You are the owner of the building he and his staff rent office space in as well as apartments. And, they hired the services of SÉCOMA, your company. Do you really think this will escape the Rwandans attention?"

"I guess you still haven't dropped me as a suspect, right?"

"I don't think you're stupid enough to display a corpse in such a manner. You are more like one of those ..." he struggled to find the right words, "... discreet businessmen. And that is something that cannot be said about many people in your sphere, especially not the men and their Chief at your company SÉCOMA. Matengo's manners leave something to be desired, to put it mildly."

"Give me a break, Joseph, since when do you care about manners?" Mayeye seemed genuinely amused.

"I have always cared about manners, it's simply that I rarely have an opportunity to practice them. But, let's leave it at that. There is also the possibility the dead man was displayed in such a manner to steer suspicion in a certain direction. If you know anything, tell me now. I merely want to be prepared for the Rwandans visit."

"I really don't know anything and I'd like to state one more time that I had nothing to do with what happened. The Rwandans can kiss my ass."

"I deeply regret that your friendly disposition towards Rwanda has slightly cooled. I'm afraid they will not show compassion for their Congolese brothers."

"Save your jokes for later, I really can do without them right now."

By then both men were standing. Mayeye went to the house bar. Above it, the picture of Kagame hung slightly askew. It usually bothered him when something was out of place, but today he ignored it and made a martini. Since Mayeye was a lover of James Bond movies and the proud owner of the entire video collection, he usually ordered a martini with the famous line, »shaken, not stirred«. He placed great emphasis on sophistication or at least what he considered it to be. However, at the moment he wasn't in the mood for proper etiquette.

"Okay, I might be able to help you if you weren't involved in the murder. You and your men should resist the temptation to come up with your own solution for solving the problem. It seems to me this case requires certain finesse. Your people, especially this Matengo, definitely don't possess this attribute. I'd like to wrap this matter up as quickly as possible," Likongo said, trying to defuse the situation.

However, Mayeye's calm composure abruptly changed. He turned towards his visitor so quickly he spilled the drink in his hand. A piercing glare fell on the commander. The 'crocodile' stepped close to Joseph and with his free hand adjusted the collar of his uniform.

"Listen to me closely, commander, it's not that you might help me, you will help me. Enough already with your suspicions."

Joseph stood quietly and deliberately stroked his collar tab with his fingertips. All pleasantness was gone from his eyes. Mayeye should know better. Usually, the Banyamulenge could rely on his instincts, but today they were absent. A grave mistake.

Likongo turned around, briefly waved one arm, and then headed for the door. "I'll be back, Thomas. You should seriously think about how you will act and what you will say when you get a visit from the Rwandans."

The next morning, news about the murder was on the front page of The New Times. Bosco brought a copy of the newspaper to his office and leaned back in his armchair.

Mysterious Murder in Gisenyi

The discovery of a dead man, presumably a European or American, in Gisenyi leaves many unanswered questions.
The dead man was found close to the border near Goma on the shore of Lake Kivu, south of Grande Barrière. The man has yet to be identified. An accident can be ruled out. The initial examination by Kigali Forensic Laboratory clearly points to a violent crime. The man had crude head injuries and severed legs. The murder, according to the spokeswoman for the prosecutor's office, was most likely not committed where the corpse was discovered.
"The facts suggest the investigation will encounter larger problems along the way. We assume this case can only be solved by conducting an investigation on both sides of the border. Contact with Kinshasa has already been established," Mrs. Umuhoza told a reporter from the New Times in an interview yesterday in her office.
"There are no similar murders in our records. The murderer is suspected of having sadistic tendencies. Nevertheless, all leads will be examined. Ritual murder has not been ruled out."
Police spokesman Dennis Mekombo describes the murder as extremely mysterious. He added that the Criminal Investigations Department has formed a special committee under Chief Inspector Jean-Bosco Kabeera's leadership in order to bring the perpetrator or perpetrators to justice.
"I would like to point out that this case is a top priority. But, the case has no relevance on overall security," Mekombo stated.
As of yet, no suspect has been arrested.

Bosco put down the paper and dialed Théo's number.
"Did you read the paper?"
"Yes, apparently *PG* considers it wise to keep a few

details from the public."

"As it probably is. I think it's time to meet with Joseph Likongo. Can you arrange that?"

"It's already taken care of. He just called and proposed we get together tomorrow at two in the afternoon."

"That's fine. I'll come over tomorrow and meet you at your office."

After a meeting with his staff, where the division of assigned tasks was once again gone over, he announced he and Théo were driving to Goma. Ariane and Fabien, as previously discussed, were to start making inquiries with rape victims in women shelters in Rwandan territory. Alphonse and Jean-Baptiste would inquire about the origin of the mask and remain behind in the office for on-call duty.

Bosco arrived in Gisenyi the next day at one o'clock in the afternoon and went directly to Théo's office on Rue de l'Indépendance. A Land Rover Freelander was parked outside the office building.

"Jambo bwana," Théo greeted him in Swahili, the *lingua franca* in eastern Africa, jokingly feigning submissiveness. "May I introduce you to our driver Prince? Commander Likongo was kind enough to provide transportation. I wasn't aware he was so accommodating, but then I'm sure he's received instructions."

Prince got up from his chair and shook Bosco's hand while removing his sunglasses with the other hand. Although the approximately five-foot-six-inches-tall man gave off an air of seriousness, he seemed to have an open mind.

"I take it you are familiar with the Kivu provinces?"

Bosco started the conversation to gain an impression of the driver. Théo had already told him about the man's abilities.

"Yes, Sir, I've had many jobs throughout the region, Rwanda and in the Congo, and I also know a few roads that are not on maps. Right now, not every area is safe. However, Commander Likongo will accompany us if it becomes necessary to go outside Goma."

"Do you know what this is about?"

"Yes, Sir, it's about the dead man found at the lake."

"Did you know him?"

"Maybe, I haven't seen what the dead man looks like."

Bosco briefly played with the idea of showing the driver a photo of the dead man but decided against it. It would be better to first consult Likongo. They would need the commander in the coming days, therefore, it would be wise not to step on his toes.

"Well then, let's get going. I'm curious to meet our colleague in Goma."

Bosco wondered why he'd never been to the Congo, but at the same time he knew the answer. It's because many Rwandans think the jungle is where the murderers of *interahamwe* roam freely around and that it starts immediately at the border. A glance at the map clearly showed that the gigantic Congolese region overwhelmed the smaller region of Rwanda. Moreover, all the militia activities in the Kivu provinces made the Congo region seem like a dangerous place.

Bosco couldn't stand when someone was prejudice, but he downright hated it when he caught himself doing it. He was convinced prejudice would not facilitate success, especially in the profession of a criminologist, which is why he made a mental note to remain as objective as possible.

Prince drove the vehicle a little over a mile before they reached the border and asked for Théo and Bosco's passports. In less than five minutes, Prince was back in the car, returning their passports. Everyone received authorization from the C.E.P.G.L. to enter the Great Lakes region.

The Autorisation Spéciale Great Lakes was established by the states bordering the Great Lakes at the request of businessmen and a certain group of people. It was supposed to encourage trade as well as allow people to cross the border without a visa.

The barricade was raised and they passed Grande Barrière unhindered. After about another mile they reached the commander's office in the center of Goma.

As they exited the vehicle, Joseph Likongo approached the car. Théo, who was on a first name basis with Likongo, kept the introduction formal.

"Bosco, this is Inspecteur Divisionnaire, Joseph Likongo, commander of the Police Nationale Congolaise in Goma."

"Come on, Théo, my name is Joseph."

Nonetheless, being introduced in that manner made him smile. Then he moved closer to Bosco.

"Joseph, this is Chief Inspector Kabeera, the current representative of the prosecutor general."

"Welcome, prosecutor. My superiors already informed me you'd be coming. I am at your disposal."

It seemed the commander wasn't all that impressed

by Bosco's title, yet he didn't show disrespect either. Bosco wasn't sure yet whether his temporary promotion to prosecutor was helpful. He had no authorization here in the Congo, but, at least, his title should make a certain impression on public authorities.

Likongo shook Bosco's hand, who in turn refrained from addressing the policeman by his first name.

"Our governments seem to place great importance on this case, commander."

"It seems that way. Even I was a little surprised about the decision."

"I'm sure this case will present us with more surprises. I'm hoping they have nothing to do with politics." *What a sly fox, quite likable, although he's hard to read.*

"Yes, the same goes for me. Please, let's go inside."

Likongo pointed to an older, somewhat dilapidated house, which apparently had been left unscathed by Mount Nyiragongo's previous magma flows. They entered the commander's ground floor office. The room was about three hundred square feet, quite comfortable, but sparsely furnished. Adjacent to a computer desk stood a conference table with only two chairs. Bosco assumed the police Chief conducted interrogations in this room. One wall was adorned with a large map of the Great Lakes region. Farther back in the room stood another larger table with four chairs. On a little side table sat a two-plate gas burner connected via hose to a gas bottle underneath. The furniture was a collection of mismatched pieces from different periods.

As if Likongo could read the minds of his visitors,

he quickly apologized for the simple furnishings of his workplace.

"I'm not really set up to receive visitors. I myself had to acquire the furniture. Our government teaches most of its servants to be modest," he explained with obvious sarcasm while at the same time smiling somewhat embarrassed and cryptically added 'most'.

They sat down at the larger table and Joseph offered tea that was brewing in a tin pot on the gas stove. Prince was asked to stay with the car. Once they were comfortable and each man had a cup of tea, Bosco pulled out a photo of the dead man and placed it on the table in front of Joseph. After only a brief glance at the photo and before Bosco could say anything Joseph surprised his visitors.

"His name is Tom Darcy. We've identified him and I already interviewed two of his employees."

Joseph pulled a photo from a folder in front of him that showed an unharmed Darcy.

"How?" Théo looked surprised.

"I was first told about the discovery of the dead man by my superiors in Kinshasa after they were informed by your prosecutor's office. When I received a photo of the deceased I immediately recognized him despite…," he struggled for the right words,"…despite the injuries to his face. He had supplied that picture when he applied for a visa." He didn't mention the fact he had identified the deceased without the photo. "He was Belgian and the owner of a film production company in Goma. The company is called TD Nature Film Production. Prince had also worked for him. Hold on a minute, you can ask him yourself."

He went to the door, asked Prince to come inside, and showed him the photo of Darcy. Silent, Prince looked at the photo and then back and forth between Likongo and Bosco.

"This is Mr. Darcy. Is he the dead man?"

"Yes. Commander Likongo mentioned you worked for Mr. Darcy before. In what capacity, may I ask?"

"I was only hired to transport a package to Kalehe and then I immediately returned to Goma."

Joseph stood up and used an index finger to point at a spot on the wall map in South Kivu near the lake between Goma and Bukavu. Both Rwandan men directed their gaze to where the commander was pointing. However, they were already familiar with the geographical location on the map.

"Do you know the contents of the delivered package?" Théo asked.

"No, I restrain myself if someone entrusts a package to me. Besides, the package was wrapped with tape."

"Do you know who it was for?"

"No, at the time, I assumed it was for a film crew working in the area. I was given a time and meeting place where I was to pass on the package to another courier."

"Did you know that courier?"

"No, but he was Congolese."

"What were the dimensions of the package?"

"Fairly small," Prince answered and outlined the size of a shoebox with his hands.

He looked around questioningly before looking only at Bosco.

"Was there something wrong with the package?"

Bosco shook his head. "No, never mind. Perhaps, later on, we can determine whether this information is of any use. Right now, I have no further questions regarding the package."

Théo and Likongo couldn't think of any questions either, so the commander asked Prince to return to his vehicle.

"When did Tom Darcy arrive in Goma?" Bosco continued the conversation by addressing Likongo.

"About two years ago. As far as I know, he only produced nature films. I hear he had excellent connections."

"Meaning, he had financial resources."

"Naturally, otherwise nothing would get accomplished here. Each member of the film crew has a C.E.P.G.L.-Authorization as well as a *laissez-passer* for North and South Kivu provinces and all have visas valid for the entire DRC. The applications and certificates are issued under the names of Tom Darcy and his team, Monsieur Piquard, Mister Dallaway, and Mister Krauskopf. The names correspond with those in the passports."

"Three employees; I thought he only had two?"

"The third man, Mr. Krauskopf, is currently on the road. We have no idea of his whereabouts. His colleagues claim not to know either."

"Have you ever seen one of his films?" Théo asked.

"Yes, they are editing several videos in their office. When I visited, I had an opportunity to watch a few clips. It was a documentary on gorillas. One evening in a bar, I encountered Monsieur Piquard and had a nice chat. He told me they were preparing for an expedition into the Garamba National Park to film white rhinoceroses."

"What was the date they wanted to leave?"

"It hadn't been scheduled yet. They still needed to find a charter plane. That's not an easy task at the moment. Look around at the airfield, there's not one machine a sane person would set foot in. Until recently, aircraft were still being patched together from scraps of others, but nowadays even those planes have become scrap. There's hardly any air traffic other than the UN transport planes and the jet servicing Kinshasa. Well, except for a few small aircraft…,"he hesitated, "transporting unknown cargo."

Although Bosco was sure what he was referring to, his slightly pained expression seemed to demand further explanation.

"You know customs needs to be updated. But, that is out of my area of expertise."

"I understand."

Théo also knew what Joseph was alluding to. The smuggling activities going on at the airport in Goma were no secret. And, the corruption of customs officials was also well-known.

"I suggest you make sure those gentlemen don't leave the area for the time being," he said.

"They can't. There's an official ban on departures due to the present security situation. I also confiscated their passports."

"Good. How do you think the dead man ended up where he was found?" Bosco asked. "According to our investigation, after he was murdered he was transported by boat to that spot. If he worked in the Congo, he could have been killed here."

Joseph, who had already thought about the same question, shrugged. "I have no idea. I find it also plausible that he was transported by boat. Nevertheless, I will search the area along the shore one more time for clues."

For some reason Bosco had the feeling this undertaking promised little success. Regardless, he nodded in agreement. "That should definitely be done, please see to it."

Now Théo was fishing. "What about his apartment?"

"I briefly looked around his home and company office. Afterwards, we sealed off both premises. I instructed my people to guard them instead of engaging a security service. They have orders not to let anybody in the office, not even the company's employees. I have also taken the office keys from Darcy's two colleagues, Mister Dallaway and Monsier Piquard."

He walked over to his desk and took a cell phone and a piece of paper out of a drawer.

"I found the cell phone on one of the desks, presumably it belongs to Darcy. I suppose he had two of them. Was there anything in his pockets?"

"No, his pockets were empty," Théo answered.

"The phone doesn't require an access code and it operates on a prepaid SIM card. I made you a list of all the telephone numbers in the phone's call registry. There are numbers to CELLCO and VODACOM CONGO as well as to Rwanda and Europe."

"Have you ever tried a number to determine who it belongs?" Bosco inquired.

"Yes, but with little success. There are no names

listed next to the numbers and many won't work without an encryption code. Every time I called one of those numbers, I heard the recorded voice of an operator, 'this number is not in service'. At the end of the directory are more numbers, each one has the letter 'Z' in front. They look like phone numbers, but the prefixes are unidentifiable if that's what they are. The call history has been deleted."

"Thank you, we will check it out."

Bosco glanced at the list. Instead of a name, each number had a letter combination in front of it. At least some of the country codes were recognizable. He immediately identified two of them, 0032 for Belgium, and 00250 for Rwanda.

"Can we take a look at his apartment?"

"Yeah, sure. It's located directly above the TD Nature Film Production . His three employees, a Belgian, a German, and an Englishman live there as well. Each man has a small two-room apartment. There are two on each floor. Darcy and the unaccounted for employee, the German, occupy the apartments on the second floor, the other two men have ones on the top floor."

"Do you know the unaccounted for man, the German?"

"Saying I know him would be an exaggeration. I have met Mr. Krauskopf only once and only briefly. He's quite an unpleasant type. He looks like the violent type. He's even taller than Darcy, but he doesn't look as athletic. He's rather fat, bald, sports a long mustache, and has the thick wrinkly neck of a bull. The Englishman and Belgian nicknamed him the *Hun*."

"Are any of these three men suspects? What do you think?"

"I'd say they are not in the clear just yet, even if we currently have nothing on them."

"Yeah, I agree."

Bosco quickly looked at Théo and then at Likongo.

"We should look at the building without giving his employees an explanation for our investigation. Is that possible?"

"No problem."

"Okay, but in case we are pressed, the official line is that we're searching for a missing person."

Both men nodded, rose, and walked out the door. Prince was already in the car and started the engine when the men joined him. Joseph occupied the passenger seat and gave the chauffeur brief instructions and Prince drove off. He knew the address.

The drive only took five minutes. The building was located near the Hôtel des Grands Lacs and was fenced. The guard, wearing the uniform of the Congolese police, saluted when he recognized the commander and waved him through, pointing to the parking lot. Prince pulled up in front of the closed office and parked the car. The large showcase windows offered a clear view of the mundane office interior. There were four desks, each with a laptop and externally connected to additional monitors.

Taking the building side entrance, they climbed the stairs leading to the upper floors. As they were ascending the steps one man after another, they heard a door on the top floor open. A woman, dressed in a skin-tight, partially see-through, glittery black dress made of cheap, stretchy fabric that barely restrained her voluptuous body, came hurrying down the staircase cussing. As she squeezed by the men, she shot them a dirty look. Théo couldn't resist grinning as he watched Bosco, whose physique almost blocked the narrow staircase, try to make room for the woman. A man shouted angrily from above, "Piss off!" and a door slammed shut. Likongo stared after her for a brief moment and then turned back to his visitors, one eyebrow suggestively raised. Considering the delicate situation, nobody commented.

"It seems at least one of the gentlemen living on the top floor is home. We should introduce ourselves. Perhaps he has some information we can use," Bosco proposed.

Likongo took the lead and gave the first of the two doors on the top floor a quick rap. The knock was immediately met with stomping. A man ripped open the door while yelling, "Damn it, now what do you…" He fell silent as soon as he saw the three men and recognized the commander.

"Mister Dallaway…"

The appearance of the resident Likongo had addressed left such an impression on the three visitors, they had to pause for breath in order to take it all in.

The commander cleared his throat. "Mister Dallaway, my colleagues and I are investigating the whereabouts of your boss, Mister Darcy," Likongo said in English, without mentioning that Bosco and Théo were Rwandans.

The Brit was about five-foot-six inches tall, quite corpulent, and wearing a loosely tied bathrobe. His thinning hair stood out in all directions with longer strands sticking to his sweaty scalp. While a pungent smell became obviously noticeable, two deep-set eyes covered by bushy eyebrows studied the visitors. He was unshaven and profuse splendiferous curled gray hair flowed harmoniously from his thick neck down his chest, visible through the partially open bathrobe. Any doubt whether the resident belonged to the species of Homo sapiens was eliminated when they smelled alcohol-laden breath mixed with stale cigarette smoke. Packed onto the tiny landing at the end of the narrow staircase, the three police officers had nowhere to go to escape the stench. Through the door, they saw a short corridor leading to a room in such a state it reminded Joseph of the condition of his home after the last volcanic eruption. At the time, he had quickly fled to reach safety. Hurriedly grabbing his most important possessions, he had left behind a mess.

Taken aback, Bosco scrutinized the man with a mixture of speechlessness and disgust.

Well, isn't he the role model of respectability, but I guess even he once had a mother who loved him.

Dallaway seemed to notice the impression he made on his visitors. He abruptly looked embarrassed and started to stammer hoarsely, "I...uh..." which sounded quite apologetic, but then he actually managed an articulate sentence. "I didn't have time to freshen up."

"That's okay, Mister Dallaway, it's only four in the afternoon," Joseph replied maliciously, the sarcasm in his voice unmistakable. The man took the commander's insult without flinching and remained silent.

"We didn't mean to disturb you, but we wanted you to know we are going to look around Mister Darcy's apartment. Where's your next door neighbor and colleague Mister Piquard?"

"I have no idea, maybe he's shopping."

"Okay, do you know the whereabouts of Mister Krauskopf?"

"No, and I don't care. He was never around and was hardly ever present for filming."

"Good to know. So, what are his responsibilities then?"

"Not a clue."

"Excuse me? I thought he was a colleague."

"Yes, but as I said, he was hardly ever here and we never had much contact with him. On the few occasions where he did make an appearance, he only spoke to Tom."

"But you must have spoken to him at some time."

"Not really. He was standoffish and rarely spoke. A conversation with him would have been impossible anyway. His English is terrible. But, we were never interested in talking to him anyway because he seemed to have little knowledge about the movie business. He constantly fumbled around with his little compact camera, a real klutz, and bugged us while we worked. We were happy when he wasn't around during filming."

Dallaway's voice was full of contempt.

"Hm, it sounds like you don't particularly care for the man."

"You presume correctly. I don't like the *Huns*, not one bit."

Bosco and Théo caught every word he said.

"What do you mean, the *Hun*?"

"Well, the Germans."

"Where were you last week, Mister Dallaway, let's say between Wednesday and Friday?" Hearing Théo's inquiry visibly unnerved the Brit.

"What's this, an interrogation? I was here in Goma the entire time. Where else would I be? There's nothing to do at the moment."

"And your colleague, Monsieur Piquard, does that apply to him as well?"

"Yes, he was here also. Actually, we wanted to visit Garamba National Park, but now ... who knows."

"Okay, but let me remind you that you are not permitted to leave the city limits. Remind your colleague as well, in case we don't see him. And, keep yourself available," Likongo warned.

"Um, okay," Dallaway grumbled. Just then, he noticed his bathrobe belt had loosened and more of his corpulent body had escaped. He quickly closed the robe and tightened the belt. Frowning, he watched the three investigators as they turned and descended the narrow staircase. On the second floor landing, Joseph pulled a key from his pocket and opened one of the two apartment doors.

Unlike the employee Dallaway, the inhabitant of this small apartment seemed to have impeccable taste. Ironed shirts hung smartly inside a closet and on the shelves were neatly folded laundry. The bed was also freshly made. On a small desk stood a black mug, presumably crafted from ebony, with carvings of monkeys on the outside. It held a few writing tools. Beside it lay a well-made, black, wooden letter opener with inlaid silver wire on the handle.

Each man looked around the sparsely furnished apartment. There wasn't much to see. One bookshelf held literature on animal life in Africa, among them Dian Fossey's book "Gorillas in the Mist", along with various literature on film production. Bosco grabbed an illustrated book on Rwanda off the shelf and noticed a wooden object hidden behind it. At first, he thought it was a bookend. When he held the brown piece of wood in his hand for closer inspection, he was stunned. He stared at the carving in the wood, a miniature lifelike representation of a puff adder, a *sumu*. The same thing had been placed as a warning in front of Dian Fossey's hut before her murder. Bosco was irritated. He was still having a hard time imagining how the murder of the Belgian was connected to Dian Fossey, but this was the second time he had encountered a link and could no longer ignore the possibility.

Turning to Likongo, he said, "I'd like to take this with me."

The commander carefully took the *sumu* from his hand and looked at it with obvious reverence. Many Africans, including those with higher education, were still mesmerized by charms used for magic. It couldn't hurt to cover all the bases. Even Likongo hadn't yet completely freed himself of this African heritage.

"Do you know the significance of the carving?"

Théo came forward and looked at it.

"Yes, it's a warning, actually a rather traditional one. This means ritual murder is still a possibility."

"Yes, unfortunately, we can't rule anything out just yet," Bosco replied absentmindedly, his mind still on the past.

Likongo handed the charm back to Bosco. "You may take it with you. I will note it in my report."

"There's not much else here to see. We should go downstairs and inspect the office," Théo suggested.

Likongo nodded in agreement. "Perhaps Mister Dallaway is presentable by now and can show us around. Let's invite him along."

Théo and Bosco went downstairs and waited outside the office. A few minutes later, they were joined by Likongo and Dallaway, who was now dressed in khaki shorts and a shirt that releases excess moisture. The designer would have gotten pleasure from seeing Mister Dallaway because it released the man's personal scent mixed with some cheap men's aftershave. The three policemen took it in stride.

"We need to inspect the laptops," Théo noted after they had a look around the office. Besides the tables with laptops and rolling storage containers, the room was furnished with freestanding shelving and a rolling cabinet. The shelves held a few books on filming techniques as well as a plastic folder with a blank label. The rolling cabinet featured a small safe with combination lock. Théo tried to move it and noticed it was affixed in place by anchors driven through the cabinet's rear panel into the wall.

"Mister Dallaway, what's the combination?"

"Sorry, I don't know. Only Darcy and Piquard open the safe."

"Too bad, but which laptop did Darcy use for work."

Dallaway pointed to the relevant desk and showed which desks he and his colleagues used.

"Can I go now?" Dallaway asked and looked at them

one by one.

"Just one more thing, Mister Dallaway," Bosco said, "would you be so kind and give us the passwords for all the laptops."

Dallaway was quick to protest and visibly outraged. "All this because of a missing person? What do you want with our laptops? What are you thinking? I only know my password, I don't know the others."

"Okay, your password then, please," Likongo answered. Dallaway complied. Snorting, he scribbled on the back of his business card in block letters the word, *Tobeornottobe*, then gave it to the police Chief.

The card read:

Festus W. Dallaway
Film Editor
TD Nature Film Production
Goma / DR Congo
Phone ++243 812 354 119
e-mail: mail@dallawayf.mgx

Joseph looked at the card and repeated the password out loud, "*Tobeornottobe*, from Shakespeare, quite an original password, Mister Dallaway. I always thought of you as an educated man. In your middle name, what does the W stand for?"

Dallaway suspiciously eyed the commander, who towered over him by a head. He actually thought of himself as educated, but he wasn't quite sure if the commander was making fun of him.

"Woodrow, just like on my passport and visa application. You should know this, you have all our papers," he answered sullenly with a bit of smugness.

"I'm sorry, the name simply escaped me. Since we've come this far, why don't you write down the e-mail addresses of your colleagues?"

The Brit hesitated briefly but concluded the information was harmless and asked for his business card back. Neatly, he wrote the addresses underneath each other:

darcyt@mail.bel
piquard.andre@mail.bel
krauske46@gxm.de

"That was very forthcoming, Mister Dallaway. Have a nice day."

After Dallaway threw a sideways glance around the office, he grumbled something and headed for the door, his flip-flops shuffling loudly until he disappeared out of sight.

In the unlocked rolling cabinet were two video cameras, gear, and other accessories. Propped up against the cabinet were a couple of tripods and spotlights.

Bosco inspected the cameras and found the slots for a memory card. Both cameras had a CF-card inserted. Joseph, who had joined him, nodded and Bosco removed the two memory cards.

"We'll let Jean-Baptiste play with them," he said to Théo.

He checked the unlabeled folder, but it was full of receipts, camera manuals, as well as lists of office supplies. The cameras were quite valuable.

Unexpectedly, an SUV pulled up outside the office and a man got out. It was Piquard, his appearance almost the exact opposite of his colleague Dallaway. He was slim, almost petite, and around five-foot-four. His face was tanned, leathery, and sported a long mustache. A grayish ponytail hung from underneath a wide-brimmed hat onto his right shoulder. He wore an almost sheer, white shirt untucked, over large cargo shorts, from which thin, sinewy legs protruded. When he saw the men in the office and recognize the commander, he came in.

"What's going on in here? I want an explanation," he hissed at Likongo in French.

"We are investigating the disappearance of your boss, Monsieur Piquard."

"And why would you need to search our office? And

who are these two gentlemen?" Piquard indicated with a nod of his head towards Bosco and Théo.

"These are colleagues of mine."

"Since when do you need help? That's a first. So, do you have more surprises in store for us?"

Likongo's patience ran out. "Let's get one thing straight, we are the ones asking the questions, Monsieur Piquard. We need the password for your laptop and the combination to the safe, if you please," the officer replied curtly and handed him a pen.

Piquard remembered the commander as more affable. He wasn't averse to taking a break during his rounds and having a beer with the *wazungu* in Goma to hear the latest gossip. However, today it seemed Likongo wasn't in the mood to exchange pleasantries. He tore off a piece of paper from a grocery bag and wrote down his password, 'tarantula', and the combination, 2399. Scowling, he handed the note to the commander. "For the record, I'm doing this under protest, commander. Who knows, perhaps Tom is hiding in the safe."

"You'll be the first to know. Your protest is duly noted," Likongo replied unmoved, then added, "We'd also like to get an overview of your video products. Do you have copies? We would like to borrow them."

The Belgian quickly gasped. With indignation in his voice and an expression between mistrust and overconfidence, he laid into the commander. "Do you have any idea how much these recordings are worth?" Piquard pointed to the safe in the open cabinet. "What do you hope to find in there? You will only find a folder containing a few CF-cards."

"We will give your work the proper appreciation."

Likongo pointed to the cabinet. "Open the safe."

Piquard made a resigned gesture, went to the safe, and opened it. He removed a folded pouch with a few memory cards stored in separate compartments. The safe held no other objects. With obvious contempt, the Belgian handed the commander the pouch.

"The CF-cards contain both clips as well as the edited videos. I hope you will treat them responsibly. They are irreplaceable."

"We certainly will, Monsieur Piquard. However, and I hate to tell you this, but we also must confiscate all the laptops. I assure you we will also treat them with the utmost care."

The three policemen left the office with the four laptops and placed them safely in the vehicle. Likongo handed Bosco the pouch with the memory cards and then went back to the office door. Piquard had a grim expression on his face as he watched Likongo lock the office door and walk away without further comment.

Turning to Bosco, Likongo said, "Please send us the material back as soon as possible if there's no reason for us to hold onto it."

"I'm sure it will take some time to go through everything, but I'll keep you updated on our progress," Bosco replied somewhat evasively.

The guard saluted as their vehicle passed through the entrance gate. His commander nodded briefly.

Breathing heavily, the man, wearing only shorts, tossed restlessly in bed only half asleep. He woke up. *Wasn't it enough? They will come and find me. I can feel it. I have to finish it. Just this one time.* As if in a trance, he went over to a bookshelf and grabbed a volume that showed great signs of wear and tear. He sat down in a chair and quietly read to himself until he dozed off in a sitting position.

6

They returned to Joseph's office to discuss their next steps. Out of the blue, Bosco asked a question.

"Oh, by the way, who's the actual owner of the house?"

Likongo had expected the question and wondered why it had taken this long to be asked. Considering he hadn't been forthcoming in disclosing Mayeye's connection to the murder victim and his relationship with Mayeye, he felt uneasy.

"The house belongs to a businessman who lives just outside the city, a certain man called Mayeye. His phone number is also on the list I gave you."

"Do you know him?"

"Yes, I inevitably have to deal with him when his people cause trouble. But, usually, he's co-operative."

"Does he rent out the building himself or does he employ someone for that task?"

"He takes care of it."

"Is there anything else you can tell me about the man?"

"Let me be frank, he's a gangster who's trying to become a big boss. His connection to Nkunda is well known. He's also the proprietor of a hotel and a nightclub, both of which are frequented mostly by foreigners."

"Is he involved in prostitution?" Théo asked.

"We don't really refer to it as such, but yes, I'm sure he is. We witnessed it this afternoon when we visited the film production company. The young women of Goma conduct their business freely and independently, but not as street hookers."

"I take it they have *pimps*?"

"Depending on the class of woman a *pimp* is not unheard of, but most women are too self-assured and work for themselves. Mayeye had been involved in that business on a larger scale, but eventually withdrew because he profits from it through his hotel. He knows I despise such business, especially when it comes to child prostitution, but so far he hasn't crossed the line."

"And where's the business conducted? Is it organized?"

"Usually in cheap sleazy hotels. Mayeye's establishment isn't among them. The use of those rooms requires a couple to pay a bit more and give the appearance of respectability. The rate for a room depends on the length of time it will be occupied. I don't get involved. We're content as long as there are no violent confrontations between rival groups and drug use doesn't increase."

"What about minors?" Bosco inquired.

"Unfortunately, they pose a problem because they're not organized. They come and go. Oftentimes, it's girls under sixteen, on rare occasions, even younger, who sell their bodies. Even for a couple of dollars."

"Where do they come from?"

"Most are from the surrounding villages and some come from a refugee camp. It is the way they support their families. I keep an eye on it. Once I find out, I put a stop to it. Not all share my sentiment. They simply don't make enough money and, at times, they use those girls to make a little extra. Naturally, the guys know what they earn and promise to look the other way."

"Who are the clients?"

"People with money."

"Foreigners!"

"Yes, they're mostly men from MONUC or the NGOs. If I suspect there's something going on involving minors, I have been known to personally pay the MONUC administration or the NGOs a visit. However, I have no leverage over them."

"And, what about Mayeye?"

"Like I said, at the moment, he has put it on the backburner. I once caught one of his men amusing himself with a thirteen-year-old. Mayeye beat him within an inch of his life and then chased the man away. As far as women are concerned, Mayeye has a soft spot. I've heard he lost a younger sister during the turmoil of war. The prostitution business is currently operated by other parties."

"We also often hear about rapes."

"Yes, it's an everyday occurrence outside Goma city limits and throughout the Kivu region. Unfortunately, this problem recently became even more prominent because AIDS-infected men believe they can be cured by having sex with a virgin. It really is incredible. Are you thinking about the bite mark?"

"Yes, we have kept rape as a motive in the back of our minds. But, a ritual murder is certainly also conceivable if Darcy had kidnapped a girl from a village, then the mask, whatever it means, would also make sense."

"That will clear Mayeye as a suspect. It's not his style to engineer such a display."

"That's probably true. My impression is that he's involved in something else."

"I see where you're going. You mean the illegal trade of commodities."

"Correct! It seems to me this Mayeye is quite a remarkable character."

"I'm sure he is, but he's also ruthless, as well as sly as a fox. He's also involved in the timber trade and the founder of SÉCOMA, a company that provides private protection and security personnel. The office is here in Goma, also in one of his buildings. The business is run by a former Sergeant of the national army, Samuel Matengo. Mayeye merely brings in jobs and reaps the benefits. Darcy had hired his company's services on a few occasions and he has SÉCOMA personnel guarding his place of business. My men are stationed there presently."

"Where is he from? Does he belong to the Banyamulenge?"

"Yes, he's from South Kivu, but has great business connections in the north through his relatives, all the way to Isiro."

Isiro is the capital of Haut-Uele district in the northeastern part of the Democratic Republic of the Congo. The district is not only known for its 'green gold' coffee plantations, but also for its gold and diamond mines.

"How about Rare Earths Elements such as coltan?"

"Perhaps. I think he's Nkunda's liaison in Isiro where he takes care of the logistics for the transport of Rare Earths Elements, gold, and diamonds. We believe he's also in charge of distribution in Goma."

Bosco was alarmed. Nkunda must undoubtedly be a nasty candidate if it was customary to hold him responsible for all crimes committed in North and

South Kivu. The self-proclaimed champion of Jesus, an Adventist, had control of all coltan mines, recruited children and made them into soldiers, and was repeatedly implicated in massacres and mass rapes committed by his men.

Particularly coltan – short for columbite and tantalite, irreplaceable minerals in the electronics industry – promised sizeable profits at a price around one hundred US dollars per kilogram. The Congo's history, which is closely connected to it vast natural resources, continues in a dramatic fashion. It started with Leopold II. who exploited the country's natural rubber and ivory with utter ruthlessness. Then, there were the raw materials of the so-called copper belt, as well as the mines in Katanga province. These sought-after commodities caused disaster for Patrice Lumumba, the man who steered the Congo to independence. Now, Rare Earths Elements set the scene for economic conflicts of interest in the Congo.

Bosco's mind wandered for a moment.

It's always the same old story. The continent's wealth is our downfall. Who will stop this madness?

"Could you arrange a meeting with this Mayeye character?"

"More than likely. He's extremely outgoing and loves idle chit-chat, although, I don't think he'll be particularly talkative about this case."

"We'll see. Sometimes, actions speak louder than words."

Bosco had an idea. If Mayeye was the type of man he suspected, a female visitor might make more progress. Ariane was blonde and great looking, therefore, ideal for interviewing such a stereotypical macho guy. However, he would have to come clean and confess it was not only her skill as a policewoman that was required. He had already complimented her several times on her analytical mind, so he was sure she would have no problem playing the role.

"Please set up the meeting for tomorrow at around three in the afternoon since we won't be back before then. I would also like to bring another team member along. She's German and fluent in English and French, however, she has no C.E.P.G.L-Authorization. If possible, I'd like to spare her the visa formalities. Can you arrange that as well?"

"I'll clear it with customs as long as you send me a copy of her passport. Here is my card with my e-mail address."

"Thank you, commander, until tomorrow then."

Bosco called Ariane as soon as they were within range of the MTN antenna.

"Ariane, can you come to Gisenyi tomorrow? I require your assistance when we visit someone in Goma."

"Yes, if you want, but is there a specific reason why you need a delicate, vulnerable woman?" she flippantly purred into her cell phone.

Bosco had grown accustomed to her sense of humor and occasionally played along.

"You're correct, Ariane. I need a delicate, vulnerable, blonde woman who can make a macho guy eat out of her hand. The man in question is Mayeye, a gangster who is supposed to be, although expressed as a compliment, somewhat difficult to handle," Bosco explained, downplaying his opinion of Mayeye. "Your presence might make him a bit more compliant and get him to open up. Granted, he's not one of those men who think with their dicks, but I wouldn't go so far as to refer to him as an outspoken gentleman either. He might be hesitant if you are not there." Then he clued her in on what they were after as well as everything he knew about Mayeye.

"All right, I guess I'll do without my superior female intellect and instead make use of my feminine wiles. Do you know my hair is actually light blonde and that I dye it a few shades darker? During previous trips to Africa, most of the children and women were fascinated by my hair, but after a while, it simply became annoying. I've never been to the Congo but I'm happy about being freed from researching rape victims. It's quite tedious. Let's see, perhaps this Mayeye guy is attractive, despite what's being said about him, after all, how can he resist my feminine charm," she replied provocatively.

Bosco grinned into the phone.

"I can tell you're already in rare form. And, the shade of your blonde hair is actually perfectly adequate. In Africa, everything not black is considered blond. Okay, I'll see you tomorrow. We'll wait for you here. Our driver Prince, will come and pick you up. Oh, and please send a copy of your passport to Joseph Likongo, the commander in Goma."

Bosco gave her Likongo's e-mail address. Ariane promised to follow through and hung up. Bosco instructed Prince to pick up Ariane and the driver left at once in order to make it to Kigali by evening.

Ariane arrived early, around noon. Initially, Bosco and

Théo had no opportunity to speak to Ariane because she and Vana hadn't seen each other in a while so they enjoyed a cup of coffee in private.

Meanwhile, Bosco and Théo used the time to discuss how to proceed.

"Théo, what do you think of Mayeye?"

"I've only heard of him. Quite an unpleasant type. In any case, we should prepare for anything."

"I hope Likongo comes prepared. We can't carry weapons and have to rely on the protection of our Congolese colleagues."

"Joseph is quite capable, trust me. So, are you sure it's a good idea to have Ariane tag along?"

"She's a cop and familiar with the risks. Moreover, she's hard to restrain. Whenever things get serious, she immediately steps into action. Besides, I don't expect to encounter any problems. Nevertheless, concerning our safety, I suggest you stay behind this time. Should we need help, you'll be much more useful here. Our meeting with Mayeye is around three o'clock. So, if we haven't returned or reported in by seven, you should call *PG*."

"Okay, I still have plenty of work to do here. We ran into trouble with *kanyanga*."

Bosco and Théo sat in the living room briefly discussing illegal distilleries and the business of beverages made from corn, cassava, sugar, and other additives when Ariane and Vana joined them. Bosco was about to take a sip of his glass of water and almost chocked when he saw Ariane. She had changed clothes and was now wearing a stunning suit. Vana stood behind her and seeing her husband's approving stare, urged him to close his mouth.

"Bosco, you may now accompany me to the car," Ariane said haughtily. Bosco rose with difficulty, winked at Théo and Vana, and followed Ariane to the car. She waved one final goodbye to Vana and Théo and took a seat in the back of the vehicle.

Shortly before the border, Bosco had Prince pull over so he could show Ariane where the body was found. Her trained eyes focused on the small cove. She pulled out her digital camera and took several photos of the area surrounding the crime scene.

Joseph had kept his word. Everything was set. Ariane received a multi-entry visa and after a short wait, they continued on to Joseph's office.

"What's your impression of the crime scene?"

Ariane was silent for a minute.

"I'd say the body was taken there by boat. The location is quite difficult to access from land and it's too close to the road. Théo's report states a fisherman discovered the body while he was out with his boat."

"Yes, the fisherman was a sixteen-year-old boy. What about him?"

"A sixteen-year-old boy doesn't go fishing alone. What was he doing there?"

"There's no information about that in the report. He probably was just fishing."

"We should have another chat with the boy."

"Likongo has people looking for him. Unfortunately, our customs agents released him."

Ariane leaned back. "Okay, I guess I can slip into the role of a blonde, gentle woman in need so I awaken his protective instincts."

Bosco remained silent. He knew her qualifications. Among others, she was trained in *Krav Maga*, the self-defense and close combat style of the Israeli Defense Force - a highly effective technique without sportive elements that solely focuses on the immobilization of an opponent. Even a powerhouse like himself wouldn't want to engage Ariane.

Likongo was waiting outside his office and immediately got in the vehicle. Bosco briefly introduced Ariane. Prince knew the destination and drove off. Still quite a distance away from Mayeye's residence, they heard a booming sound. As they advanced, the noise turned out to be an improperly adjusted bass from oversized loudspeakers. Shortly thereafter, they recognized the song, "Shida za Dunia", by Ugandan musician Jose Chameleone and his band. Bosco knew the song well because it was his eldest son's favorite band. Ariane was also a fan of Chameleone's throaty voice. The one time she had seen them at the *Cadillac* nightclub she stated, "My goodness, when Joe Cocker hears that he'll want to retire."

The song told the story of a loser who couldn't get anything right. Even when he tried to hang himself, the rope broke. In the end, while citing Martin Luther King, "Everything done in the world is done by hope", his young son pulls him into a consoling embrace.

Soon after, they pulled up to the protected entrance of Mayeye's residence. The guard briefly glanced in the car, nodded at Joseph, and let them pass. In front of the entrance of the mud brick structure, they exited the vehicle and were met by another guard. He was a brutish looking Congolese in a uniform with the SÉCOMA insignia, who leered lewdly at Ariane.

Grinning broadly, he walked over to Ariane while ignoring the two police officers and Prince, who was still sitting in the car.

"Who do we have here? This will be the most enjoyable body search of my life." He brazenly put his meaty paws on Ariane's shoulders. "I'm sorry, sweetie, it's mandatory."

It happened quickly. Ariane turned one arm with lightning speed outward, sending the guard immediately to his knees, and finally to the ground moaning. As he was about to reach for his gun the sound of clapping hands came from behind him. A laughing Mayeye stood in the entrance in black trousers, a white shirt, and a loud green jacket, and his ever-present sunglasses. Amused, he addressed the guard lying on the ground. "If you touch her again I'll cut off your balls."

The frightened guard removed his hand from his gun at once. Despite the smiling face on the man of the house, no one doubted the seriousness of the threat that presumably had been put into practice on occasions.

With a somewhat exaggerated welcoming gesture and eyes trained on Ariane, Mayeye invited his visitors to enter the premises. "My deepest apologies, it seems I have neglected to teach my men proper manners. Please follow me."

Bosco and Likongo received a brief condescending look. Deliberately stepping over the guard still lying on the ground, Ariane made sure the heel of one of her shoes ripped a hole in a pant leg. The venomous stare of the humiliated guard followed her until she entered the house. Bosco and Joseph followed discreetly behind, but not before giving Prince a sign to stay in the car, ready.

Apart from the somewhat stylistically challenged interior, Mayeye had made an effort to create a pleasant atmosphere for their meeting. Nevertheless, the visitors did not forget who they were dealing with. On the mahogany table were glasses, plates, silverware, and a large wooden bowl with mangoes and bananas. The shelf behind the bar offered a collection of untouched bottles of booze. To his irritation, Bosco noticed the picture portraying the president was now perfectly aligned.

A president cannot always choose his friends. He simply has to put up with them.

With an inviting gesture, Mayeye offered his visitors a seat. He took command of his beloved over-sized armchair and leaned deliberately back in a relaxed pose. The young woman Joseph encountered on his previous visit came from the kitchen with a water-filled glass jug in hand and filled their glasses. Mayeye removed his sunglasses and stared icily at Bosco.

There are three possible scenarios when two such characters meet: they can be sympathetic, indifferent, or they can't stand each other. It was obvious Bosco and his host silently opted for the third scenario. Both men knew it was all they had in common.

Likongo detected the increased tension in the room and smiled nervously. Ariane, who was convinced room interiors said a lot about the resident, discreetly took in her surroundings.

"Well, Monsieur Chief Inspector Kabeera, what brings you here?" Mayeye started the conversation, placing emphasis on *Monsieur Chief Inspector* as if it was a contemptible title. The commander intervened before Bosco could reply and educated Mayeye.

"I'd like to point out Chief Inspector Kabeera is acting on behalf of the prosecutor general."

"Oh, my apologies, prosecutor, I was unaware," Mayeye said, briefly folding his hands. His insincere rueful expression was reminiscent of a dachshund that had lost its stick. Mayeye attempted to smile. "I've been informed you're entrusted with the investigation into the murder of the dead Belgian. What a tragic incident, it's truly regrettable. How can I be of service to you? I hope you don't think me or my men had anything to do with this matter. I'm sure the commander can attest to the fact that we always observe the law."

Likongo didn't react to the brazen display of camaraderie.

Ariane crossed her legs. The movement didn't go unnoticed by the Banyamulenge. He immediately focused on his female visitor, giving her his undivided attention. Bosco had no objection since it gave him an opportunity to study the gangster inconspicuously. Ariane knew the role she had to play and seized the moment, crossed her arms, and started the interview.

"Rest assured, Monsieur Mayeye," she said somewhat stilted, "we haven't connected anyone to the murder, yet. But, given that you had a business relationship with the deceased it is obvious we have to ask you a few questions." Ariane paused briefly until Mayeye nodded slightly without commenting. "You are the owner of the building that houses the office of TD Nature Film Production, as well Darcy's and his employees' apartments. Is that correct?"

"Yes, it is. And the rent is always paid on time."

Ariane used his forthrightness and expanded her inquiry. "Is the rent paid via bank transfer?"

"Are you kidding? You can't trust any local bank. I always send one of my men to pick up the rent in cash and to sign the receipt."

"Is that common practice for all your business dealings?"

"Of course."

Bosco cleared his throat. "I hope you're not evading taxes, Monsieur Mayeye."

Mayeye was momentarily speechless. Even his dark skin color couldn't hide the blood rushing to his head thanks to Bosco's provocation. Mayeye locked on with a hate-filled look. Likongo suppressed a laugh and struggled to maintain a straight face. Mayeye noticed and cast a hostile glance in his direction. He sat up straight in his chair, leaned forward, and went on the offensive.

"Actually, it's none of your business," he snapped at Bosco. His gaze traveled to Likongo and he added a bit more restrained, "But, since we're in the presence of a state representative my answer is a resounding no, Chief Inspector, excuse me, prosecutor."

An obvious lie and everyone knew it. Mayeye clearly was easily provoked, but the visitors noticed he became more attentive.

"But, you also have, or rather, had other business dealings with Mister Darcy," Ariane continued the interview after making brief eye contact with Bosco.

Mayeye reclined, folded his hands, and smiled at Ariane. "Oh come on, *Mademoiselle*, you already know this. His film production company hired the services of my company SÉCOMA, as you are well aware. I'm hoping his employees continue using my company's services."

Ariane briefly considered correcting him for addressing her as *Mademoiselle* but refrained in order to keep the conversation moving forward.

"And, what do those services include?"

"SÉCOMA security personnel guard the office of TD Nature Film Production ; however, currently the commander has replaced them with his own people. In addition, Darcy's staff also requires protection while out shooting films. You should watch one of their films. The scenery of Africa's nature is breathtaking," he gushed excitedly, rolling his eyes. It almost made him seem sympathetic, even Joseph briefly forgot he was dealing with the *crocodile*. "As a Congolese, I couldn't be prouder. I love our wildlife. And, apart from a few exceptions, I am a vegetarian," he blurted in obvious delight while lecherously glancing sideways at Ariane. His hand twitched as if he wanted to pat her legs. Apparently, her contemptuous look was misinterpreted or he simply ignored it. Mayeye's ego had no room for self-doubt when it came to his effect on women. As it turned out, Bosco's impression of him was correct.

"I've vigorously supported the artistic creations of film team ," he added and laughed, showing a row of white teeth.

Quite the actor, Ariane thought.

"Do you know anyone else Darcy was in contact with?" Bosco asked, drawing attention back to him.

Mayeye glanced briefly at him and then gazed upward as if he was thinking.

"I don't remember. We are only security personnel, we don't control our clients. I'm sure you understand, but discretion is an extremely important business principle of ours."

"Of course, we understand, Mister Mayeye. But, perhaps you can tell us your men's last assignment for him."

"I don't get involved with individual assignments, but I believe it took place somewhere between Goma and Bukavu. Capitaine Matengo is in charge organizing and planning assignments."

"Capitaine? He's not a sergeant?" Likongo inquired.

"He was a sergeant in the army, but I promoted him. SÉCOMA is structured militarily. And, it motivates the employees. Granted, he's not the brightest bulb in the chandelier, but he and I go back a long time and he's loyal to me. That's extremely important and they ensure I am not bothered by people. This is the reason I have three sergeants. They can take charge of any extra assignment."

Ariane couldn't hold back an imperceptible smile. *Divide et impera, what do you know, an African Machiavelli.*

"Okay, so how many men were involved with that assignment and what are their present locations?" Once again, Bosco took over the questioning.

"According to the invoice, it required two of my people. As far as I know, they are on vacation," Mayeye lied outright. The two men had disappeared around the same time Darcy's body had been found. Since he actually had no idea of their current whereabouts he didn't want to speculate. It was likely his two men had something to do with Darcy's death, which would cause more trouble for him over the course of the investigation.

"I think they went home to their villages."

"We would like a word with them when their vacation is over."

"I'm sure that can be arranged. I will ask Capitaine Matengo to recall them."

"Just one more question, Monsieur Mayeye. Apart from video production, has Darcy used your services for any other business?"

The Congolese didn't take long to think.

"No, he has not."

"Can you think of a reason why he was mutilated in that manner?"

Mayeye shrugged indifferently and said, "I don't have the faintest idea. Maybe he acted inappropriately while visiting a village or perhaps he ran into a gang when he was filming in the jungle. Don't forget, this is the Congo. We still have plenty of deranged characters running around. But, nothing will change as long as the people in Kinshasa won't govern and develop the country."

He almost sounded pro-nationalistic even though his visitors knew he was one of the forces that feared such development and sought to prevent it by any means.

Bosco felt the man had become increasingly relaxed compared to the beginning of the interview. Either they hadn't asked the right questions yet or he actually had nothing to do with the murder. Nevertheless, he couldn't shake the feeling the Banyamulenge knew more about the case, but he decided it was enough for now.

I'm sure we'll meet again.

"Well, Mister Mayeye, thank you for seeing us."

Everyone rose. Joseph's relief was obvious. Once they were outside, they noticed the previously unruly guard had left his post. Prince had already turned the car around and no one looked back as they passed the entrance gate.

After the car was out of sight, Mayeye scrolled to a specific number in his cell phone directory and pressed the call button.

"Piquard," the recipient answered.

"Do you know Darcy's been found?"

"No, where is he?"

"He's the dead man that was found at the lake."

Piquard fell silent for a moment. He had heard about the dead man but hadn't connected it to Darcy's disappearance.

"Where did you get this information? Likongo was here with two other police officers. They searched the premises and took the laptops, but didn't tell us anything."

Mayeye didn't reveal that he had known about Darcy's death for a while now. "Likongo is working with Rwandan investigators. Stay calm. Is there anything incriminating on the laptops?"

"What do you think? We have nothing to hide. I obviously don't know what Darcy kept on his laptop, but he and Krauskopf were involved in other business dealings. I always assumed he was dealing...". Piquard faltered. It didn't seem wise to involve the other man on the line in that business. Therefore, he didn't say *with you* and said, "...was involved in smuggling raw material. Those two never included us and never talked about it. I don't think he has anything compromising on his laptop. Remember, he was extremely cautious. What about Krauskopf? He hasn't reported in either."

"Hopefully, he went into hiding. Two of my men are also missing. I'm looking into the situation."

"What are your plans?"

"You'll hear from me."

Mayeye pressed the disconnect button. Piquard appeared clueless. Yet, he also wished he didn't know everything he knew.

> *Isn't it enough already? How am I supposed to go on living?* Trembling, his hand grabbed the books that provided him with comfort. His rapid pulse subsided and his irregular breathing gradually gave way to a normal rhythm.

7

Under the yoke of the Belgian King Leopold II and in the wake of the Belgian protectorate until the Congo's independence in 1960, unspeakable atrocities were committed against the population while the eyes of the world watched. Those who delve deeply into the Congo's painful history cannot help but go to Belgium to find clues. Built by Leopold, the former colonial museum in Tervuren, a small suburb of Brussels, is an impressive testament to the reign of the Belgian king. Today, it is home to the Musée Royal de l'Afrique Central, where one the most breathtaking collection of recovered historical pieces of art from the former colony is on display. Today, academics working there were sought-after experts in Congolese history and culture.

Alphonse and Jean-Baptiste were already busy contacting several museums and appropriate research institutions in order to research the origin of the mask. It was wooden and had a menacing expression with crooked teeth protruding from its mouth. Showing photos of the mask to street vendors in *Le petit village de l'artisanat* was fruitless as they mostly sold newer masks of no historical or cultural significance to tourists. However, a few believed the mask wasn't from the Kivu region. During their investigation, the policemen relied not only on African sources but also contacted outside experts, particularly from museums in Europe.

It was the following Saturday, a week after Darcy's body had been discovered. For a change, Alphonse was in the office. He still had some work to do on the missing person case they had neglected because of the highly publicized murder case. New information had arrived from Kinshasa he wanted to check out. His work phone rung.

"Butera, CID Kigali. Who am I speaking with?"

"Le Roux," the caller answered. Alphonse could not immediately place the name and remained silent for a second. The man at the other end added, "Docteur Le Roux in Tervuren," and immediately continued somewhat awkwardly, "Uh, I apologize for taking so long to get back to you, but, unfortunately, I was at a convention. I have taken a look at the photos of the mask you sent me."

He had that certain quiver in his voice scientists get when they're onto a new discovery. Alphonse, understanding what the call was about, replied reverently. "Thank you for calling, Docteur Le Roux. I hope we didn't inconvenience you or take too much time from your busy schedule."

"Not at all, the mask is an extremely interesting and quite a unique specimen. It bears distinctive characteristics that allow us to form an expert opinion. We will send you a written report. Because of the urgency of your request, I wanted to notify you verbally in advance as well as by e-mail, of course, it is still supposition."

During previous investigations, Alphonse gained experience dealing with scientists and was aware of their propensity for minute details. Expecting a long-winded lecture on masks, he had already gotten comfortable but eagerly straightened up again.

"That's very forthcoming of you, Docteur Le Roux. So far, we have learned little during our investigation.

We are grateful for any information."

"My colleagues and I agree that from a purely artisanal point of view, the craftsmanship isn't uncommon, however, we couldn't find any masks in East Africa matching the style."

Le Roux paused briefly. Alphonse couldn't think of an appropriate comment, yet for some reason he felt compelled to say something.

"Really?"

"It's a so-called frontal mask, also called face mask."

"Interesting!" Alphonse sounded subdued. Le Roux must have known this knowledge hadn't escaped the CID in Kigali, but he nevertheless expected more enthusiasm and quickly added, "As opposed to a helmet mask that covers the entire head."

"I understand."

"The mask seems to be quite old. Close-ups of the patina suggest the mask wasn't often used in recent years. Since we only have a photo, we cannot identify the wood, but typically, the material is a soft wood. We know mask carvers only use wood from freshly felled trees, which would make it easier to determine the age of the mask. But, of course, there have been instances when already crafted old wood items had been reused. But, I don't think you're interested in that artistic aspect."

Alphonse didn't want to encourage a lengthy lecture on the art of African woodcarving by the academic. Therefore, he refrained from commenting, certain Le Roux was prepared to give a detailed presentation.

"Generally speaking, determining if a mask's origin is in East Africa is not an easy feat. Rumor has it East Africa has little to offer in terms of art. When it comes to masks, and looking at it in purely quantitative terms, apart from the perfected craftsmanship of the Makonde or even the Yao and Rotse ethnic group in Zambia, West and Central Africa seem to offer more. Particularly noteworthy is the art of making masks in Côte d'Ivoire."

Le Roux was clearly in his element and increasingly excited. Alphonse realized the scientist's lecture would go on for a while longer, so he reclined again with a barely audible sigh and anxiously regarded his wristwatch. He had a ticket for the national team's practice game for the upcoming match against Zimbabwe at the Amahoro Stadium today. He definitely didn't want to miss the game.

"That's good to know, Docteur Le Roux."

"The mask cannot with certainty be assigned to any tribal area. The Lega settled in areas of the eastern Congo and Rwanda. The artistry of the Lega is dominated by masks of the Bwami society. However, these masks aren't used in a classic way like face masks; instead, they're propped up and displayed or worn on the arm. Its importance lies in identifying the wearer as a member of the Bwami society. The mask you found is still unknown to us in East Africa."

"That certainly explains why not one person had anything to say about it," Alphonse's reply let the expert know he was paying close attention.

Le Roux expected nothing less and wouldn't be distracted. "However, we also know tribes had no problem incorporating their neighbor's style into their hand-crafted works of art. Your mask seems to verify this."

Le Roux paused a moment, seemingly wanting to

give his listener the opportunity to digest everything and to make sure he was open for more insights.

"But, we are positive about the mask's purpose."

"Really? In your opinion, Docteur Le Roux, what would that be?"

Alphonse sat up again, all ears.

"The Pende tribe in the remote Congo province of Western Kasai has masks with similar facial expressions; however, they are adorned with straw hair. The easily seen white spots are most likely ritual kaolin. But, the same can be found on other masks such as those from the Lega tribe and can therefore not be used as an identifying unique feature," he added while resolutely ignoring the question.

Alphonse refrained from repeating the question and instead decided to show interest in Le Roux's apparent favorite subject. "Is there information on these artists?"

"That's a good question, monsieur. However, art dealers have been clever enough to keep the names of the artists secret, if they know them. The most beautiful exhibits were exported after the World War I by the colonial authorities from Africa. In 1935, a German, Erich Himmelsbach, attempted to honor Negro artists in his dissertation."

Alphonse realized he couldn't suppress the scientist's passionate explanation. Consulting his wristwatch again, he wondered how he could prod the expert into ending his presentation. With little hope, he launched an attempt and asked specific questions to steer the conversation in the desired direction.

"This ritually-used kaolin, Docteur Le Roux, must have something to do with the mask's function. Is my assumption correct?"

"That's exactly the point, my friend. Kaolin, also known as white clay, is a finely granulated white rock, primarily consisting of kaolinite. It is a weathering product of feldspar, the main component in granite rocks. This weathering only takes place in tropical conditions. There are also deposits in Rwanda. I looked at a geological map of Rwanda. Near Kigali, just across the bridge spanning the Nyabarongo River, on the road to Butare is a strip mine where they extract kaolin. I suppose it is used for manufacturing porcelain."

"How does kaolin relate to this case?"

"*Bear with me*; I'm getting to that. The generally consensus is that white kaolin connects the world to the realm of the dead. White represents the color of death."

Alphonse was excited. It sounded as if Le Roux was finally getting to the pertinent information.

"The mask's vicious and terrifying expression as well as its protruding teeth are quite common and suggest one purpose."If they would be talking in person the scientist could've seen Alphonse's smile, however, he only heard his quietly voiced expectant question. "And, that would be?"

Alphonse had a sudden craving for a cigarette. He was the only one among his colleagues who hadn't yet managed to give up smoking. Cradling the handset in between his shoulder and chin, he fished for a smoke in his pocket and lost control of the handset. It tumbled to the ground, the curly cord yanking the base after it. Cursing under his breath, he picked up the heavy unit and handset. Apart from the brass, everyone else still used the old German made black W48 phones from the 60s. He heard Le Roux's voice coming from the handset.

"Monsieur Butera, What's going on? Can you hear me?"

Alphonse placed the device back on his desk and decided to forgo the cigarette. "Excuse me, Docteur Le Roux, the handset slipped and fell."

"Oh, okay, so where were we?"

Although he asked, he immediately continued where he had left off. "You see, masks are often used in secret societies, therefore not much is known about their ritual significance. Indigenous groups place great importance on confidentiality. This is less true for people belonging to secret societies, but it always applies to rituals. For example, we know masks are used for initiating young people. In addition, there are masks that represent specific duties, for example, a policeman or judge. Whatever authority a mask represents is thus transferred to the one wearing it. But, the wearer is not solely responsible."

Alphonse heard him breathe with great enthusiasm.

"For some time now we've been discussing the interrelated features in African art. Our previous opinions on the styles of individual tribes are perhaps too one-sided. But, unfortunately, it is quite difficult to find appropriate research material. The origins of masks traded by art dealers are often not clear and researching them exceeds our budget. The majority of African art is made of wood, which poses a problem because in tropical Africa the material is subject to heavy degradation."

"Which means what?"

"This means tropical East Africa originally had many more artifacts made of wood. There is speculation that Islamic influence made its way south and put an end to the art of mask making due to religious reasons. This also rings true for Christianized countries such as central Congo and Rwanda. What a shame!"

His voice betrayed his obvious outrage.

"You're quite right, Docteur Le Roux."

Without asking any further questions, Alphonse slumped back in his chair.

"Therefore, we are of course extremely delighted to find such a specimen from that region. I would give anything to look at and inspect the actual mask. Unfortunately, and I'm sure you can sympathize, my travel funds for this year are already exhausted due to budget cuts."

This fact seemed to increase his outrage even more. Snorts and huffs were clearly audible over the phone.

Alphonse took advantage of the brief silence and quickly restated his question before Le Roux could start up again. "What was the mask used for, Docteur Le Roux?"

"Oh, I beg your pardon; I believe I've gone into too much detail, Monsieur Butera."

"Not at all, Docteur Le Roux, your account was extremely informative," Alphonse replied with rolling eyes, glancing at the time again.

"Could you tell me how you came by this mask? You haven't given me any background information."

Alphonse saw his chance to regain control of the conversation. In his estimation, Le Roux was a rather sensitive man so he decided to confront him with a harsh reality.

"We found the body of a dead man whose skull had been split in half and whose legs had been severed. The mask covered his face, if you can refer to the shapeless mass of flesh..." he hissed *shapeless mass of flesh* into the tightly held mouthpiece, "...as a face."

His description of the victim had its effect. Alphonse enjoyed a little triumph when Le Roux remained silent for a moment.

"That's dreadful, simply, simply...horrible!" Le Roux exclaimed. "I've never heard of such a case. But, let's get back to the rituals..."

"Docteur le Roux! What's the mask used for?"

"I apologize. I lost my train of thought. Most likely, the mask was used by an executioner."

"Excuse me?"

"As I said, the mask is worn when enforcing death sentences. Whoever is chosen as the executioner puts the mask on over his face and in so doing loses his identity. From that moment on he represents the instrument of justice."

Now it was Alphonse turn to take a deep breath. He had not expected such information. "We're deeply indebted to you, Docteur Le Roux. That is an extremely valuable clue."

"Don't mention it; I am at your disposal whenever the need arises. If you need an accurate determination of age and a certificate of authenticity, we have the latest state-of-the-art analysis and infrared spectroscopy equipment. Naturally for that we would need the original piece."

"Thanks for the offer. We will certainly get in touch with you should it become necessary. But for now, your expertise will be just fine."

"It has been my pleasure. I wish you good luck with your investigation. I will e-mail the summary of our expert opinion to you now."

"Thank you, Docteur Le Roux. Have a nice weekend."

Although in a good mood, he inadvertently slammed the phone down.

Okay, should I call Bosco now or later?

He decided not to bother his boss on the weekend. A short while later the expected e-mail arrived. He printed four copies, placed them in a folder, and forwarded the e-mail to Théo. The Inspector was last in the CID to leave headquarters and as he pulled away in his little private car the guard on duty waved at him. It took ten minutes to reach Amahoro Stadium in Remera, just in time to hear Rwanda's national anthem played.

On Monday, Alphonse went directly to see Bosco, who in turn immediately assembled the team and handed out the folders with the expert opinion of Le Roux and his colleagues. Théo participated via speakerphone. Everyone perused the report by the experts from Tervuren.

"Okay, so he was executed, is that what the report is asserting?" a raspy voice asked over the speaker.

"We didn't really need the mask to tell us that. Every intentional murder, in a way, is a type of execution."

Everyone reread the e-mail, the same information Alphonse had received during the phone call.

Finally, Ariane spoke. "That's not entirely correct, Théo. Not every intentional murder can be described as an execution. Let's suppose the mask was placed on his face in order to draw our attention to something else."

"Okay, and what do you think that is?" Fabien asked.

"The mask is not placed on the perpetrator. According to the report, the executioner wears the mask. It is possible the murderer wanted to point this out."

At first, everyone looked puzzled at Ariane and then at Bosco, who was listening intently to his team's conversation.

"There are easier ways to point something like that out. If we regard this as a working hypothesis, then the murderer considered the dead man a criminal and we might be dealing with an act of vengeance in connection with other crimes. And, if that is true, then our case is even more complicated than it already is."

"This doesn't mean we steer our investigation in another direction," Alphonse remarked.

"That's right and we cannot yet assign any importance to the mask with certainty. Therefore, we continue as planned for right now. Let's disregard the possibility of a ritual murder. As long as there is no concrete evidence pointing to it, we continue following the coltan-lead as well as the bite marks. Have we made any progress there?"

"Unfortunately, no," Fabien replied. "We visited a few Rwandan centers for rape victims. Most of them were abused in connection with the genocide. We even encountered a boy in Cyangugu who was abused by a white pedophile. The man has been identified and he's currently in prison."

"As for the coltan, we're still waiting on the map with the locations of deposits," Alphonse informed.

"Good. Ariane and Fabien, I think it's time you look around Bukavu. The murder case is a bit more relevant in the Congo. I already informed Joseph Likongo you will be there investigating the murder."

He addressed the young policeman.

"Jean-Baptiste, have you gone through the pouch with the CF-cards that we received from Piquard yet?"

"Yes, I have, but there was nothing useful. The two memory chips from the cameras were blank. The memory cards from the pouch contain protected material and edited videos from Kenya, Tanzania, Uganda, and Rwanda. All of it looked professional, but there's nothing there that would help us."

"I want you to take a close look at all the filmmakers' laptops. See if you can crack the passwords for Darcy and Krauskopf's laptops. Once you're in, make a list of the data and a short summary, as well as note recent Internet sites visited and e-mail correspondences, providing there are any."

Bosco turned to Alphonse. "Alphonse, get in touch with Commander Likongo and have him send you copies of the four nature filmmakers' visa data and ask INTERPOL whether anyone faces charges or if anyone has ever been the focus of an investigation."

Bosco's team rose and left the office while discussing the case.

Yet again, in increasingly shorter intervals, the desperate man was driven to his books to find peace during his sleepless nights. Countless hours crept by until he fell asleep.

8

Ariane and Fabien left early. They commandeered a small Suzuki SUV from the police vehicle pool and headed to Cyangugu. From there, they planned to drive across the border into the Congo and on to Bukavu. Fabien was behind the steering wheel. The two cities were connected by a bridge over a narrow inlet of Lake Kivu. The lake water flowed approximately two miles further south to a dam built to generate electricity and then emptied into the border river Ruzizi.

After a quick look at Ariane's visa and Fabien's C.E.P.G.L.-Authorization, they were waved through the border crossing without further delay.

Bukavu, still terrorized by Nkunda and his rebels until 2004, was once again in the hands of the UN troops, MONUC. Unrest continued, mostly fueled by the militia of the *Mayi-Mayi*. The *Mayi-Mayi* (swahili for water), were guerilla troops under the command of local resident leaders. Originally, they were a freedom movement, connected by the *dawa* (the holy water), fighting the colonial administration of German East Africa. The absurd belief promised invincibility during battle, provided they followed certain rules. The *Mayi-Mayi* were feared. In their madness, they threw themselves into the opponent's line of fire without regard for their lives. Those struck down by a bullet had simply failed to follow the rules. For example, it was forbidden to have intercourse with a woman before a battle. However, rape during raids was not against the rules. When Nkunda withdrew to North Kivu, the militia returned. Despite numerous assaults by Nkunda's marauding soldiers, they were relatively disciplined compared to the militias. Once given free reign, the *Mayi-Mayi* as well as the Hutu militia attacked the populace. This led to the 2005 UN resolution with a strict mandate, allowing MONUC armed forces to use deadly force against militias. Together they succeeded in disarming twelve thousand rogue fighters.

Bukavu was the capital of South Kivu province. From a distance, the panorama presented the city of about seven hundred thousand inhabitants with its villas as a seaside resort for the wealthy. Back in colonial times, Bukavu was a favorite vacation resort for diplomats. The southwesterly located city of Mbogwe stood in the shadow of the more than six thousand five hundred foot high towering plateau. The elongated peninsulas resembled the imprint of a left hand with a missing ring and middle finger. The five spits extended north into Lake Kivu. Located on the western peninsula, i.e., the pinky finger, also called *La Botte* (the boot), due to its shape, was the Palais Royal, the Cabinet du Gouverneur, the Palais de Justice, as well as other administrative buildings.

Fabien purposefully steered the vehicle down Avenue Lumumba in the direction of the peninsula. After passing the still visible picturesque Cathédrale Notre-Dame de la Paix de Bukavu, he guided the car onto the narrow promontory that connected the *boot* with the city center. After a third of a mile, they headed in a westerly direction along the coastal road Boulevard Reine Elisabeth. The road followed the outline of the coast for a quarter of a mile and then veered off to the east. After another two hundred yards, they stopped in front of a house surrounded by a high wall. A sign on the plain steel front door revealed the house was the seat of the NGO Mamas for Africa.

The NGO Mamas for Africa, was founded in 1999. The organization's objective was to improve the living conditions of single women and their families as well as to provide psychological care for traumatized victims of sexual violence.

Fabien asked Ariane to perform the questioning alone while he waited in the car. He had called ahead to announce their arrival and although no direct reference had been made, he was left with feeling that a man wasn't particularly welcome.

An African woman answered Ariane's knock on the door and invited her in. The head of the house welcomed her warmly. Ariane stated her request and showed the picture of Darcy.

"I don't think we can be of any help to you. None of the women here were raped by a white man. I guess it wouldn't hurt to show them the photo and see if anyone has ever seen the man. Please follow me."

They entered a room where ten women sat in front of sewing machines. The woman in charge introduced Ariane, passed the photo of Darcy to the women and speaking in Lingála, explained the reason for her visit. The women remained silent as the photo went from one woman to the next, each shaking their heads. Ariane and the head of the house had returned to the foyer and were exchanging a few final words when one of the previous women joined them and spoke to the manager in a language she didn't understand. Addressing Ariane, the woman in charge translated.

"Forgive me, but I forgot there's a woman in Bukavu who was fathered by a white man."

"Is that so unusual?"

The woman in charge cringed. It seemed as if she had said something better left unspoken.

"Well, it's just...you know how people gossip. We don't like to take part in it. But, since you came right out and asked, I might as well tell you. It is rumored her mother..."

"...was raped?"

"I'm ashamed."

Ariane placed her hand on the woman's shoulder in a reassuring manner. "I won't tell her you talked about her. What's her name?"

"Her name is Marie Kamanda. She lives in the Ibanda district near Notre Dame Cathedral. Once a week she comes and gives the women here lessons in French."

"Do you know her actual address?"

"She lives in the house below the cathedral hill with her son and an elderly aunt. I've never been there, but I know she goes almost every day around lunchtime to the cathedral."

"What does she look like?"

"She's about your height and a light complexion, obviously. The women here adore her. She is quite beautiful."

Ariane thanked her and said goodbye.

The two police officers sat for almost an hour on the steps above the main entrance of the cathedral before spotting Marie Kamanda. Their informant had definitely not exaggerated. The woman in question was an extraordinarily beautiful creature. Her hair was loosely pinned up and covered by an indigo blue and white headscarf, with a few strands of black hair escaping down her neck. A traditional wraparound skirt, a *pagne,* encircled her body. As many Africans do, she walked with a smooth gait, proud and upright, the result of carrying goods on their heads since early childhood. Ariane observed the woman closely as she approached unhurriedly.

I don't think I could ever move with such elegance.

She squinted at Fabien, who sat there deliberately feigning disinterest.

From a light-colored face, a pair of friendly blue eyes looked at the couple in the process of rising. Apart from them, no other person waited nearby. Ariane approached the woman.

"Madame Kamanda?"

Although astonished by the inquiry, she replied without hostility,

"Yes?"

Her voice was so gentle it was unimaginable it could ever become loud and belligerent.

"Madame, we are police officers from Kigali and are investigating a challenging case. I was wondering if you could spare a moment."

"Of course, although I'm not sure how I could be of help."

"I wanted to ask you if you know this man." Ariane handed her the photo of Darcy.

Carefully she studied the photo, visibly excited, as if she wanted to absorb the image.

"Do you know the man? His name is Tom Darcy."

Suspicious, the Congolese woman eyed the two

police officers. Ariane and Fabien knew the look. The entire population of Africa had zero trust in government institutions, especially the police. Waiting patiently, Ariane endured the woman's scrutinous look. After a brief moment of uncertainty, the Congolese woman said, "Come with me, I don't live far."

Ariane and Fabien exchanged a quick look. They were relieved the woman didn't ask why they came to her. In silence, they followed the woman down the hill on which the cathedral stood. A few minutes later, they arrived at a tiny house surrounded by a wall adorned by lush bougainvillea. Marie Kamanda led them around the side of the house to the back garden. An elderly woman sat on the patio, apparently keeping an eye on the five-year-old boy playing with a ball on the manicured lawn.

"Excuse my aunt, she only speaks Lingála."

The old woman realizing the remark was meant for her, smiled, a little embarrassed. She got up, went into the house, and returned with two glasses and a bottle of water. Marie Kamanda pointed to the group of chairs.

"Please take a seat. I'll be back in a moment."

They looked at the beautiful garden with its numerous banana trees, vegetable, and flowerbeds. The playing boy squinted shyly at the white woman. Eventually, curiosity won out and he slowly approached without taking his eyes off Ariane. Smiling insecurely, he snuggled between the old lady's knees. After a few minutes, Marie Kamanda returned to the patio. She placed a wrinkled, faded black and white photo with serrated edges on the table and pointed to a man.

"My father!"

Ariane held her breath. The photo was of two men with rifles in their hands, leaning against an open ATV, apparently happy and full of laughter. They wore jungle camouflage and laced boots. Although the man Marie Kamanda pointed to was quite young, it was definitely Tom Darcy. It seemed back then he had shaved his head almost bald. Ariane handed the photo to Fabien, who looked at it briefly and then turned his gaze to the Congolese woman.

"Where did you get the photo?"

"My mother gave it to me before she passed away. She told me he was my father."

"Have you ever met him in person?"

"Not as far as I can remember."

Fabien returned the photo to Ariane, who glanced at it again and then asked, "Is there anything else you can remember about your father?"

"As I grew older and began to ask about my father, she spoke of him. Every time she came back from town, she had money. It helped us survive. She never said where the money came from and I never asked. I'm sure my father had already left the Congo."

"Forgive me for asking, but do you think Darcy might have..." She hesitated because she didn't want to ask so bluntly the question they were interested in. "I mean, what kind of relationship did your mother have with Tom Darcy?"

A shadow passed over her face as if she fought off bad memories. For a moment, the sparkle in her eyes disappeared.

"You want to know if I'm the result of rape."

"Are you?"

"I...I don't really know. My mother never said anything bad about him. Many raped mothers either disowned their children or kicked them out of the house entirely. There's usually no future here for a woman who has been raped. My mother loved me. I'm half-white and I was always considered something special in the village where we lived at the time. She never admitted to being raped. I believe she was hoping he'd return one day. Even if someone believed my mother was raped, we were never stigmatized due to our financial status. I was always able to attend school. She provided me after her death with enough money to buy this house."

Ariane wasn't sure how to ask. Perhaps Darcy had supplied the money or maybe her mother had worked as a prostitute. She decided to dispense with the question since its clarification was presently not relevant.

"How do you earn a living?"

"I have a piece of land in our home village. I lease it to a relative and live off the income. I also give French lessons."

Ariane briefly nibbled on her lower lip. Questioning her was a bit uncomfortable. Delving into someone's private life always left her feeling this way, even if she was only doing her job. It simply was a duty she didn't enjoy. Nevertheless, she was professional enough to know a concrete description of the perpetrator speeds up the elimination of other possible suspects.

"Are you married?" Fabien asked.

"I'm a widow. My husband was killed by guerillas."

The answer sounded definitive. Ariane winced at

Fabian's question. *Yet another Congolese tragedy. Is there anyone whose life hasn't been ruined by those thugs?*

She glanced briefly at Fabien. They silently agreed not to ask any more questions along those lines. Ariane shook off her dark thoughts.

"Let's get back to Tom Darcy. Did your mother tell you who he is and what he does for a living?"

"Yes. Before I was born, he belonged to *The White Giants*. He was one of the youngest mercenaries in the mercenary Republic of the Congo. I don't know what he did afterwards, nor do I know where he was living at the time."

Ariane was stunned and remained silent. She wasn't sure what she had expected, but she would have never thought of Darcy as a former mercenary soldier.

"In what year were you born?"
"1968."

The history of the Congo was, and still is, stained by hard to believe events that no person could have ever dreamt up. The greatest absurdities of all occurred in 1967 during the several weeks-long reign of the mercenary soldiers, the time of *The White Giants*.

After Katanga province gained its independence in 1960, Moise Tsombé, an ally of the Belgian mining company Union Minière du Haut Katanga, was in charge of the resource-rich province's secession from Lumumba's government. At times, he had employed more than one thousand mercenaries for defensive measures. Tired of the wishy-washy UN troops, Lumumba asked the Russians for help, who saw an opportunity to expand their influence in Africa. The Belgians and in the background, the Americans, found it necessary to intervene. They supported Mobutu, Chief of staff of the former Congolese Army, Force Publique. This resulted in a coup against Lumumba, who was deported to Katanga and murdered by Belgian and Congolese agents. During subsequent political confrontations, the UN forces also turned against followers of Lumumba and backed Mobutu, Chief of staff of the Congolese Army. Eventually, Mobutu gained the upper hand during ensuing fights for power and forced Tsombé into exile. After deposing the already elected President Kasavubu, Mobutu only had one problem left to deal with: Tsombé's mercenaries. They were a motley crew of Belgians, Englishmen, Germans, South Africans, French, and Irish. Their leader was the former British officer Mike Hoare, nicknamed *Mad Mike*. Another member was the winner of the Iron Cross, the notorious German Siegfried Müller, in Germany also known as *Kongo-Müller*. With extreme ruthlessness, they defeated the Simba - rebellion, followers of Lumumba. From then on, they continued their uninhibited lust for murder under the presumption of invincibility. The population referred to them as *The White Giants* or *Les Affreux* (the dreadful). No one dared oppose them.

After their leader Tsombé had gone into exile, they feared for their sinecures because Mobutu planned to dispose of them. A few, such as *Kongo-Müller*, left the country. Others enlisted under the command of mercenary leader Jean Schramme and took part in the 1967 occupation of the area surrounding the town of Bukavu. They proclaimed it independent and named it the mercenary Republic of the Congo. They presented Mobutu's government with an ultimatum. The aim: to return Tsombé from exile and reinstated him as president.

The German journalist Randolph Braumann, called by colleagues as *Kongo-Randy*, offered to draft the government declaration. At the time, press reporting overflowed with abysmal accounts of events. In reality, some instances were actually worse. Following a meeting with Mobutu along the shores of a river in the Congo, where corpses still floated downstream, Braumann voiced an insight.

"There is no certainty except that the current flows broadly and powerfully from the heart of darkness into the Atlantic."

In addition, he saw

"Dead black men turned white in the heat."

Mobutu moved with a tenfold superior force and besieged the occupying forces in Bukavu. The ensuing battle caused numerous fatalities, including civilians. Another mercenary leader, a Frenchman, Bob Denard, who was born in Bordeaux as Gilbert Bourgeaux, approached from Angola trying to rescue the besieged, but he also failed to vanquish Mobutu's troops. Eventually, those left alive fled to Rwanda. Although Mobutu demanded their extradition, the then Rwandan President Grégoire Kayibanda decided to let them leave the country on a Sabena flight.

Ariane didn't want to leave the woman in the dark.

"Tom Darcy is dead. He was murdered."

Unemotional, Marie Kamanda looked the white woman straight in the eyes. The melancholy gaze seemed inappropriate for such sparkling blue eyes.

"Many people have been killed, whites and blacks. I guess he took part in it and was found guilty. God forgive him!"

It didn't seem as if she was interested in the circumstances of his death, therefore, Ariane withheld the details. She couldn't help but feel sympathy for the woman. As a foreign body, neither white nor black, she lived in a world Europeans would consider traumatic, yet for her, it was an everyday brutal reality. Was it possible she was a murderess or, perhaps, she hired someone to murder her father? Was Darcy her mother's rapist? It was hard to fathom, but Ariane couldn't and didn't want to form an opinion yet. She decided first to firmly establish the woman's identity.

"Would you mind if I take a sample of your saliva, as well as take a picture of you?"

"What do you need it for?"

"I need definite proof you are Darcy's daughter. A DNA test can tell us that."

"Is it important to you?"

"I can't say yet, perhaps, but isn't it important to you?"

Marie Kamanda nodded.

"When was the last time you ate?"

"Around eight this morning."

Her watch read twelve, a DNA test required no food one hour prior. Ariane looked at Fabien, who in turn pulled two swab tubes from a plastic bag. Ariane popped open the sterilizing tube and used each swab to take samples of the woman's saliva. Her colleague immediately sealed the tubes so the samples wouldn't be tainted. Then they said goodbye and started their return journey.

"What do you think of her story, Fabien?"

"Perhaps she withheld a few things."

"Why do you say that?"

"Whether Darcy had raped her mother or not, we must also consider he raped her as well. It wouldn't be the first time a father molested his daughter, especially when she looks like Marie Kamanda."

Ariane was silent for a moment. She hadn't thought of that possibility.

"Why didn't you ask her?"

"First off, women here aren't known to admit something like that and, secondly, it might have made her reluctant to speak."

"You're right, but it would have been nice to gnaw on it on the drive home. She would make a great suspect if she had been raped. I even find it unlikely her mother was raped by Darcy. Granted, mercenaries during that period were some seriously bad guys, but they had an honor code of sorts, even if it was due to pragmatic reasons. As a rule, they didn't rape women indiscriminately. Instead, they frequented brothels. Naturally, women working in a brothel also become pregnant, meaning her mother could've been a prostitute.

"Back then, Darcy was young and inexperienced. Those guys ran through the bush full of adrenaline, convinced of their superiority. It stands to reason that another man could have put his hands on her."

"It's a possibility. But, if she wasn't victimized by Darcy it doesn't matter what really happened. What matters is what she believes and whether she thinks Darcy was accountable."

"How could she have organized Darcy's murder and transported him to Gisenyi?"

"Money can get anything accomplished here. Even I could find and hire a hit man."

"Are you thinking of Mayeye and his SÉCOMA guys?"

"No, in this case, not likely. They were in business together."

"Okay, but the woman seems to have the means to hire a contract killer, perhaps even with the murdered man's money? I don't know, it sounds a bit far-fetched, but anything is possible here."

Fabien fell silent. They left the border checkpoint behind and crossed the bridge into Rwanda. He drove cautiously along the winding road leading to the center of Cyangugu and was soon on the freeway to Butare.

"So far, we haven't made any progress on the old bite mark," Fabien said continuing the conversation.

"Forget about them for now. We'll wait and see what INTERPOL has to say."

The conversation faded away again, both caught up in their thoughts. Fabien turned the radio volume up a bit. The on-air topic was about the average growth of the population, which for Rwanda was estimated at 2.7 percent. In Kigali, the number had already reached eight percent. A discussion on the settlement policy, also referred to as *slum upgrading*, was praised, yet at the same time, it was also criticized, predominately from abroad. Entire neighborhoods were razed. The moderator spoke Kinyarwanda and Fabien translated for Ariane, but she refrained from commenting.Ariane closed her eyes. Population growth and motherhood; a sensitive issue near and dear to her. On a personal level, she never encountered a shortage of suitors, but none were marriage material and she wasn't willing to be dependent on someone. In the background, the unheard ticking of her biological clock was running out and made sure her status didn't change. An engraved plaque of a German consular officer in one of those countries regarding the population growth in less developed countries flashed through her head. It read as follows:

"The problem here is that men are always ready and women are always willing."

This was considered a racist remark and he was terminated. The situation couldn't be explained so easily, even if it was close to the heart of the problem. Any type of birth control was nonexistent. Men wasted no thought on the problem and women were too afraid to say no to unprotected sex — a reason for the rampant HIV epidemic. And, the situation was only exacerbated by African heads of state who trivialized the problem or simply denied it altogether. They even claimed white people intentionally spread the HIV virus. President Jammeh of Gambia, gained notoriety by creating his own personal herb and banana mixture to cure those who had contracted AIDS and instructed the Ministry of Health to administer his mixture. A look at Africa's situation in 2005 shows how misguided he was!

Ariane and Fabien made only one fuel stop in Nyanza and after a six-hour drive, finally arrived in Kigali. Fabien dropped Ariane off at her apartment on Avenue des Grands Lacs. The guard opened the gate to the condominium's parking lot and gave a friendly wave.

9

The CID made a room available for Jean-Baptiste to work undisturbed on the seized laptops.

When the young Constable had finished his training as an IT specialist, he had applied for the newly created position at the CID. Although he had only completed the basic training program in criminology, he was already a sought-after partner in the CID, given that most of his colleagues were technologically behind the times and overwhelmed.

For three days straight, he worked on the laptops and was repeatedly interrupted to take care of other tasks. The contents of the hard drives of Dallaway and Piquard's computers, to which he had the passwords, were rather disappointing. He could neither find anything revealing in the files nor any useful Internet connections. The search history on both laptops was not deleted. Both men obviously enjoyed pornographic websites. In addition to a few links to various online shops, they also saved the link to their company. Clicking the link opened the website to background music and showed wildlife and nature photos and short video clips together with genuine sounds of animals and nature. A box marked *contact*, connected the user to the e-mail address: NFP@gxmail.com.

No additional contact information was provided. However, they had already received Darcy's and his co-workers' private e-mail addresses from Dallaway.

The findings revealed little, but he did find e-mails for old reservations Dallaway and Piquard had made for a hotel in Brussels, as well as a hotel reservation

Dallaway had made in London. At least the two men had an alibi for that time if needed. There was no evidence Krauskopf had traveled.

It almost seemed as if they operated like legionnaires and broke off all personal contact with their home countries. Both men also used the same program for editing videos, yet besides a seemingly finished video about gorillas, no other videos were stored. Before he could examine Darcy and Krauskopf's laptops, he first had to acquire the passwords. Jean-Baptiste knew most people used easily remembered passwords. The higher the education level, the greater the vocabulary and a wider range of possible passwords. Nevertheless, that still left endless possibilities. Considering how the man had been described, he expected Darcy's password to be less profane than Krauskopf's. Jean-Baptiste diligently worked first on Darcy's laptop. If there was anything to be found it had to be on his device.

As a rule, he first used a program to reset the password, which worked most of the time. Of interest in this regard was the list of phone numbers with the meaningless letter combinations in front in Darcy's cell phone directory. If he cracked that encryption, it might lead to the laptop's password.

He had no problem detecting the type of encryption, although a layman would have had a harder time. The system was based on placing a password at the end and under the row of an alphabetical number combination and then exchanging the above lying row of an alphabetical number combination with the letters of the password. All letter combinations adhered to the sequence of the alphabet, starting with A, and then arranged in order while omitting the letters of the password. The only prerequisite was that a password could not contain two of the same letter. Longer encrypted messages required the use of a coded alphabet. Encrypted names were easy to remember.

Quite unprofessional. Every Boy Scout knows that.

Now, he went to work on the list of phone numbers. Likongo had already verified Thomas Mayeye's number. In front of the phone number was the letter combination Z_CNYWDS. Since Jean-Baptiste was a computer nerd, he had a natural penchant for number and letter combinations. It didn't take long to notice the number of letters in the combination matched the characters of Mayeye's first name, Thomas. The prefix Z was merely to designate its place in the phone's directory. He placed the encryption key under Mayeye's name. Thus, C stands for T, H stands for N, and so on.

```
A B C D E F G H I J K L M N O P Q R S T U V W X Y Z
    D           N       W   Y       S C
```

It took two hours before he had written a small program to determine the password by entering the above criteria.

On the monitor appeared the flashing letters

BISCLAVRET

and the encrypted alphabet:

A B C D E F G H I J K L M N O P Q R S T U V W X Y Z
D F G H J K M N O P Q U W X Y Z **B I S C L A V R E T**

Now, what's that supposed to mean? Is it a technical term?

An Internet search revealed it was the story of a British nobleman in 1170, who, through his wife's betrayal, transformed into a werewolf.

Realizing the owner's first name was used to identify his phone number, the rest was easy. For example, someone named Hugo bore the encryption code, NLMY. Dialing any of those numbers would not make a connection without a secondary code, except for a few cases where it wasn't deemed necessary, such as Mayeye's number.

Jean-Baptiste checked if the password would grant him access to the laptop.

"Bingo," he exclaimed, as he entered the word BISCLAVRET after powering on the laptop and the operating system started.

Using the system's search function to access Word, Excel, and pdf files led him to a directory labeled TD with the desired properties.

A search revealed the contents of the pdf and Word files were downloaded documents from the Internet, mainly dealing with photography and motion picture technology.

However, an Excel file looked promising. Under the heading *Daily Allowances*, were sums paid out from the previous year: $50 USD per day for Piquard and Dallaway and $100 USD per day for Krauskopf.

A second table labeled *House Rent* listed sums of $1000 USD per month going back two years, each with a note, *paid in cash.Those four gentlemen are great tenants.*

The third table, *KBS-Account*, listed five different entries: 5,000,000 – 1,000,000 – 2,700,000 –1,600,000 – 8,000,000 – each in US dollars and marked with a date. The last entry date was two weeks before Darcy's murder. An amount for 1,464,000 US dollars without a date stood next to the letter combination CNYWDS that he had already identified as Mayeye's code. Those were obviously remittances. Jean-Baptiste whistled softly through his teeth.

Mayeye, aren't you handsomely remunerated.

His brain was working in overdrive.

It seemed Darcy had been well off, but what did KBS stand for? Were the contributions to Mayeye payment for SÉCOMA security service?

Always the easiest and obvious first, he had learned. However, usual training procedures didn't always produce results. Meanwhile, beads of sweat gathered on his forehead. It was hot inside the room and the fan did nothing to alleviate the sultry heat that prevailed at the beginning of the rainy season. Jean-Baptiste felt thirsty. After taking a sip of water from a Source de Nil bottle, he placed his feet up on the windowsill, closed his eyes, and slightly rocked his office chair for a moment.

Two minutes later, he purposely spun his chair back around to his desk and reexamined the laptop and, to his surprise, stumbled on an unprotected e-mail account. In Darcy's inbox were receipts for a few online tickets to Brussels, as well as one to Kinshasa.

Then, Jean-Baptiste tried to access Krauskopf's laptop. Halfheartedly, he started entering German words he knew from the menu at *La Galette*, such as sauerkraut, schnitzel, currywurst, but, unsurprisingly, wasn't successful.

It's obviously not that simple.

It appeared the password reset program led to a quicker success because unlike Darcy's computer, the security program had not been set. After several attempts with different programs, the problem was solved and he started the operating system without a password.

As was the case with Dallaway and Piquard, the search of Krauskopf's laptop failed to reveal much. There wasn't much there, no personal e-mails whatsoever. Apparently, the device was hardly used, which could be explained by Krauskopf's infrequent presence in the office in Goma. Compared to Piquard and Dallaway, there was no software installed to show it was used for film production. There were only a few shots of animals, where the quality was greatly inferior to the photos of his two colleagues. The internet protocol included activity for TD Nature Film Production and, as with Dallaway and Piquard, links to pornographic websites. Jean-Baptiste decided not to look and put the device to sleep.

Decoding Darcy's cell phone numbers turned out to be more difficult. He suspected one or more digits of the stored numbers were encoded with a number. The connections would then be deciphered with a simple number. Maybe it required one or two digits, for example, the first or the last two, to add or to subtract a number, or conceivably more complicated than that, perhaps even multiply or divide the number by a specific factor in order to get the actual phone number. In essence, there were endless possibilities and almost hopeless. At any rate, it would require a great deal of time.

"I have to come up with a different solution," he muttered, somewhat disappointed. He decided to show his current results to his colleagues. Carrying five copies of his two-page A4 summary with an index of Darcy's laptop in hand, he left the room in search of his co-workers.

He found them sitting in the conference room in front of a large magnetic board that displayed all known facts as well as photos of their suspects and the murder victim. Many clues had question marks next to them in felt pen — a constant annoyance to the members of the investigation team.

After Jean-Baptiste handed out the copies, a few minutes of silence ensued while everyone familiarized themselves with the report.

"Ok, Jean-Baptiste, the information might not seem useful at the moment, but I'm sure it will come in handy later on," Bosco said, ending the silence. "If the amounts in the list under *KBS - Account* are actual sales of film recordings, I'll have to change my opinion about the production of nature films. The transferred amounts to Mayeye are too large to be payments for his security company's services. And, we know they are definitely not. He already told us he collects the fee for SÉCOMA's services in cash."

"Considering the amounts listed under *Daily Allowance*, I am wondering about their annual salaries. There's no mention of those figures. Apparently, producing nature films is a lucrative business," Ariane added, stunned when she finally registered the sums on Darcy's spreadsheets.

"I want to know what Krauskopf's actual function is in the company since there is no evidence he performs any type of production work. To me, he's a phantom," Fabien said.

Everyone nodded in agreement.

"Yes, I also have a feeling these guys aren't on the up and up," Alphonse commented on the newest findings.

"You're right, Alphonse. Given that Krauskopf received double the daily allowance as the other two, I'm really interested in his job description," Bosco said, dominating the discussion again. "We'll continue our surveillance of these gentlemen. I'm hoping Joseph will play along. Let's summarize. First, there is no evidence the film producers are involved in criminal activities. Second, all four had literally no e-mail communications from their home countries. Third, what is Krauskopf's function? Four, what does the letter abbreviation KBS stand for? Five, whose phone numbers are so important they needed to be encrypted? I want to add: Was contact with Mayeye limited to his security service and is the amount $1,464,000 USD for said service appropriate?"

"It would be interesting to know how the videos are distributed as well as to whom," Ariane remarked.

Fabien looked at Jean-Baptiste. "Can't they be transferred via online server and an agency then puts them on the market?"

"It's unlikely with such a huge amount of data. Even compressed they are too large for East Africa's network."

"This doesn't help." Bosco spoke again. "We must figure out who the phone numbers belong to, as well as the importance of Darcy's numbers with the Z in front. If the list contains customer data, why is it encrypted?"

All eyes were on the Constable.

"I suspect the numbers with the Z in front aren't actual phone numbers."

"So, what are they?" Bosco asked.

"Perhaps login codes for web storage, so-called *clouds*, or maybe they're bank account numbers. I'll keep at it, but as I said, it's better if we find another lead. It might take me a while."

Looking at his colleagues' faces, Bosco knew the mood had reached a low point. He was aware they needed some success for overall morale. His investigation reports to the *General* should eventually indicate progress. Granted, he could document all the work they had already performed, but Mugambage was not keen on details, and he was hardly willing to read more than a one-page summary of the key facts.

"If that's all the questions, I guess it's time to get back to work. Let's return the laptops except Darcy's and the cameras and CF-cards. Perhaps then they'll believe we are no longer interested and feel safe if they have something to hide. I also want to let Likongo know we complied with the terms."

Jean-Baptiste took notes during the meeting and stated, "I'm going to make a new summary and distribute new copies. Should I send one to Likongo as well?"

Bosco thought briefly and nodded.

"I've got some news too," Alphonse said. "The map of coltan and cassiterite deposits I asked for came in today. I had no idea there were so many."

Alphonse unfolded the map. It was a normal topographical map in the scale of 1:200,000. Red circles indicated areas with rare raw resources. Most of the circles were in the Congolese Kivu provinces. Everyone bent over the map until Ariane spoke up.

"I know a German geologist here who works on behalf of the BGR, the German Institute for Geosciences and Natural Resources, performing so-called mineralogical fingerprints. His office is in the Museum of Geology on Avenue de la Justice. Perhaps he can help us."

"What are mineralogical fingerprints?"

Bosco had asked the question, but looking at everyone's expressions, Ariane knew they also had no idea.

"I asked him the same question. As he explained, scientists have been working for some time on determining the origin of minerals. It's a way to prevent the trade of valuable raw materials such as so-called blood diamonds and coltan that come from deposits controlled by criminal groups. We all know that's how they finance weapons."

"Okay, I want you to get in touch with him. Take the map and samples. Let's see if he can provide anything significant," Bosco said with little conviction.

The group broke up without much enthusiasm. Everyone was frustrated and longing for a breakthrough in their investigation.

"Fabien, wait," Ariane called after her colleague who had just walked past her. She took out her cell phone and searched for a number. Robert Marx, BGR Hannover. They had met at *La Galette*. Ever since, seemingly innocent meetings in Kigali were clearly staged.

The man answered on the first ring.

"Ariane, long time no hear!" he joked in pidgin English.

"Tell me about all the evil going on in Rwanda?"

"Hello, Robert. Well, until recently, it had been rather quiet. Then, naturally, something extremely bad happened. Perhaps you've heard about the dead man found in Gisenyi."

"Sure I have. Is there anything new?"

"That's why I'm calling. Do you have time to see me? You might be able to help."

"Sure, I'm at the office."

"Okay, I'll be right over."

Fabien had been listening. "I'll get a car."

Soon, they were on their way to Avenue de la Justice. The office was located on the first floor of an older building near the Richard Kandt House. Kandt, the founder of Kigali, became a resident in 1908 of the German province of Rwanda.

Robert Marx had been in Kigali for one year. From there, he undertook extensive excursions to, primarily, sample Rare Earths Elements from mines in the region. Several times, he encountered armed guerrillas, but every time he managed to buy his freedom without revealing his true purpose for being in the region. That would have been a death sentence. His sample collection was now quite extensive and he was regarded as an expert, especially when it came to the coveted mineral coltan.

The term Rare Earths Elements incorporates elements whose chemical properties make them especially valuable to the electronics industry. These are metallic elements, thus, the correct designation as Rare Earths Elements. Overall, in the earth's upper crust, they are not exactly uncommon, as the term suggests. Areas of deposits with high concentrations are rare, which is what makes them extremely lucrative and cost-effective. Deposits of coltan can be found in the eastern part of the Congo and to a lesser extent in Rwanda. Coltan is a combination of the metal oxides columbite and tantalite. Tantalum is extracted from tantalite, a rare earth metal required for the miniaturization of capacitors in mobile phones and laptops. Since there is no state regulatory authority in eastern Congo, the mines are controlled and exploited by local militias in the relevant area. Most mines are occupied by Laurent Nkunda's Rassemblement Congolais pour la Démocratie the Rassemblement, who in turn uses the mines' proceeds to finance weapons as well as to pay his soldiers. This not only results in massive ecological destruction but also to slavish oppression of the local population. Trade and transportation, mostly through Kigali to Dar es Salaam, Tanzania, is organized by intermediaries at the Rwandan border. Bypassing the United Nations embargo is an easier problem.

Ariane and Fabien found the door bearing the sign *Dr. R. Marx, M.Sc., Geologist*. After a brief knock, the scientist answered the door. Ariane introduced Fabien and Marx pointed to a visitors table with a pot of coffee and three cups. They all took a seat.

"Okay, so how can I help?"

"In connection with our investigation into the murder of the man found in Gisenyi, we're interested in the origin of a coltan sample," Ariane explained in English, showing consideration for Fabien. She placed a cylindrical glass tube with a label from the Rwandan forensic lab on the table. Marx regarded the inscription: *Coltan, most likely ferrotantalite*. Underneath was a handwritten remark: *Murder Victim T. Darcy, location: Gisenyi, Great Barrier, 20050813*. Scrutinizing the tube, he walked over to his desk where he kept his microscope.

He laid the sample underneath and gave his initial assessment after a quick glance. "The sample doesn't originate from a primary deposit; instead, it comes from a *placer*."

Ariane and Fabien looked at him questioningly. "What do you mean?"

"Look at the magnification. The grains are clearly rounded, meaning they were subject to water movement. If the sample originated from a primary deposit, i.e., the place where it formed, it would have a crystalline form. The ore is retrieved from river sand, which is where these raw materials accumulate into so-called *placer* due to their greater specific weight, either by panning or by means of industrial conveyor belts.

The two CID colleagues regarded the eight times magnification of the matt black grains and nodded in unison.

"And how do you determine the origin?" Fabien asked.

"That's not so easy. For that, a few analyses would be necessary, which can only be done with the mass spectrometer in Hannover. Takes about a week. I'd send the sample today with DHL. If we've already catalogued the sample's deposit area, we'd only have to check our database and then we'd know where it originated."

10

Two men working for Mayeye's company, SÉCOMA, took care of special assignments. They came in a fast motorboat in the middle of the night and docked near the old warehouse. Their equipment consisted of Maglite high-power flashlights and their weapon of choice, AK-47.

The AK-47, also called Kalashnikov, in reference to its Russian designer, is the most produced weapon in the world. The traded weapon is referred to in the military as a *Awtomat Kalaschnikowa, obrasza 47* and numerous variations have been produced since 1947. It is particularly easy to handle and therefore happily issued to child soldiers, the *kadoko,* in African conflict areas. Frequently, this perfidious manner of abusing and manipulating young children turns them into soulless killers during hostilities with difficult to repair psychological damage.

In addition, each man carried a gun the HK USP Elite nine millimeter, in a holster attached to his belt. Unlike many other special assignments, they didn't expect to use their guns. Each man also dragged a ten-gallon canister of gasoline the short distance from the shore to the clearing where the warehouse and outbuildings stood. Having arrived at their target, the men first quickly inspected the abandoned building and then poured gasoline on the sidewalls. In only a few seconds, the licking flames turned the dry wood into a blazing inferno. The arsonists, aware of the success of their short deployment, did not wait for the end of their mission. As the boat rapidly plowed across the lake towards Goma, the wood framing of the old building collapsed, turning the plot of land into a raging pyre.

The CID had put Alphonse in charge of maintaining Interpol's database and was the only one granted access. In 1949, the United Nations authority granted consultative status to NGOs. Rwanda has been a member since 1974. Although access to INTERPOL's database via the internet has been possible since 2002, the Rwandan communications network was still under construction. Granted, the network allowed e-mail traffic, but transferring large amounts of data still posed a problem.

The following Monday Alphonse arrived early at the office and once again tried to establish an Internet connection to INTERPOL in Lyon. Fortunately, INTERPOL's home page popped up immediately on his monitor with its logo and objective, *Connecting Police For A Saver Wold*. He clicked the publicly accessible link, *Wanted Persons,* on the right-hand side of the page.

One by one, he entered the names of Darcy and his co-workers, but without results. Presently, no one was searching for the four men, meaning their names wouldn't be in the *Red Notices* column. Logging into the *Nominal Database* turned out to be promising. All four employees of TD Nature Film Production had awakened the interests of the investigative authority. There was a dossier on each man that listed all the findings of the local authorities in Germany, Belgium, and the UK.

First, he took a closer look at Darcy's dossier. The photo showed a kneeling, youthful man holding a young dog by the collar.

> DARCY, TOM
> IDENTITY PARTICULARS:

Name	: DARCY
First name	: TOM
Gender	: Male
Date of birth	: 09/15/1945
Place of birth	: Namour, Belgium
Languages	: French, English, Walloon, Swahili
Nationality	: Belgian
Height	: 1.85 m
Eye Color	: blue
Hair color	: blond
Fam. Status	: single, no known relationship
Father	: Bruno Darcy, died 1960
Mother	: Emilie, nee Drost, died giving birth to T.D.
Siblings	: none
Profession	: dog breeder

DISTINGUISHING MARKS:
Tattoo, red rooster left arm (Coq Hardi depicted in Walloon flag).
Hairless furrow along the left temple, probably natural and not due to injury.

OTHER:
A Walloon nationalist, most likely violent, no previous criminal record. Good physical condition, strong physique.

CHARGES:
No current charges, suspicion of criminal activity.

CRIMINAL HISTORY:
Fined for a minor offense; see summarized

biography.

SUMMARIZED BIOGRAPHY:
Until 1963:
Lived in orphanage, dropped out of school despite good grades.
Received a small inheritance.
1964:
Breeding herding dogs breed, *Bouvier des Ardennes* in a village near Brussels.
Attempted to train fighting dogs. After an incident, where a visitor was severely injured by one of the dogs, he paid a fine and decided to quit the business.
Has contact with Walloon nationalists.
Changed residences with sympathizers.
Added to Interpol's database.
1964 - 1975:
Whereabouts unknown.
1975 - 1985:
Residence, Madrid, profession unknown.
Frequent travel, presumably to East Africa at times.
1985 - to date:
Whereabouts unknown.

Alphonse added:

2003 - 2005:
Whereabouts Goma / DRC
Owner and CEO of TD. Nature Film Production.

08/13/2005:
Found dead in Rwanda, victim of a violent crime.
Investigation ongoing.

Piquards dossier contained no photo.

PIQUARD, ANDRÉ
IDENTITY PARTICULARS:

Name	: PIQUARD
First name	: ANDRÉ
Gender	: Male
Date of birth	: 08/24/1950
Place of birth	: Liège, Belgium
Languages	: French, English, Walloon, German
Nationality	: Belgian
Height	: 1.65 m
Eye color	: blue-gray
Hair color	: light brown, starting to gray
Fam. Status	: single, no known relationship
Father	: Pierre Piquard, died 1974
Mother	: Clara, nee Lachet, died 1976
Siblings	: none
Profession	: photographer

DISTINGUISHING MARKS:
None.

OTHER:
Lean physique, but in good shape.

CHARGES:
No current charges.

CRIMINAL HISTORY:
None in Europe; see summarized Biography.

SUMMARIZED BIOGRAPHY:
Until 1966
Secondary level, education with diploma.
1966 - 1968:
Photographer apprenticeship

1968:
Cameraman in a small studio in Liège. Freelancer at parties; passport photos, etc.
1968 - 1989:
Extensive travel, especially to Asia and Africa. Lectured in Belgium and Germany.
1989:
Prosecuted in Cambodia for having sex with children. He provided witnesses who testified he was only involved in taking certain pictures. He paid a steep fine for sending pornographic videos and photos to Festus Dallaway (see dossier on Festus Dallaway). Added to Interpol's database.
1989 - to date:
No information, last residence unknown.

Alphonse added:

2003 - 2005:
Whereabouts, Goma / DRC.
Cameraman and film editor for TD Nature Film Production (see dossier on Tom Darcy).

After reading Darcy and Piquard's illustrious biographies, Dallaway's was no surprise. The photo showed a young man in a suit and tie, hair neatly parted so it covered the already visible bald spots.

DALLAWAY, FESTUS WOODROW
IDENTITY PARTICULARS:

Name	: DALLAWAY
First name	: FESTUS WOODROW
Gender	: Male
Date of birth	: 01/30/1954
Place of birth	: Manchester, United Kingdom
Languages	: English
Nationality	: British
Height	: 1.70 m
Eye color	: gray
Hair color	: reddish-blond
Fam. Status	: single, no known relationship
Father	: unknown
Mother	: Janet Dallaway, died 1980
Siblings	: none
Profession	: film editor, photographer

DISTINGUISHING MARKS:
None.

OTHER:
Heavyset, obese, suffers from hypertension, presumably an alcoholic.

CHARGES:
No current charges.

CRIMINAL HISTORY:
Prison sentence, see summarized Biography.

SUMMARIZED BIOGRAPHY:

Until 1970:
Secondary level education.
1970-1972:
Photographer and film editor, apprenticeship in Manchester.

From 1972:
Sold self-produced pornographic photos and movies.
1989:
Trip to Southeast Asia, where he presumably made first contact with André Piquard (see dossier on André Piquard).
Indicted for money laundering; served prison time.
Added to Interpol's database.
1995 to date:
Presumed to be involved with Piquard in the porn industry.
Current whereabouts unknown.

Alphonse entered another addendum:

2003 - 2005:
Whereabouts Goma / DRC.
Photographer and film editor for TD Nature Film Production. (see dossier on Tom Darcy)

It turned out Krauskopf was the worst candidate. His dossier contained two photos that obviously came from some police booking. The photograph from the front showed a grim-looking man with piercing eyes. Although his skull was cleanly shaven, he sported a mustache that snaked around the corners of his mouth and down his chin, just like the photo on his visa. His muscular body was recognizable by his thick neck as well as his broad and powerful shoulders. The second photo showed his face in profile, revealing an earring and two distinctive folds in his bull neck.

KRAUSKOPF, ERNST
IDENTITY PARTICULARS:

Name	: KRAUSKOPF
First name	: ERNST, nicknamed the 'Hun'
Gender	: Male
Date of birth	: 06/22/1946
Place of birth	: Aachen, Federal Republic of Germany
Languages	: German, some English
Nationality	: German
Height	: 2.05 m
Eyes	: brown
Hair color	: blond, suffers androgenic alopecia early balding
Fam. Status	: single, no known relationship
Father	: unknown
Mother	: Karin Krauskopf, died 1979
Siblings	: none
Profession	: none

DISTINGUISHING MARKS:
Double-S tattoo on right upper arm (Nazi Rune), as well as other tattoos.

OTHER:
Extremely violent, dangerous.

CHARGES:
No current charges.

CRIMINAL HISTORY:
Served prison time, see summarized Biography.

SUMMARIZED BIOGRPHY:
1956:
Dropped out of school.
1957:
Prone to violent behavior, enrolled in home for maladjusted teenagers.

1964 - 1975:
Dismissed, odd jobs, bouncer, pimp. trained in kickboxing.
Repeatedly involved in brawls.
1976 - 1982:
Added to Interpol's database.
Served a prison sentence for involuntary manslaughter, victim - pimp.
1983:
Presumably first contact with Walloon nationalists in Liège (see dossier on Tom Darcy).
1983 to date:
Current whereabouts unknown.

Alphonse also updated his record:

2003 - 08/2005:
Whereabouts: Goma / DRC; employee at TD Nature Film Production.(see dossier on Tom Darcy)
Current: 08/13/2005 : missing.

Alphonse looked contemptuously at the dossier photos. *These guys are a nightmare to any society. As though we don't have enough deranged people running around here, we now also have to deal with the dregs of Western countries.*

Apart from their regular meetings each Monday, every CID employee with a good reason could request a meeting. Alphonse knew his time had arrived and called one colleague after another. In the conference room, he handed out copies of the four dossiers. Everyone studied the contents thoroughly.

Bosco cleared his throat. "Okay, what's your opinion?"

"This doesn't help at all. We can merely state that

these, uh...gentlemen fit a certain milieu, identifying them not only as nature lovers," Fabien stated.

Ariane couldn't help herself and chuckled. All eyes were drawn immediately to her.

"Sorry, but I had to laugh because of Krauskopf's nickname. The Brits cannot stop labeling us Germans as the *huns* in order to brand us as barbarians. One year, my parents sent me to an English boarding school and behind my back, my classmates called me the *hun*."

"How did you respond?" Bosco asked.

"I once addressed the subject in history class and explained to the Brits where their origins lie. The pathetic Brits have a hard time coming to terms with the fact their royal family are descended from Germans. That's why after World War I, they changed their name from *Saxe-Coburg and Gotha* to *Windsor*. And, let's not forget they are also genetically handicapped through raiding Vikings."

"How did your English classmates respond to that?" the Constable inquired.

"Well, they ascribed it back to Emperor Wilhelm II's famous *Hun - speech*. In reference to the Boxer Rebellion in 1900 in Beijing, and while posing it as a threat, he compared the German soldiers to King Etzel's hordes of Huns. My classmates were somewhat embarrassed and they stopped calling me the *Hun*."

The group was amused.

"Now you know who you're dealing with, so tread lightly. But, back to the subject," she said, directing the conversation again. "Concerning Krauskopf, I'm sure the comparison is quite appropriate. No one involved in that scene retains friendships. Speaking plainly, these characters are likely to make numerous enemies over the course of their exciting careers."

"At least in their home countries. But, I don't believe any of those enemies would go through the trouble of coming to the Congo to settle an old score," Fabien remarked.

Ariane spoke again. "Darcy's dossier doesn't mention the scar on his arm. Either it was overlooked or it happened later. That would mean they don't only have friends here. While it seems, except for Krauskopf, they're currently running a legitimate business, there's still certain doubt."

Bosco nodded. "Therefore, we must take a closer look at their operation from here. I am more and more convinced the gentlemen also had their fingers in an entirely different pie. Jean-Baptiste, are you making any progress with the telephone numbers?"

The Constable shook his head. Being unable to solve the problem was eroding his confidence.

"No, but I've been thinking about the amount of money that was apparently transferred to Mayeye alias CNYWDS."

"What about it?"

"The amount of $1,464,000 USD is exactly eight percent of the amount Darcy listed under KBS, 18.3 million US dollars. To me, it looks like a share disbursement."

They all looked dumbfounded at the young Constable.

Bosco scratched his head, a little embarrassed. "I guess our knowledge of numbers is limited to our payroll."

The introverted Constable couldn't help the cocky remark "Well, the number on my paycheck is so easily manageable that I repeatedly seek new challenges."

Bosco's eyebrows rose imperceptibly before joining the understanding laughter of his team.

Ever since the conversation with Mayeye, he had become Bosco's favorite for further investigation. It seemed the gained insight strengthened his opinion that the Congolese should remain at the center of their investigations.

"It seems Mayeye worked on commission. But doing what? Providing security at a shooting location? That's a bit unusual and the amounts are too large. I think we should take another look at this guy."

Nobody disagreed.

11

Apart from the fact that people killed in eastern Congo were often buried in mass graves, the funeral ceremony at the cemetery in Burhiba, north of Bukavu, seemed ordinary. The only fact an attentive observer would have noticed was that the mourners were small in stature while the size of the wooden box lowered into the grave was significantly longer than those present. But then, the population of the country had long since stopped caring about the affairs of others and even less about a funeral.

Ariane and Bosco drove to Gisenyi. Théo and Prince were expecting them. Previously, they had agreed Théo would remain in Gisenyi.

"I've just learned Joseph is currently away on urgent business. I couldn't even reach him," Théo said as he welcomed them.

"I guess we'll have to manage without him. Prince, can you take us to Mayeye?"

"Shouldn't we call ahead and announce ourselves?"

Prince's dubious expression didn't escape them. Bosco hesitated momentarily and eventually decided to throw caution to the wind.

"I believe we'll pay him a surprise visit."

Prince nodded and refrained from further comments. However, Théo voiced his concern.

"Bosco, that guy is dangerous."

"I know, but he won't chance being hunted by both the Congolese government and Rwanda."

"I hope you're right. I'll remain in the office where you can reach me anytime. Call me immediately if you encounter any problems. If need be, I can request help from Joseph's deputy in Goma."

"Sounds good, nevertheless, try to reach Likongo and tell him our whereabouts."

"Will do. But, watch your back, don't provoke Mayeye unnecessarily."

Bosco climbed into the car's front passenger seat. Ariane sat on the rear bench. Prince drove the shortest route through Goma. Heavy rain started to fall. The summit of Mount Nyiragongo lay hidden behind towering, menacing grayish black clouds. Instead of a volcanic eruption of lava, a torrent of muddy water now seemed to spill over the crater's rim. The dirt road, unable to deal with the onslaught, was defenseless against the corrosive encounter. The windshield wipers barely kept pace with the torrent, blurring the view ahead. Due to limited visibility, Prince was forced to drive slowly. Nevertheless, the situation didn't seem to faze him. Focused, he maneuvered the vehicle down the road filled with deep ruts, potholes and black sand, clay, and gravel the water had displaced. The deep rumbling and sharp cracking noise of lightning over Lake Kivu created an eerie atmosphere. Many pedestrians, mostly young people, but also women, elderly men, and children, with loads on their heads, rubber boots or flip-flops on their feet, and wet clinging clothes, wandered towards unknown destinations. Men pushed bikes down the street with large bundles of wooden beams balanced on the bar. Most young people cumbersomely pushed their *tshukudu*, the African version of a scooter made out of wood, with sacks of goods resting on the footboard towards Goma.

Ariane was lost in thought. *I wonder what they are transporting in those sacks and where?*

"Prince, what are they transporting in the sacks? Are they smugglers?"

"It's *makala*, charcoal, Madame. Some deliver to camps, others sell it in Goma. From there *makala* is smuggled into Rwanda. Hundreds of thousands of refugees here have nothing to cook with, so it is a good business. Especially popular is hardwood. It has a greater heating value, but then it also costs more."

"How much does it cost?"

"Around thirty dollars a sack."

"Hardwood? You mean tropical tree wood. Where does it come from?"

"They cut down trees in the rainforest and build charcoal piles on site."

"That's permitted?"

"Of course not, it's against the law. But, nobody pays attention."

Ariane exhaled.

"Who transports the cut wood from the rainforest?"

"Those are also refugees. Most work for the rebels. They run a large scale business and hand out concessions in the areas they have influence."

"In essence, the rainforest is going up in smoke."

"Correct, Madame." Prince's voice lacked emotion. Their eyes met briefly in the rearview mirror. It seemed her outrage wasn't shared.

Ariane suspected he had also adopted Africa's generally accepted point of view that tomorrow's problems were rather abstract in nature. More important were everyday issues, which all too often came down to mere survival.

Disheartened, she directed her gaze back to the road. Even though Prince proved to be a cautious driver, pedestrians dodged out of the way, petrified. No one expected to be shown consideration. Repeatedly, they were forced to slow down behind a loaded trailer without an opportunity to pass.

For almost a half hour, they were stuck behind a two-axle version of a Magirus-Deutz Jupiter transporter traveling at a snail's pace. The worn dual tires of the rear axle labored up the slight incline, repeatedly losing traction, and spinning out of control. The driver of the transport seemed unfamiliar with the vehicle's old technology. Even with the tumultuous downpour, loud grinding of the transporter's unsynchronized transmission could be heard at regular intervals. In the cargo area, mostly young fighters dressed in worn camouflage sat under a heavily tattered tarpaulin, virtually unprotected against the bad weather. Poor visibility made it impossible to tell if they were the Congo's regular army soldiers or guerillas. Almost all had a fetish bag or a hairy paw of an animal hanging around their necks. They clutched their weapons and looked sullenly at four-wheel drive SUV stuck behind them. Ariane had donned a raincoat.

So as not to draw attention, she pulled the hood low over her forehead. If recognized as a foreigner, being stopped either by guerilla troops or regular police was expected. The sole objective was to claim a *fee*, preferably in dollars. Those who knew the practice always carried a few dollar bills. The uninitiated had to go through the hassle of an inspection, only to end up paying a *fee* anyway. Not all of Likongo's people participated in the practice.

After a turn, they suddenly found themselves alone on the descending road. Due to their previous visit, they knew Mayeye's house was located along the lakeshore. Shortly thereafter, the turbulent water could be seen through the wall of rain.

Suddenly, the clouds parted as if a curtain had slid open on its rod, allowing the sun to make an appearance and presented the landscape in all its beauty. Only a tiny cloud remained over the summit of Mount Nyiragongo. Upon reaching the entrance to Mayeye's property, Lake Kivu glittered peacefully in the afternoon sun before them. As the guard approached, Prince lowered the passenger window for Bosco.

"Are you expected?"

"We need to speak to your boss," Bosco replied, ignoring the question.

The man thought for a moment. He remembered them from their previous visit and decided to call Mayeye.

"He wants to speak to you in person." The guard handed him his walkie-talkie.

"Kabeera!"

"What do you want?" The voice on the other end sounded resentful.

"To talk with you."

"Where's Joseph?"

"He'll be here later. There was other business he needed to attend to first."

"You're out of your jurisdiction and have no authority here."

"We are authorized by your Government to

investigate. You should answer a few of our questions."

There was a long pause on the other line.

"Let me speak to the guard."

The man grabbed the walkie-talkie and while speaking quietly and gesticulating, he repeatedly looked at the vehicle.

"He will see you. You know the way," he said brusquely and pointed to the building.

Prince pulled into the courtyard and stopped in front of the already open entrance door. Since no other guard was present, they entered the house and walked down the short hallway straight to Mayeye's living room. The door was open so they went in. Bosco sensed danger and an uneasy feeling crept over Ariane. Out of nowhere, three armed men appeared behind them. One of the three was the guard Ariane had already had the misfortune to meet. All the three grinned maliciously and aimed their guns at them.

"Move it, hands behind your head."

Bosco and Ariane did as they were told. The door of the walk-through room opened and Mayeye entered the living room. This time, he was dressed in cargo pants, matching khaki shirt, and black lace-up boots.

"You should not have come here, Kabeera."

"We are unarmed and our only purpose is to ask a few questions."

"You're not here to ask questions," Mayeye replied, this time hostilely. "As for weapons, that can be changed. We wouldn't want Joseph to think we killed you in cold blood."

While Bosco tried to calm the situation verbally,

Ariane thought feverishly about how to get it under control. Apparently, they unknowingly placed the criminal under intense pressure and he panicked. The man was certainly not joking.

Mayeye signaled his henchmen and led the way to the door of the second room. Bosco and Ariane felt gun muzzles prodding their backs. Ariane tensed her body. However, it wasn't the right time yet to fight back. With difficulty, she suppressed her developing fear. Was escaping her bourgeois life worth it, to end up here? Suddenly, Hamburg seemed infinitely far away. She had freely chosen to take part in the exchange program. Now, a determined criminal had taken over as the director of her life. Image after image popped into her mind - her life flashing before her - ships on the Elbe, rough swells of the North Sea, and faces of family members and friends. Would they even be able to visit her grave?

Damn it, Bruce Willis is never around when you need him.

One by one, they entered the servants' wing and descended the stairs to the basement. Bosco was right behind Mayeye. Ariane briefly touched him and gestured inconspicuously with her chin towards Mayeye when he glanced at her. Bosco also correctly assessed the situation and was completely focused, ready to fight back. He understood Ariane's intent and discreetly nodded. *Now!* The man behind Ariane blocked the path of the two men following.

Krav Maga gun defense from behind.

Fast as lightning, she whipped her whole body around. One of the criminal's arms ended up locked in the crook of her arm. Using her elbow, she pushed his shoulder joint downward while simultaneously ripping the gun away with her other hand and without hesitation immediately shot the next man. Mortally wounded, he crumpled into a heap on the stairs. As the third man used the moment to seek cover back up the staircase, she rammed her knee into the disarmed man's abdomen and struck him over the head with his gun for good measure. The wind immediately went out of him. In the dim light, she recognized her special friend lying unconscious on the steps at her feet, bleeding heavily from a laceration on his head.

Mayeye had fully relied on his three paladins and kept his gun holstered. Even before he had completely turned around, Bosco threw his whole weight on him. Although the Congolese man was much taller, he stood no chance against Bosco's powerful muscular body. After a brief tussle, he managed to relieve the Banyamulenge of his weapon. Ariane was about to grab the gun of the man she had shot dead when the third man shot blindly from above into the dark stairwell. The shot missed Ariane but struck Bosco painfully in the upper arm. He winced and instinctively ducked. The diversion worked and Mayeye successfully freed himself. Before Bosco could aim, Mayeye disappeared into the hallway, his retreating footsteps echoing off the walls.

Ariane noticed Bosco was wounded. Before she could ask if he was okay, he said while checking if Mayeye's gun was loaded, "I'll take care of Mayeye, you eliminate the guy upstairs."

Not waiting for a reply, Bosco turned and disappeared into the tunnel. Holding the gun ready, he cautiously groped his way down the dark passage that became increasingly brighter. A wet musty odor filled the air, signaling the nearness of the lake.

Ariane, in the meantime, wondered how to neutralize the man on the stairs. Above, someone turned off the power and it became almost dark. Turning towards the stairs, she suddenly heard a noise and a huge shadow in front of her continued to grow larger. The man she knocked unconsciousness regained his senses sooner than anticipated. Before she could react, her attacker slapped the gun out of her hand. Two great paws wrapped around her neck and deprived her of air. Hot breath reeking of alcohol and tobacco assaulted her.

"Now I have peace and quiet to deal with you."

I won't last much longer. Krav Maga choke defense.

Using all her strength, she seized both of the man's thumbs and twisted them outward until his forearms gave way, followed by two successive powerful kicks to the groin. Groaning, the attacker doubled over. While pushing his head even further down, she brought up her knee and rammed it into his face. The man screamed in agony. Ariane took two steps backward and reached down, her hand groping for the nearby gun. Her eyes had finally grown accustomed to the darkness when suddenly the man charged, screaming with rage. Ariane fired twice in quick succession. One of the shots hit the man in the heart. He stood there a moment, frozen on the bottom step. Ariane stepped aside just in time. Her attacker toppled forward and hit the cool concrete floor with a loud thud.

It seemed the third man had decided to flee. For a brief moment, an eerie silence engulfed the area, abruptly followed by the unmistakable rat-tat-tat of machine gun fire coming from somewhere on the grounds. In between, the dull pops of a gun being fired could be heard. Ariane decided to follow Bosco. Cautiously, she made her way down the tunnel where he had disappeared.

Bosco pursued Mayeye into the tunnel where he had vanished, towards the gradually brightening light. Turning the light off was meant to benefit Mayeye, but the darkness also protected his pursuer. The exit of the tunnel was now clearly visible. When Bosco was fifty feet from his target, he heard the typical initial misfire of an outboard motor that sprang to life on the second attempt and immediately roared as the boat took off.

I cannot let him escape.

Bosco ran out of the tunnel and found himself in an open grotto with a slipway where a boat could be pulled ashore. A short distance away, he spotted the retreating open motorboat. In addition to Mayeye, there was another man aboard driving the boat. The boat had not traveled far yet when the Banyamulenge turned and recognized Bosco. Mayeye immediately aimed an AK-47 at Bosco, who in turn had already assumed a shooting stance and fired several shots. Hit in the left shoulder, the criminal fell to his seat. He staggered back up and struggled to maintain his balance while attempting to aim at Bosco with his right arm.

A fast approaching noise signaled the approach of another motorboat. Mayeye's helmsman recognized the danger and gunned the outboard motor digging the boat's stern deep into the swells. Mayeye held on for dear life. The second boat neared and Bosco saw

Joseph Likongo at the helm with three other men, each holding a German-made Heckler & Koch G3 automatic rifle at the ready. Once within range of Mayeye's motorboat, they opened fire on the vessel. The rounds repeatedly hit the boat as well as the outboard motor. Iridescent fuel spread across the water's surface and ignited soon after. Another series of shots punctured the second tank. The leaking fuel immediately erupted into a wall of fire. The lake was now in flames. Both criminals attempted to grab their AK-47s but were quickly hit with several bullets. Mayeye's face contorted as the rifle slipped from his grasp and both hands moved to his chest. The man at the wheel collapsed and ceased moving. The boat lurched slightly and made an abrupt uncontrolled turn. Mayeye tipped forward and sideways overboard, disappearing into the lake's dark water. The mortally wounded man behind the controls sent the leaderless motorboat racing at high speed directly at a rocky promontory. A huge explosion destroyed the vehicle and turned it into a burning torch. Bosco, Ariane, as well as Likongo and his team, even some of Mayeye's overwhelmed men, if they were still alive, stared spellbound as the rest of Mayeye's boat slowly sank out of sight. Some of the flames united with water and black plumes of smoke began to rise.

Ariane reached the exit of the tunnel and admired Likongo's intervention.

"Well, I guess that's over and done with."

"Let's go back up to our car," Bosco said.

Prince sat behind the wheel as if he had never left his seat. Ariane waved hello.

"I see you made it to safety."

"The thugs had me pinned me down for a while, but once Likongo and his men arrived, they quickly lost interest in me."

The commander walked up to them.

"That was a close call, colleagues. You should have waited for me."

Bosco's didn't have a clear conscience.

"I didn't believe he was that deeply involved in the case. I don't think your presence would have made a difference. He still would've tried to kill us before attempting to escape. Actually, I'm rather glad you weren't here. By the way, what kept you?"

Joseph chuckled briefly. "Perhaps you're right. I was on my way to Idjwi. I had turned off my cell phone because there is no reception on Idjwi. Before I left my service provider's coverage area, I turned it back on to check for messages. That's when Théo reached me and let me know what was going on. Plus, I received a call from Prince and knew my presence was urgently needed. I turned around straightaway and alerted my men."

"What was your business on Idjwi?"

"A mining company reported a fire. A few of my people are on site investigating. I presume it was arson. But, as of yet, I don't know anything concrete since my men cannot reach me on my cell."

"Why didn't Mayeye call his men at SÉCOMA for help?"

"He might have tried. I had the house immediately surrounded. My people make sure they only drink tea and are ready at all times. It looks as if Mayeye lost his cool. Oh well, I had to do some clean up here anyway."

Ariane and Bosco were treated by a female police officer. Bosco's wound was harmless, but his jacket was ruined. Ariane merely suffered an abrasion on her hand during the scuffle on the narrow staircase.

"Thank you, Joseph," Ariane said. "And to hell with you, Bruce Willis," she added, mumbling in German.

"What was that?"

"Oh, nothing, I was simply thinking out loud."

Slightly perplexed, Joseph smiled, but sensed Ariane's presence. She glanced at him warmly.

What a nice change, a black man as a white knight.

Bosco noticed the charged atmosphere and was somewhat confused for a moment, then smiled discreetly.

"Joseph..." He immediately realized he had slipped and in his usual familiar way, addressed the commander by his first name, something he had avoided so far. "I'd like to take a closer look at the grounds."

"Sure, Bosco, go ahead and look around. I have two of my men stationed on the roof terrace keeping an eye on the surrounding area."

While Joseph's men loaded the guards' bodies into the back of a pickup truck, they observed a dead body being offloaded from a boat. They had found Mayeye's corpse and brought it ashore. Joseph went and came back with a wallet.

"Here it is, four hundred dollars, almost dry, and one credit card. There was nothing else."

Bosco and Ariane looked at the card. It had the inscription of the Kanton Bank Stein AG, Switzerland, as well as a logo with the letters KBS. Ariane clucked quietly.

"Now we know what the KBS abbreviation stands for on the list of Darcy's suspected money transfers. It seems both were clients of the same bank."

Bosco grabbed the credit card and looked at it closely. "It seems Switzerland doesn't particularly care where their clients' money comes from. Even Mobutu had been considered a friend of Switzerland. Apparently, Darcy and Mayeye also left their retirement accounts there. It would be nice to know what they're going to do with all that money."

"It'll go in probate. I don't think it'll pose too many problems for the Swiss bankers," Ariane pointed out. "Mobutu wasn't the only autocrat who managed government funds in Switzerland. That also reminds me, Switzerland remains the largest recipient of foreign aid."

The song "Indépendance cha-cha-cha" sprang from Joseph's cell phone. Bosco and Ariane watched his face increasingly hardened while talking on the phone in Lingála.

"One of my men is back from Idjwi. Several dead bodies were found in the fire, which means I have to go. My people here will take care of Mayeye's estate. They have instructions to assist you. I'm going to stop by my office and then I'm off to the island. Hold on to the wallet and include it in your report."

After Joseph introduced them to the officer in charge, he climbed into his car and drove off towards Goma. Ariane and Bosco entered Mayeye's residence. A frightened elderly couple and the young woman who had served them during their previous visit sat at the kitchen table. The elderly only spoke Lingála. The eighteen-year-old girl was their granddaughter and spoke French. Bosco decided to have Ariane talk to her.

"How long have you been employed by Mayeye?"

"Three years."

"Did you have a...a personal relationship with him?"

Detached, the young woman looked her squarely in the eye.

"Are you asking if I climbed into bed with him? No! My grandparents and I come from the same village as Thomas. He was friends with my parents."

"Why was? Where are your parents now?"

"They were murdered by Mayi-Mayi militants."

Ariane immediately regretted her question. She had often refrained from such inquiries unless they were absolutely necessary. In the Congo, almost every family had suffered the loss of one or more relatives during the numerous wars or raids. She was astonished by the composure of the young woman.

It seems they have become accustomed to violent deaths.

Awkwardly, she conveyed her sympathy.

"Did Mayeye receive many visitors?"

"Not many, but he saw some people regularly."

"White people?"

"Whites and africans. Even Nkunda visited every so often."

Ariane pulled Darcy's photo out of her pocket.

"Do you know this man?"

She looked at the photo and nodded. "Yes, it's Mister Darcy."

"And how often was he here?"

"I don't know exactly, but several times, at least."

"Did you ever overhear what he and Mayeye talked

about?"

"It was mostly about money and business. I only heard bits and pieces of their conversations."

"Do you know what type of business?"

"Darcy produced videos, which everyone knows."

"Was? Are you saying you know he's dead?"

"Yes, that news spread like wildfire."

"Please try to remember what exactly he was doing here and what was being discussed."

The young woman thought for a moment. "He often borrowed one of Thomas' motorboats and took it out on the lake. Most times, he didn't return until the next morning."

"So, Mayeye has, or rather had, several motorboats?"

"Yes, two."

"Where is the second one?"

"No idea. I believe Mister Darcy recently borrowed it."

"Do you know where he took the boat?"

She paused again, thinking. "They repeatedly mentioned Idjwi island. Apparently, SÉCOMA encountered some problems with the island's population."

Ariane turned toward Bosco, who was silently listening to their exchange. "Any objections to giving this family the four hundred dollars?"

Bosco thought for a moment and nodded.

Ariane handed the girl the four hundred dollars and one of her business cards.

"Thank you for your cooperation. You may go home now. And, if you think of anything else, please give me or Commander Likongo a call."

The young woman accompanied her to the kitchen

door. "Madame, he wasn't all that bad of a man. He provided well for us."

Ariane answered with a friendly nod.

What can I say to that? It's her perspective.

They went upstairs. It had three rooms: a bedroom, a sort of private study, and another room with a bed and cupboard. It didn't appear anyone was using the room. The master bedroom featured a huge bed, a wardrobe, and a dresser. The floor was covered with a heavy carpet. Looking out the bedroom window offered a clear view of the entrance gate. The furniture was stacked with clothes, shoes, and underwear. Some clothing lay on the floor next to a partially packed open suitcase.

The floor of the study was littered with several editions of The New Times. The edition featuring the press release about the discovery of the dead man in Gisenyi was among them. On the desk, which had a rather old chair before it, was a computer with its housing open. The hard drive had been removed.

Ariane looked at Bosco and commented. "It looks like it was getting too hot for him."

"It sure does," Bosco replied. "Mayeye was getting ready to flee."

12

> "Peace is not the absence of war,
> peace is a virtue, a state of mind,
> a disposition for benevolence, confidence,
> justice."
> (Benedictus de Spinoza, Dutch philosopher,
> 1632 - 1677)

1992, a village in eastern Congo.

Nowhere else other than in the Congo had temporary absence of war little to do with actual peace. Nevertheless, the people of the village didn't regard the current situation as an opportunity to rest. Instead, they went about work as they had always done. However, now they thought of it as prosperity instead of mere survival.

"Papa, I'm going to try to shoot something for dinner," the boy whispered into the ear of his deaf father. He nodded at him. His father's old carbine was no longer true in its aim, but he was familiar with it. "Go, my boy, take my binoculars and rifle. Watch yourself," the old man admonished. "We'll prepare the meal." When the son shouldered the rifle, his mother and younger sister waved at him and then went to work preparing the cassava.

The jungle bordered the village. The boy had oftentimes accompanied the men of the village on hunts. Recently, hunting had become increasingly problematic. Soldiers and guerrillas roamed the jungle and shot anything that moved. On top of that, the constant clashes in the eastern Congo had led to a massive wildlife migration to quieter regions in neighboring countries. Two hours later, he still hadn't killed an animal. He debated whether he should go deeper into the jungle when he spotted a gazelle in a small clearing. Cautiously, he crept closer for an advantageous firing position. The silence was abruptly broken by shots being fired, followed by the immediate reply of the apocalyptic rat-tat-tat-tat of machine guns, all of which came from the direction of the village. The gazelle promptly ran into the bush and disappeared out of sight. Overcome with fear, the boy ran to the jungle's edge. He was greeted by a scene that made his blood run cold.

The marauding mob hadn't given the people a chance to flee. Many villagers' lifeless bodies lay on the open ground and while the huts burned, their killers loaded supplies and domestic animals into several pickups. Helpless and unable to do anything, he grabbed the binoculars and tried in vain to find his family. He focused the field glasses on a man standing in an open jeep directing the mob. Tears blurred his eyes. Suddenly, two men grabbed him from behind. His fierce resistance was ineffective. They dragged him to one of the pickups where several young men already sat, their hands securely bound. Five of them were from his village, although they were significantly older. He hardly ever had contact with them. Either way, apparently they had been instructed to remain quiet. The others he didn't know, which led him to assume their village wasn't the first to be raided.

A short time later, their vehicle joined an unruly convoy making its way loudly through the bush. A brief look back told the boy his village no longer existed.

No one stood in their way. All vehicles were filled with armed men smoking, drinking, and horsing around, all the while assaulting the tranquility of the bush with loud music from portable radios. The ten prisoners barely had room to move. After a five-hour journey through the jungle, they finally reached the center of a tent compound and a few bamboo structures. Two men roughly ordered them to disembark and line up in a row.

The leader of the group stood in front with his legs apart and his fists on his hips. Beads of sweat decorated his forehead. He tried to transform his sneer into a smile, but his cold gaze overshadowed it.

"Men!" he began in Lingála as his gaze traveled down the row of men. "Mobutu has abandoned us and we have to rely on ourselves from now on. Starting immediately, you are members of our liberation movement. I am Commander *Predator*. My orders will be obeyed without protest. You will be one of ours and well taken care of; however, insubordination is punishable by death. First, you must undergo military training and prove yourself. Those who do will join us in the fight against our enemies. All others will work in our mines, also an honorable duty. Regardless, all of you will fight for your future!"

He didn't mention who the enemies were or what future they were fighting for, and nobody dared to ask.

"You, over there, step forward!" He pointed to the first man on the right in the row of prisoners. The one addressed, a big and strong-looking boy, looked shyly around, and then followed the order.

"As of now, you're a sergeant and on active duty. Your name is *Evil Spirit*. Repeat your rank and name!" The young man repeated in a trembling voice, "I am Sergeant *Evil Spirit*."

One by one, each man stepped forward and did the same with his newly given nom de guerre. The boy who was out hunting was the youngest. When it was his turn, the commander approached and patted him on the cheek.

"You're still very young. We will make a good soldier out of you. What name do you want?"

The boy lowered his head and stubbornly replied, "My name is Prince."

The commander laughed loudly, looked over at his men with a bemused expression and his mouth twisted into a wide grin. "Did you hear that? His name is Prince." His followers laughed dutifully along. The commander turned back to the boy.

"As you wish. We will call you *Prince of the Killing Bunch*, PKB for short, okay?"

At that moment, although Prince had difficulty suppressing his inner outrage, he eventually managed to nod his resignation.

Commander *Predator* assumed his previous stance and announced, "Now, we will show you your quarters. You may not leave camp without permission! Is that clear?"

The timid murmur rippling through the group of young men signaled their understanding. A man ordered them to follow and led them to an open shelter made of rough-hewed trees and a corrugated iron roof. The floor was covered with straw mats.

"This is where you sleep. Out there…," he gestured

with one arm at the surrounding jungle, "you can expect to encounter Simba's law, survival of the fittest. Many who came here have attempted to escape and failed. Do not try it. You are only safe with us."

Another gesture told them they could refresh themselves at the rainwater barrel. Each new recruit was also handed a plastic bottle of stale water to drink. Afterwards, everyone searched for a place to sleep.

After dusk, the moist heat of the night provided little cooling. Despite intrusive loud noises of the drunk and boisterous militia, Prince and his fellow captives soon fell asleep. Even the guard assigned to keep an eye on them succumbed to his inebriation and dozed off while sitting against a tree.

Young Prince was determined from the outset. No one would turn him into *Prince of the Killing Bunch*. Simba's law wouldn't discourage him. After another hour, it suddenly became quiet as the last of the noisy crowd finally fell asleep. Only the loud croaking of nocturnal panther toads with their large vocal sacs resounded through the dark jungle, betraying the proximity of a body of water. Silently Prince stood up, took his bottle with the remaining water, and crept to the dozing guard. Without disturbing the man, he stole the guard's long knife from a sheath lying next to him as well as a small flashlight. To confirm his departure had not been discovered, he looked around briefly before quickly fleeing the camp and disappearing into the bush.

13

The missing Belgian NGO consultant, called Isaam Kabija, was in charge of agricultural issues in the Kivu regions. He came from a Tutsi family from North Kivu and worked on several projects, both in Rwanda and the Congo. Once his regular visits to report in at headquarters, Head Office Kigali, abruptly stopped, the director in charge informed the police, who in turn started a missing person file and sent copies to all other police departments.

A few weeks earlier, they had their annual employees' get-together at the organization's headquarters and as usual, they enjoyed food, drink, and ongoing conversations until the wee morning hours. Employees were permitted to bring family members or friends. At the last gathering, Isaam was accompanied by a Belgian who had introduced himself as a producer of nature films. They had met on Idjwi island, where they had become fast friends. That evening, the event progressed as usual, some took photos to capture the occasion, and everyone had been in a good mood without the urge to drink excessively.

Ariane entered the police station and like every day, she glanced at the notice board in the vestibule where pictures of missing persons hung. Considering she was a foreigner, she showed more interest in news updates than most working in the building, especially since they often announced events her local colleagues already knew about. Her eyes briefly scanned the missing persons' reports. Good-looking guy she thought and went to her office to work on the dead man in Gisenyi case. As soon as she opened the file and saw the attached photo of the murdered man on top, shivers ran down her spine. In the photo of the missing person, they had missed something.

She dashed downstairs into the vestibule, ripped the missing person report from the wall, and rushed back upstairs. What had been overlooked was the person standing in the background, partially obscured by the body of the missing person. Although the picture quality was mediocre and lacked deep focus, as is often the case in portraits, she identified the man with the hairless furrow on his head.

"Bosco, our victim in Gisenyi must have known the missing person," she exclaimed as soon as she opened her boss's office door, interrupting his phone discussion with Théo.

Bosco glanced up.

"Hold on, Théo, please stay on the line, I'll put you on speaker."

He looked at the photo.

"We seem to have a lead. I have to check it out right now. I'll call you back later."

"No problem. Call me at home if it gets too late."

Bosco hung up and briefly looked to Ariane, who was still standing in front of his desk.

"We need to find out who took the picture, as well as the location. Go ahead and give his employer another call."

Ariane went back to her office and dialed the phone number they had on file in the station's information system for the Belgian organization.

The head of the NGO answered curtly. "Marchal! Who am I speaking with?"

"Ariane Manstein, CID Kigali. Monsieur Marchal, I would like to speak to you briefly. It's about your missing advisor."

"Oh, I hope you have good news."

"It seems we're making a little progress. Would it be okay for us to come by and take up a little of your precious time?"

"Why certainly, I shall be expecting you."

"Thank you, we will be there in thirty minutes."

Shortly thereafter, they were on their way to the city center. The office of the Belgian NGO was located on a narrow side street off Avenue Paul VI. Monsieur Antoine Marchal received them immediately in his office. Although they knew from the police database that he was well into his sixties, he, nevertheless, seemed vivacious. Bosco introduced himself and Ariane. Marchal merely glanced at their police badges. His office decor consisted of fine tropical woods and the walls were covered with family photos and photos taken on safaris. On the shelves, wooden sculptures by African artists rested in between books. One wall featured a wooden mask whose gloomy expression immediately attracted the visitors' attention. Curious, they inspected the piece of art.

"Do you know about the art of African masks, Monsieur Marchal?"

Marchal briefly glanced at the mask and then somewhat questioningly eyed the two police officers. "No, I'm not overly versed on the subject. I bought that mask from a dealer in Angola. He even explained its meaning. Quite sinister looking, don't you think? Assuming he didn't lie to me, that mask belongs to the Chokwe tribe and it represents *Kalunga*, supreme power." He leaned back with his arms crossed in front of him and looked complacently at the mask. Smiling, he gave Bosco a sidelong glance and said, "It cost me quite a pretty penny. Once I retire, I will occupy myself with getting to know African art in more detail." Not wanting to prolong talking about the mask, he sat up properly again and inquired about the purpose of their visit.

"You said you have news about the whereabouts of our co-worker?" He pointed to two empty chairs at a neighboring table. Ariane and Bosco sat down.

Bosco replied. "No, Monsieur Marchal, sorry to have to disappoint you, but we have discovered a lead. In the photo you gave us, a man is standing in the background. Our reason for coming here is to learn a bit more about him. In particular, in what way is he related to your organization?"

Bosco took the photo from his file and pointed to the man in the background, without revealing he had already been identified as Tom Darcy.

Marchal took the photograph, looked at it briefly, cleared his throat, and fidgeted in his oversized armchair.

The two police officers suddenly felt as if something in the picture was making him uncomfortable.

"I asked a co-worker to provide you with a more suitable photo. I couldn't find a good picture in my private photo album and the photo in his personnel file is too old. I wasn't even aware of a second person in the picture."

"Where was the photo taken?"

"That was out back in the garden, at our annual company party. He does not work for our organization. Isaam introduced him as his friend Tom. He claimed he was a producer of nature films and spoke French. I assumed he was Belgian by his dialect, but I didn't ask him about it. I don't recall his last name."

"Did you see him talk to anyone else?"

"I really didn't pay any attention to him after we were introduced. As I said, Isaam introduced him to me and a few of our colleagues by his first name, then..." He thought for a moment. "I cannot remember. Oh yeah, Isaam also mentioned he met him on Idjwi island, which is where we consult on agricultural issues."

"But, he had to have spoken with someone besides Isaam," Ariane interjected.

"That's certainly possible. If you wish, I can ask around the project offices. Many people know Isaam, some are even his friends."

"That's kind of you, we would be most obliged," Bosco said. "You would really be helping us out. However, is there anything you else you might have noticed about the man? Are there more pictures?"

"No, I didn't notice anything out of the ordinary. Perhaps his clothes were a bit too formal compared to those of our employees, who prefer to dress more casually. In regard to photos, yes, we certainly took lots of pictures, and my colleagues have given me theirs. Each year we make a photo album of our festive gathering, which I'm in charge of," he added and offered an embarrassed smile as if he wanted to apologize for having to deal with such a trivial task in his position.

Ariane and Bosco smiled sympathetically in return.

"So far, I have only glanced through them. If you like, we can look at them together. The photos are stored on my laptop."

"That would be great, Monsieur Marchal," Bosco said.

The Belgian asked his two visitors to a table in the corner of the room, where he placed his laptop and connected it to a large external monitor. He started his device and rearranged the monitor so all had a good view.

"I hope you're not pressed for time, there are about five hundred pictures," he remarked.

Without waiting for an answer, he started showing the pictures in the program's slideshow feature. Every now and then, they manually stopped at a certain photo and zoomed in to catch details. Overall, it took ninety minutes. The result was startling. While everyone else present was in numerous pictures, often in a friendly embrace with a co-worker with glasses in their hands, the man who was introduced as Tom didn't show up in any of the many photos.

"I admit, I might have overlooked him in the photo I gave you, but not seeing him in any others is a bit strange," Marchal commented hesitantly about the presentation as he leaned back.

"Well, I think some people have good reasons for not wanting to be captured on film and are extremely vigilant to make sure it doesn't happen. I don't know whether you noticed, but the photo your employee provided us with shows him merely by accident. It's the one time he obviously failed to notice that a camera was directed at him," Bosco replied.

"I find it strange you don't have a photo of him,

even with your employee. How do you explain this?"

"I myself only took a few pictures and my co-workers only sent me the ones they chose for the album. It's quite possible this Tom is in some of the photos I don't have. Considering he isn't involved with our organization and most of my colleagues probably don't even know him, it makes sense they didn't choose photos with him in them. May I ask why the CID is so interested in this man? Has he broken the law?"

"No, at least not that we know of. We're interested because he was found dead," Bosco said dryly without going into the circumstances.

Marchal was visibly shocked. "Oh my goodness, how did it happen? Was it an accident?" He looked questioningly at Bosco.

"We wouldn't be here if he died in an accident, Monsieur Marchal."

"Yes, yes, of course. Since it has been so peaceful in Rwanda lately, it is easy to forget we live in a dangerous region. Do you think the man's death is connected to Isaam's disappearance?"

"Perhaps, we're still in the initial stage of our investigation," Bosco replied. He glanced at Ariane and, seeing she didn't have any further question, turned back to Marchal. "Thank you, Monsieur Marchal. Please call us if a colleague stumbles across a photo with him in it or perhaps has other information on the man."

„Also, we would like a copy of Isaam's personnel file," Ariane said.

"I also have his file on my laptop. If you have a USB stick, I'll copy it for you," he offered. Ariane fumbled with the USB stick on her keychain and handed it to Marchal. After downloading the data, he accompanied Ariane and Bosco to the door. With a somewhat embarrassed glance, he said in a halting voice, "There's one thing you might find interesting that a lot of people who work here don't know." Without waiting for a response, he continued. "Isaam is gay. Not that it's an issue in our organization, as long as it doesn't affect work performance. However, we keep such knowledge private because homosexuality in Africa is still heavily stigmatized. Naturally, that little tidbit is not mentioned in his personnel file. We never had reason to suspect he used his work in any way to establish relevant contacts."

Bosco and Ariane exchanged a brief look. Bosco replied, barely able to control his anger, "It's nice you finally decided to share such important information with us. I hope there isn't anything else we should know about. This new information changes the way we look at our case significantly and it shines a different light on the disappearance of your employee."

"Please forgive me. My dilemma is that I am infringing on the privacy of my staff when I provide you with information. But rest assured you have my full support."

"Was there any indication Tom was gay?"

"Not that I remember. I only met him briefly. Isaam had a completely laid-back way of dealing with people. How would any of us know?"

"But you and perhaps other co-workers know he's gay. Wouldn't you have suspected Tom of being intimate with Isaam?"

"The thought might have crossed my mind, but I was busy that day. I don't care about it one way or another. And, I don't know about other co-workers sexual preferences."

"Okay, Monsieur Marchal, let's leave it at that for now. It is possible we'll contact you again about this matter," Bosco said, ending the conversation.

"Of course, Chief Inspector, I am at your disposal anytime."

On the way back to the office, both police officers were deep in thought. Ariane glanced sideways at Bosco, who was driving.

"I think this new development complicates our case even further. It seems we have to consider completely new scenarios."

Bosco remained silent for a moment. "Yes, unfortunately, and we definitely have to spend more time on the missing person case. I can't help but think Isaam's disappearance is somehow connected to Darcy's murder."

14

Back in the office, Bosco sat at his desk, leaned back, and stared at the ceiling. Due to a new regulation, the ceiling fan was set on the lowest setting and stirred the warm air without noticeably affecting the stuffy atmosphere. The installation of air conditioning had already been discussed, yet it had been repeatedly postponed due to the ongoing energy crisis, currently at its peak. The state energy and water utility company, ELECTROGAZ, had been struggling for some time due to the continuing drought. Because of the drought, reservoir levels in the north had dropped and the water could not drive the turbines.

Bosco couldn't stop thinking about Idjwi island. The girl in Mayeye's house also mentioned the island in connection with Darcy. He leafed through the case file and reread Théo's report. The fisherman who had discovered Darcy also lived on the island. The name he had given was Ota Benga. The interrogation report didn't give any further details. Allegedly, Ota Benga spotted the dead man from his boat and had immediately informed the border patrol, who then called the police. For some reason, Bosco felt something was missing in the official report, which was made by the staff in the public prosecutor's office. Unfortunately, he could no longer remember the exact wording of Théo's report.

Ariane entered and wanted to discuss the crime scene photos again.

"One moment, Ariane, first I have to ask Théo about something." He picked up the phone and turned on the speaker so Ariane could listen. Théo picked up immediately. After informing him about the new information, Bosco asked his question.

"Théo, do you still have a copy of your report?"

"Yes, of course, I always keep them. It wouldn't be the first time some important paperwork disappeared."

"Great! I'm interested in the section containing the fisherman's statement. Would you read it to me, please?"

"One second, I have the report right here." During the pause, Bosco heard the rustling of paper as pages were turned, before Théo came back on the line.

"Okay, here it goes. A fisherman by the name of Ota Benga, a Congolese Twa, saw a lifeless body lying on shore from his boat…"

"You said Twa? That's not in the official report we received from Mugambage's office. Unbelievable! Damn all political correctness! The prosecutor's office staff conveniently withheld the fisherman's ethnic origin."

Théo was silent for a moment, then humbly apologized.

"Sorry, Bosco, I should have noticed. I guess I didn't find the fact important."

"At least you didn't avoid describing him as a Twa. Is there proof of his identity?"

"No, the border guards asked, but fishermen don't exactly have a reason to carry their papers with them. He was a boy no more than sixteen years of age. He's around four-foot-six inches tall and slender. I guess they didn't think he could've been he involved in such a murder."

"Actually, that should have been our call."

Ariane chimed in. "I noticed something when I took a second look at the crime scene photos. To me, it looks as if you cannot even see that area from the lake. The corpse was lying under a tree with low-hanging branches that should have blocked the view, providing the boy wasn't near shore."

Bosco frowned. "I admit I didn't even pay attention to it."

"Uh, hold on," came over the intercom. Again, Bosco and Ariane heard the rustling of pages being flipped before he spoke again. "There's nothing in the report stating how far out he was when he saw the dead man and or whether the fisherman came ashore. The shoreline is steep in that area. I don't think anyone would voluntarily pick that spot to climb up to the road."

Bosco could still picture the steep embankment he scrambled down during his visit to the site. Ariane brainstormed.

"If he was in that spot, what was he doing there? We should ask the border guards on duty where he moored the boat."

"You could be right," Bosco said. He caught himself reverently eyeing Ariane from the side. She was looking, lost in thought out the window, and did not notice. Even if she was mistaken, she was asking the right questions.

On the other end of the line, Théo remained silent.

"Théo, is it possible we overlooked something?"

"That's always a possibility! Damn it, Bosco, when did we get old? We'll take our boat at once and check it out. I'll call you back."

Ariane turned toward Bosco. "No reason to make a

face, it doesn't mean I'm right."

"Of course, but I still have to consider it," he said, resolutely. Bosco was a bit upset with himself. Granted, mistakes happen, but he should've noticed.

Ariane's cell phone called. The caller id displayed the name Richard.

"Hello, Richard, you have news from Hannover?"

"Yes, the report is on its way as we speak. We were lucky. The area of deposit has already been certified. It's a mine on Idjwi."

"Fantastic, that's what I wanted to hear. It fits perfectly with the direction our investigation is taking. Thank you so much, we're in your debt!"

Bosco listened in and tried getting her attention by waving his arms.

"Chief Inspector Kabeera also says thank."

"Okay, I can think of something. How about you guys treat me to a meal?"

"Sounds good, but after we close the case."

"No problem, just let me know."

Bosco grabbed the Rwanda Natural Resources Authority map with all the coltan deposit sites and unfolded it. Among the red marked coltan and cassiterite deposit sites were locations on Idjwi island.

As soon as Bosco arrived at his office the next morning, Théo called. "It's as Ariane suspected. You cannot see the spot out on the water. I also questioned one of the border agents again. He states the Twa was moored on the Congolese side when he reported the discovery."

"Well then, I'd say we have enough reason to take a look around that island."

The fire Joseph had mentioned, was it connected to the case? Bosco felt a sense of urgency. In such situations, he always a popped a piece of gum in his mouth, it was a clear signal to his colleagues and his wife that he was in hunting mode.

"Théo, ask Joseph if he can arrange a boat trip. We need to take a look around Idjwi."

15

The apathetic armed guards at the entrance gate waved him through. He was expected. The young man entered the old warehouse near the lake. The spacious property containing a house, two smaller adjacent outbuildings, rented by a mining company, had been fenced-in. Apparently, the house held valuable devices that needed protection. The room he entered was dark. Suddenly, a spotlight directed at his face temporarily blinded him. Instinctively, he raised an arm to protect his eyes.

"Tom, is that you?" he shouted into the darkness.

He could barely make out the outline of what looked like a stage with no identifiable equipment. Without warning, a strong arm came from behind and wrapped around his neck, pulling him down. As he tried in vain to free himself, he felt the slight sting from a needle in his upper arm. His last sensation was of his body lying on the ground, from which he continuously drifted farther and farther away until finally, dark nothingness.

In the southern half of Lake of Kivu was Idjwi island, which journalists often called *The forgotten Island*. This might, as with other areas in East Africa, have been true before the turn of the century, but since hunting for industrial nations' Rare Earths Elements began, Idjwi also gained partial recognition in the world. On the island were sites that mined the coveted raw materials, whose prices fetched record prices on stock exchanges.

Idjwi island belonged to the Democratic Republic

of Congo, its location was about seven to ten miles from the eastern shoreline of Rwanda and approximately the same distance to the western shoreline of North and South Kivu provinces of the Congo. The southern tip of Idjwi was only separated from the Rwandan mainland by a narrow waterway about a half a mile wide. Inhabitants of the island, which produced agricultural products, sold their goods at markets in the Congolese coastal towns of Bukavu, Goma, and Kalehe.

The entire area of the eastern Congo was rich in mineral deposits and was the cause for the struggles throughout the entire history of this vast country. While a South African company operated mines on Idjwi with technical aids, there were countless other mines where Rare Earths Elements such as coltan, as well as tin ore cassiterite, gold, and diamonds, operated without oversight and by means of manual labor. As in all illegitimately operated mines, diggers or *creuseurs*, as they were called in francophone Africa, working conditions were deplorable. Living conditions of the population in the surrounding areas of these mines weren't any better. The miners lived in primitive settlements that provided extremely poor hygienic standards. Using wood to make coal as well as for the construction of dwellings left a large part of the rainforest barren. Women offered unprotected sex, ideal conditions for spreading infections and AIDS. The waters from which drinking water was derived, gradually evolved into chemical time bombs. Mercury, which was used to extract gold from the soil, was highly toxic. This was done with the so-called amalgam method, where mercury was added to a pan filled with grains of sediment that surrounded gold. Then, through gravity separation, valuable gold nuggets could be removed. The remaining mixture of sediment grains and mercury was drained into the nearest body of water. In order to attract pure gold, the next step required heating the gold so that the remaining mercury would evaporate, during which workers inhaled the fumes.

Part of the population on Idjwi was made up of the Batwa pygmy people, who were referred to in the Great Lakes region, which Lake Kivu was part of, as Twa. Presumably, Twa were the original inhabitants of Rwanda, before the Hutu and the Tutsi outnumbered them. Although socially the Twa always ranked the lowest, the coexistence of the three ethnic groups, in the beginning, was problem free and each one adopted the customs and rituals of whoever ruled. During the Tutsi monarchies, the Twa were entertainers at the royal court.

With the exception of the senior executives of the South African mine group Shaka Resources Inc., the soldiers of the regular Congolese army, FARDC, as well as a few employees of NGOs, mostly island residents, had hardly any contact with people from the mainland. Rather, they saw themselves as the inhabitants of the *Island of the Forgotten*.

There were no automobiles on the island. Those without a two-wheeler were dependent on the numerous motorbike taxis. The connection to the mainland was maintained by the Nyamizi, a barge, in the small town of Kashovu. The small settlement in the south of the island was equipped only with a primitive jetty, making the mooring of the barge an adventure for the captain each time. From here, the Nyamizi operated regularly from the island to the two capitals of Kivu, Bukavu in the south and Goma in the north.

Surprisingly, the ruling system of the *mwami* persevered autonomously into the 21st century. The island managed to stay out of mainland conflicts. Many refugees fleeing Rwanda (at first the Tutsi and later on the Hutu) found refuge on the island and discontinued hostilities. There were organsided in two so-called *collectivités-chefferies* (Collectivity Chieftaincies), one in the north and one in the south, each presided over by a *mwami*. Conversely, the Twa had a président who represented their interests.

The increasingly progressive deforestation in the region majorly affected living conditions. As a result, the Twa habitat was severely limited, forcing them from their once natural environment, the rainforest. Considering their main livelihood consisted of hunting, they turned to other means of support. So, on Idjwi island as well as on the adjacent Congolese mainland, Twa communities were established where they devoted themselves to fishing and agriculture. Nevertheless, even here their new habitat was greatly reduced by commercial and private interests who claimed increasingly more and more land for themselves.

Their situation worsened not long ago when a few *wazungu,* together with armed Congolese men, made their home on the land of an abandoned mining company. Ruthlessly, they started terrorizing the Twa and decimated whatever wildlife was still alive. When one of the *wazungu* Congolese helpers was caught and lost his life in a trap the Twa had set to protect their territory, their group took one of the Twa working a field and killed him.

The fragile peace under which the Twa community lived their lives abruptly ended. Admittedly, foreigners didn't dare attack the fortified pygmy people in their villages because they feared their traps and poisoned arrows. Regardless, the Twa habitat had been severely restricted. Therefore, they decided to end the interference by giving a clear warning to the *wazungu* office in Goma, a *sumu*.

> *How can I go on living like this? It must end.* Like the numerous sleepless nights before, he grabbed one of his books, leaned back in an armchair, and began to read until his eyelids became too heavy to remain open. Finally asleep, the book slipped from his hand and landed on the floor.

16

Goma, eastern Congo. It was a busy evening at the Coco Jambo Club. Many foreigners and Africans sat at the bar, occupied tables, or danced with the numerous girls present to African rhythms. The two men arrived separately. The *mzungu* came by taxi, briefly looked around, and choose a table in the far corner with a clear view of the entrance. The nightclub was dimly lit and he wanted the man he had an appointment with to find him easily. One of the numerous female servers spotted him and approached his table. He immediately ordered two Mützig beers without even acknowledging her provocative packaging. She returned with the beers and he placed cash on the table. A brief nod indicated he didn't want the change. Shortly afterwards, an African entered who spotted him immediately and headed resolutely for the table. Casually, the man sitting pushed out one of the chairs surrounding the table and pointed to the newly ordered beer.

"Bonsoir, Capitaine, do sit down."

"Don't address me as *Capitaine* in here. What do you want? Why so conspiratorial?"

"Because I prefer not to be seen with you."

The African briefly looked around. "Okay, get to the point."

"I have a small job for you." The *mzungu* explained the details.

As the two men spoke, they failed to notice they were being watched closely. The young man noticed the *mzungu*, whom he knew, while dancing with a girl, yet decided not to greet him. He also immediately recognized the Congolese as he approached the foreigner's table. Overwhelmed by memories that haunted him since the age of thirteen, he inadvertently pulled the girl tighter against him. She accepted it with indifference but looked surprised when she realized her dance partner's attention wasn't on her. With difficulty, the young man held back the tears and buried his face in the girl's curly hair. Once he regained his composure, he knew his future life had only one objective. He would not lose sight of the man.

The man addressed as Capitaine took a sip from his bottle. After a few moments to think about the offer, he finally looked at the foreigner. "You call that a small job? It'll cost you."

"How about ten percent?"

"Ten percent of what?"

"Approximately one million US dollars," the other man lied.

"How about twenty percent?"

"Fifteen, plus an additional sign on bonus of ten thousand," the *mzungu* haggled.

The African took another sip from his bottle and agreed to take the job after a short pause. He pulled a business card from his wallet, wrote something on the back, and handed it to his companion. "Since Mayeye is dead, it's now my responsibility to find jobs. Here's my bank account. I'll be waiting for the sign on bonus. Without another glance, he left the nightclub and entered his car. A vehicle followed undetected to his house. Meanwhile, the *mzungu* enjoyed the rest of his beer before leaving a few minutes later.

It was still early in the morning when Joseph slowly pulled his boat into the shallow water of the northern shore of Idjwi island. The outboard motor was already off and in the tilted position as the hull screeched against the sand before coming to a standstill. A frightening premonition came over him. The owner of the property and head of the South African mining group, Konzern Shaka Resources Inc., approached him.

"So good of you to come. We are all quite shocked."

Together, they walked to the site of the fire. The charred wooden beams lay haphazardly on top of each other. In the middle of the square, where a warehouse and two other buildings had previously stood, loomed two supporting beams pointing skyward like beacons that had partially survived the inferno due to their hardness. The usually grassy area was now covered in white ash. Only black skeletonized remains of the surrounding bushes and shrubs stuck out of the ground. A misshapen fused together row of steel wire marked the boundary of the formerly enclosed area.

The director pointed to a group of men in deep discussion standing adjacent to the property. They were Joseph's staff, who concealed the view of a number of bodies lying on the ground. When Joseph and the director approached they snapped to attention, saluted, and stepped aside. Stacked in a row were ten corpses, nine Africans, and one white man with his legs removed. In addition to the ten bodies, there was an extra set of legs, also belonging to a white man. One of the men approached Joseph.

"The bodies were buried behind those bushes over

there. One of the men discovered disturbed soil while taking a piss."

Joseph recognized the dead *mzungu*. It didn't take much imagination to connect the missing torso to the severed legs. He believed he had seen the dead man in a SÉCOMA uniform before in Goma. The condition of the bodies was hard to look at even for seasoned men.

Joseph turned to the director and showed him the photo of Darcy.

"Do you know this man?"

"Yes, I do. He leases the property."

"Do you have any means of contacting the mainland?"

"Yes, I have a satellite phone."

He reached into his pocket and handed Joseph the device. By now, he knew Bosco's phone number by heart.

"Bosco, it's Joseph."

"Hello, Joseph. I'm glad you called. We've been trying to reach you. What do you need?"

"I need you here on Idjwi. We've found several dead bodies, including Krauskopf, as well as two severed legs of a *mzungu*. I think they are the missing parts of Darcy's remains. A violent massacre occurred here. I suggest you drive to Kibuye. It'll be the fastest. I'll meet you there with my boat."

Bosco had heard enough and asked no further questions.

"Bosco, it's clear this fire is connected to your case. Now I have to involve the forensic pathologist from MONUC. This case is getting too complex and exceeds our capabilities."

"Kinshasa is okay with it?"

"I have no idea and I am not going to ask them for permission. I really don't care what they want. But, I'll arrange it so you will be here first."

"Thank you, Joseph. We're on our way. I guess we can be in Kibuye in about two and a half to three hours. I'll have Natalia Baranyanca, our medical examiner, accompany us. You can liaise with MONUC's people."

Joseph handed the satellite phone back to the director. "I have to get to Kibuye to pick up my colleagues. I'll be back in approximately five hours. We need to cover the dead with a tarp or whatnot. Do you have anything like that?"

"Hm," the director thought for a moment, "we have a couple large tents. I believe one is big enough."

Joseph gave his men a few instructions before starting the outboard motor. After a two-hour cruise, he reached Kibuye and moored the boat on Bethanie Guesthouse's small jetty on the outermost tip of the bay within sight of Idjwi. It would still be a while before Bosco and his team would arrive. He ordered a cup of coffee from the guesthouse restaurant and called Bosco to tell him where he was berthed. A short time later, the Rwandans arrived at the guesthouse. Before they departed, Joseph informed the general at MONUC, with a request to send experts in forensic examination. As it turned out, MONUC had already been informed about the dead in Gisenyi and about the investigation in the DRC. Apparently, the order from Kinshasa not to get involved was met with little understanding and a cover-up was suspected. Hence, the general of the troops was reticent at first, but after a brief discussion, he eventually agreed.

Around noon, Joseph, Bosco, Ariane, Natalia, and Fabien, set off for Idjwi.

Meanwhile, a tent had been erected over the dead. The director of the mine had also set up a diesel generator for a mobile air conditioning unit.

One of Joseph's men greeted them.

"We've inspected everything, but can't quite make sense of the event. The razed warehouse has lots of items made of steel and except for a few chain links we were unable to identify anything else."

Natalia pointed questioningly at the tent.

"Yes, there are ten."

Bosco nodded at her. "See you later."

Silently they walked and inspected the markers where Joseph's men had made discoveries.

"This is the spot where Darcy must have been murdered," Bosco murmured. Trepidation was written on his face as they studied the debris field.

Fabien stood helplessly in front of the towering steel girder that had braved the flames. At the foot was a lump of molten metal that had seeped deep into the gravelly ground. With some force, he managed to wrestle the heavy piece of molten metal encased with pieces of gravel out of the ground. Now it was obvious there were two different metals. Part of the object framed another piece that seemed heat resistant. The frame portion had a different appearance. Using a penknife, Fabien scratched the surface. The material was soft.

Bosco was curious and joined him.

"That's lead! Didn't Darcy's body show traces of

lead?" Questioningly, Fabien looked up at Bosco.

"That's right. Take a sample for lab comparison."

Joseph approached. "Let's go to the tent."

The bodies were still lined up side by side, the smell of decay almost unbearable. Everyone covered their nose with a cloth.

Natalia had already taken a good look. "I have no doubt these legs belong to Darcy's corpse," she said as she met the investigators. "The cleaved areas of the severed legs match the stumps of Darcy's corpse. Here, look at this." She pointed to a picture on her camera screen and a photo she brought from the institute. "Surprisingly, the one identified as Krauskopf only has one relatively small wound below the right clavicle besides the severed legs. All the dead, except for Krauskopf, are Africans, including two women. Two men have on the SÉCOMA company uniform. One had his throat cut and the other has a wound in the area of the heart. Two other men had their heads cut off." She pointed to two strongly decomposed corpses with severed heads. "One man has a huge chest wound. Except for Krauskopf and the two uniformed men, all are naked and show evidence they were subjected to brutal torture. The men had their genitals cut off, the two women their breasts. One woman's upper body was also slashed. The traces of decay differ from body to body. We have lots of work ahead of us. I hope the people from MONUC arrive soon."

Fabien joined Bosco.

"What do you think; are those ghosts of the past?" Bosco understood what Fabien meant. He thought about the murderous gangs of *interahamwe*, those who to date still hid behind the so-called freedom movement of the Forces démocratiques de liberation du Rwanda.

Bosco shook his head.

"Okay, the FDLR are into murdering, but they do not go through the trouble of covering their tracks and burying their victims."

Ariane, as usual, armed with her camera, photographed each detail. Natalia took samples to safeguard the DNA.

A short while later, the boat carrying the experts from MONUC arrived. Joseph quickly introduced Natalia. The experts immediately started their investigation. Due to the provisional conditions, urgency was required because the temperature necessitated a fast reburial. To speed things up, the director of the mine had already contacted a *mwami* who offered to help identify the victims and to rebury the bodies. Meanwhile, the CID team busily re-examined the terrain.

"The fire didn't leave much standing," Fabien stated.

"Yes, unfortunately, but I believe it was intentional. The warehouse inventory is puzzling," Bosco said. "What do you think, Ariane?"

"Well, it definitely wasn't a mechanic's workshop. You might find it hard to imagine, but people were tortured to death here."

"What's the connection to Darcy and the *Hun*?"

Natalia joined them. "We will know soon enough. Krauskopf's wound below the right collarbone is quite interesting, not to mention his strange contorted posture. One of the SÉCOMA men was also found in this position. The wound the *Hun* suffered was unlikely fatal."

"So, how did he die? Don't tell me..."

"Looks like it. Unlike the edges of the cuts on Darcy's stumps, the *Hun's* show less bleeding."

Ariane groaned. "Unreal. Someone has done quite a job here."

"All of it doesn't fit together," Bosco said. "We have the *wazungu* and uniformed men on one side and on the other, the horribly mutilated."

Joseph listened wordlessly. "Bosco, we should talk about how we're going to proceed."

"Quite right, Joseph. Please get a hold of this Ota Benga. We need to speak with him."

"Okay, I'll get the *mwami* involved."

"By the way, what's your opinion of the director of the mine? Can you help us compile a list of all known facts about him?"

"He hasn't come to our attention yet. His company acquired all necessary licenses and he enjoys a certain preferential treatment in Kinshasa." With a meaningful glance, he added, "For whatever reason. They are certainly concerned about their employees' well-being."

"Where does he live?"

"In Kashovo. He makes property inspections on his own motorbike. Occasionally, he is in Goma."

"Okay, at least he seems cooperative. Whoever performed this horrific massacre knew what they were doing, knew the surroundings, and covered their tracks. But, I think there is more than one perpetrator."

Stunned, Joseph and the entire team looked at Bosco.

Ariane asked, "Do you suspect Mayeye had something to do with it?"

"The thought crossed my mind. However, there are also other possibilities."

"I can picture it easily," Fabien remarked. "Darcy and the *Hun* have been up to no good here and then were killed for it. Mayeye had his fingers in it and wanted to get rid of pesky witnesses."

"Let's see what the forensic examination turns up. That should tell us more, but until then we have to investigate here on Idjwi," Bosco said ending the discussion.

Back in Kigali, they worked under intense pressure. Bosco wrote a report for the prosecutor, who he previously informed by phone. Natalia wrote a report on the forensic examinations. She and the people of MONUC agreed to compare notes. Ariane and Fabien wrote a report on the crime scene.

17

Dazed, the young man emerged from unconsciousness. He was hanging completely naked over a slightly elevated wooden platform. Steel cuffs fastened to taut chains attached to the scaffolding encased his neck, wrists, and ankles, reducing his mobility. He was suffering severe headaches. The cuffs' metal edges cut into his flesh. A bright spotlight shone directly on him.

"Right now, you have no idea why you're here, but you will soon find out," he heard a male voice say in broken English from the darkness.

Croaking incomprehensibly, he tried to connect with the voice.

"What are you doing to me? Where's Tom? I have an appointment with him."

"Nobody here named Tom. It's just you and me. I want to play a game and you're my partner."

The voice sounded brutal. The captive immediately sensed the threat grow unbearable.

"Why, what would be the point?"

"That's not important."

The captive tried hopelessly to move. The cuffs dug further into his flesh. However, he felt the pain helped him counter unconsciousness. Feverish and bathed in sweat, he prayed for the nightmare to end. There was only one hope. Tom would soon come and free him. He was convinced of it. The man stepped out of the darkness and Isaam saw he was speaking to a physically large *mzungu*. He had covered his head with a black mask made of cloth and was dressed in knee-length pants and a sleeveless jacket. His bulging upper arms sported numerous tattoos. The man's lifeless eyes stared at his prisoner through the slits in the cloth. Now the giant's masked head came close to his victim. Isaam closed his eyes and tugged on the chains again. The tormentor's hot breath escaped from the mask's mouth slit.

He wants to kill me.

The masked man stepped back into the darkness. At first softly, then ever increasingly louder, a chorus accompanied by dramatic sounds of various concert instruments pierced the room. Puzzled, he opened his eyes again, but the glaring spotlight made it impossible to see anything. What followed was sheer horror. Abruptly, out of the darkness, a leather strip studded with short nails, whipped his body repeatedly and in no time was covered in blood. The pain was excruciating. The tortured body reared up several times before succumbing to unconsciousness shortly thereafter.

The morning after the crime scene inspection on Idjwi, Ariane found an official letter from the KFL in her inbox. Initially, she was a bit perplexed because the results from Idjwi were not yet available. Natalia's handwritten note cleared things up:

Ariane, a DNA analysis confirmed that the Congolese, Marie Kamanda, is a descendant of Tom Darcy. Enclosed is the certificate in quadruplicate.

Greetings, Natalia.

"Fabien!"

Her colleague, who sat across from her with his head

stuck in his laptop, peeked over the monitor's edge.

"She's Darcy's daughter. Natalia sent me the DNA results."

"We should tell her."

"Of course, but not by mail. Could you contact the Belgian consulate and inquire whether she and her son are eligible for Belgian citizenship."

"Why?"

"Maybe they'll want to emigrate if they have the opportunity. I don't think a woman wants to live here willingly, considering all the robberies and raping going on in the Congo."

Fabien wasn't quite sure how to respond. Whites always believed it was better not to live in Africa.

"This is their home."

Ariane was aware she had touched one of Fabien's sensitive nerves.

"Yes, I understand, but you also know what the conditions are."

"You firmly believe she had nothing to do with her father's murder?"

Ariane was glad Fabien didn't want to debate the quality of life in Africa. "Yes, but we'll continue to keep an eye on her as long as the case is unsolved."

"All right, I'll get in touch with the embassy."

"I could go alone and tell her."

Fabien needed a moment to find the right words.

"I...I don't think it's a good idea. I better tag along."

Ariane offered one of her girlish smiles.

"Are you my protector, Fabien?"

Her colleague was a little embarrassed. Ariane was unaware everyone at the CID had orders to ensure her protection.

"No, I believe you can handle yourself just fine. But, come on, this is the Congo!"

She stifled the desire to point out that he just confirmed her assessment of the conditions in the Congo.

"Okay, we'll go together. Perhaps you can first obtain the applications, so we can take them along."

Fabien left for the Belgian Consulate. It wasn't his first visit and he was familiar with the staff.

"Hello, Fabien, are you traveling to Europe again?"

The woman at the front desk was an attractive female Rwandese he had spoken with often. Fabien felt her friendliness wasn't merely professionalism. She liked him and each time he wanted to ask her to dinner but repeatedly chickened out.

"No, Joselyne, we want to help a woman and her son, apply for Belgian citizenship. She is the daughter of a deceased Belgian."

"Does she live here in Kigali?"

"No, she is Congolese and lives in Bukavu. We are going to see her soon and would like to know what requirements must be met."

"She should go to the Belgian Embassy in the Congo."

"You know the Belgians only have representation in Kinshasa and Lubumbashi. We really would like to save her the trip."

"She needs a notarized birth certificate from a Belgian or international agency. Certification from a Congolese agency won't do. What's her name?"

"Marie Kamanda."

"And, the father is Tom Darcy?"

"Yes, but..."

"She was already here and submitted an application. We are presently processing the request."

"How is that possible? Did she have a birth certificate?"

"Yes, everything was in order."

"May I see the document?"

"Um...I guess it's okay since you're a policeman. Wait a moment."

She stepped into her office, returned with a file, and found the document after briefly rifling through it.

Fabien studied the document. It was issued by MONUC's lab in Goma and seemed genuine.

"Huh, we didn't expect her to do this so soon. Was someone with her?"

"Nobody came inside with her, but a vehicle was waiting for her."

"What kind of vehicle?"

"A black SUV, a Toyota I think."

"Could you make out who was sitting in the car?"

"Yes, by chance. I was getting something from my car when she got out the vehicle and walked to the entrance. I saw two Africans, one driving and one in the backseat. Why, is something wrong?"

"No, not that I know. I was merely curious. So, when will her passport be ready?"

"In approximately five days. Tomorrow afternoon she finds out if her application was approved. I presume she'll get the passport two to three days later."

"Has she asked for it to be delivered?"

"No, she wants to pick it up in person."

"How did she behave? Did anything stand out?"

Joselyn thought a moment. "Well, come to think of

it, she seemed rather nervous and terse. She is quite an attractive woman. Are you interested in her?"

"Joselyn! She might be good looking, but a man can also have other reasons to be curious about a woman."

"Okay, a cop, maybe."

Fabien wasn't in the mood to prolong the conversation.

"Thank you, Joselyn, I'll see you."

"I certainly hope so. Call me."

Joselyn leaned on the front desk with her elbows. Smiling and flirting suggestively, she provided him a view of her feminine assets. Her subtle décolleté certainly was enough to spark a man's imagination. She was conscious of the fact and showed it sparingly, but when necessary, spontaneously and goal-oriented.

Men! Most can't stop ogling, but he averts his gaze.

Although Fabien looked kindly back at her, he had no inclination to flirt with her. His mind was on Marie Kamanda - and for good reason.

"I'm sure I will," he said absentmindedly and waved briefly before exiting the embassy.

Fabien went straight to Bosco's office. Interrupting his conversation with Ariane, he informed them about the Congolese's application for citizenship at the Belgian embassy.

"I find the Congolese's action somewhat odd," he said concluding his report.

However, he wasn't the only one with that opinion. Bosco used the department's phone and turned the speaker on. "I'm going to call Natalia. Perhaps she knows why MONUC issued her a Belgian birth certificate."

"Hey, Natalia, it's Bosco. I have a question: Did you give your colleagues at MONUC Marie Kamanda's DNA results?"

"Yes, we agreed to compare all results. You already have her birth certificate. I also sent the results of the examination and the DNA analyses on Darcy's torso and the newly discovered severed legs. They also sent me their findings on all the other murder victims. So, everything has been double-checked and we have arrived at same conclusions. We're writing up our joint report. Identifying the bodies wasn't difficult. The women were prostitutes from the region around Bukavu. The men were also from the same area. The two men in uniform were employees of SÉCOMA in Goma. Joseph Likongo is trying to learn more about them. By the way, concerning the *Hun* and one of the men in uniform, both had a high dose of strychnine in their blood."

"And, what does that mean?" Ariane spoke up. "We used that stuff as rat poison.

"Here, we have indigenous tribes who use poison derived from a nut tree called *strychnos usambarensis*. It kills animals instantly."

"Indigenous tribes? You mean like the Twa?"

"Yes, Twa or Ituri pygmy people. Both use barbless but notched arrowheads. An arrow like that usually breaks when you try to pull it out."

"This Ota Benga, who discovered the corpse, is Twa. I take it there aren't any arrowheads in the wounds?"

"No, they were removed. But, the wound canal certainly matches and you can see they were subsequently disturbed."

"How does the poison act?"

"It causes convulsions. We recognized it by the contorted positions of the bodies. The venom also causes immediate paralysis. It causes skeletal and respiratory muscles to permanently contract, which eventually leads to death, depending on the concentration. However, that venom is only used by tribes who live in the jungle, the *impunyu*. The Congolese was probably killed instantly, but Krauskopf...? He certainly was incapacitated, but considering his body mass and the comparatively harmless wound, I don't think he perished quickly. He must have been super strong. I'm convinced he was still conscious when his legs were amputated. Quite vicious."

"One more question. The way it looks, the UN laboratory also issued her a birth certificate. However, Marie Kamanda has applied for Belgian citizenship with the birth certificate issued by MONUC. Do me a favor and get back in touch with your colleagues and ask who exactly issued the birth certificate as well as to whom it was given?"

"That shouldn't be a problem. I'll call you right back."

Annoyed, Bosco frowned.

"This new development doesn't come at a good time. Joseph called. He wants us along when he goes to the island to interrogate the Twa who found Darcy. I hope we resolve this quickly."

Meanwhile, Jean-Baptiste and Alphonse joined them and offered their opinions. Ariane was restless. Natalia called back after thirty minutes.

"Bosco, MONUC did not issue a certificate, but the

lab was broken into and many valuables were stolen. They didn't discover that blank official documents were missing until I called, including genealogical documents and the official stamp of the MONUC laboratory. Ergo, the birth certificate is a fake."

The new development was alarming. Everyone thought about what it meant. Fabien looked at Ariane questioningly. Her tongue was dry and she tried to organize her thoughts.

"It makes no sense. Why take a fake birth certificate to the embassy. She knew we were looking into her lineage, why not come to us."

The group paused for a moment, lost in their thoughts. In his usual shy manner, Jean-Baptiste spoke up. In private, it meant he was sometimes not heard or simply ignored. Yet his colleagues at the CID had long since learned to listen to him because he seldom said anything without having given it serious thought. The remark, which he made without emphasis, caused Alphonse to stare desperately at the ceiling, Fabien to scratch his head, Bosco's brows to furrow deeply, and Ariane to pale.

"Darcy also had a Swiss bank account. Isn't the Congolese his rightful heir?"

Ariane groaned.

"You're right, damn it, you're right again. I believe we are not the only ones with a problem now. Fabien, you said she arrived with two Africans."

"Yes, but Joselyne didn't recognize them."

"Let's assume the worst. Someone wants to empty Darcy's account and is using her to transfer the money."

"This case continuously presents us with

unexpected twists and turns," Bosco interjected. "We might as well take your worst case scenario into consideration. But, I remind everyone we still have a murder to solve. We cannot fall behind on our investigation."

Ariane gave Bosco an angry look.

"You're not going to look into it? Bosco, we are also bound to prevent crime."

"All right," he said soothingly. "But why would she go along with it? Granted, she is a good suspect, but Joseph is in charge of investigating the burglary in Goma. We can't step on his toes."

"Who knows why, but she does have a young son," Ariane replied, sounding discouraged.

"Are you suggesting she's being blackmailed?"

"Why, is that so far-fetched?" she snapped at her colleagues, looking angry again. The men flinched. They had never seen Ariane act this way. Everyone was aware of the possibility. For a moment, they remained silent.

"I'm starting to sweat just thinking you could be right." Fabien broke the silence.

Ariane couldn't help herself and said what was on her mind. "You might as well sweat a little. Remember, it was invented in Africa and is one of the most successful survival concepts of the human race."

Ariane's argument seemed reasonable. Bosco had to admit they couldn't ignore the fact that Marie Kamanda might be in danger, even if it was in Rwanda.

"Okay, I see no other way than to split up. I'll ask Théo to accompany Joseph and me to Idjwi to interrogate the Twa. Ariane, you and Fabien leave now for Bukavu and check out Marie Kamanda, providing she's there. And, make sure her boy is there too. Jean-Baptiste and Alphonse, you two stay in touch with the Belgian consulate, just in case Ariane and Fabien don't find the Congolese in Bukavu."

"Shall we arrest her?" Alphonse asked.

"No, ask her to come to the station to answer a few questions. She can even bring someone along if she likes. If she doesn't cooperate, you can pressure her into coming."

"But, if she's accompanied and it turns out we are right about our suspicion, it's possible her companion or companions will be armed."

"It's possible, so take along help. To be safe, I'll assign two armed colleagues. They should, however, remain in the background and only intervene if absolutely necessary."

Ariane and Fabien were already at the door when Bosco called after them. "Please check in with Alphonse every five hours."

18

The spacious fenced grounds with the old warehouse and the two outbuildings of the South African mining group, Shaka Resources Inc. was on a spit on the north end of Idjwi island and was accessible only by a narrow strip of land. The building was originally temporary storage for cassiterite and coltan, the processed degradation products of the mines on the island. The building had stood empty for quite some time now, ever since transportation logistics became better organized and didn't require such long storage periods. Vegetation had again spread from the lake a hundred yards away to the fence and gradually took ownership of the building.

Then, the *wazungu* and helpers showed up and leased the property and buildings. The mining company, which operated several mines in the area, was only too happy to have found someone willing to renovate the buildings.In the following months, after the new tenants had made themselves at home, more and more people disappeared. Although a few families showed concern, it wasn't unusual in the eastern Congo. It was also uncommon to report a missing person if the person was not missed. The general assumption was that the missing had left for China to do business. While Western governmental and nongovernmental organizations provided help and technical support under the condition of good governance, Chinese companies were already doing good business. The living conditions of the Congolese staff were, in their words, an internal affair that they didn't want to interfere in. Dealing with

China was quite lucrative for many Congolese. They managed to set up shops in China with local partners and from there, organized trade with the Congo. Many African countries had been enjoying business relations with China for quite some time. The cheap Chinese products flooding the continent were a testament to it. Many Congolese regarded China as the Promised Land. Those left behind believed, respectively, wanted to believe, those who had gone missing went on to a better future and that one day they would be back, knocking on the hut door with lots of money in hand.

"Gahiji, we need to talk."

The *président* of the small Twa settlement pointed to a stool in front of his hut. He wore the traditional token of his status, a hat made from the coat of a wildcat, and gravely regarded his visitor, whom he had asked to see.

The addressed party sat down. Only 28 years old, he was a loner without family, but already an experienced *impunyu*, the term for the last hunters and forest dwellers of the Twa. Because of his late mother, whose hut he used, there was a small connection to the Twa settlement on the island. His father had been from a village in north Rwanda where he also grew up. Their ancestors had intermarried with Hutu, making him physically, especially in height, stand out from the rest of the Twa in the village. He was strictly against abandoning the original Twa way of life, as so many inevitably had done. He didn't work in the fields or fish on *sambaza* boats. He devoted himself to the traditional way of hunting, even if it was becoming increasing harder, and fishing from shore. The *président* knew Gahiji didn't accept the farmers' authority, yet they enjoyed respectful interaction with each other. Since the Chief no longer hunted or used his boat, he made it available to whichever hunter would share his killed game with him. After the common exchange of pleasantries, the *président* voiced his concerns.

"Isaam has been gone now for several days and our warning has been ignored. We should look around the stranger's warehouse. It's been too long since we've paid any attention to his activities. I want to know what they're up to over there. This new friend of his, Tom... you once mentioned you knew him. Who is he?"

Gahiji nodded and told him his story.

"I'll take care of it," he concluded, "but I could use some help."

The *président* nodded. "Pick a few men, but please be careful. We cannot win a war against SÉCOMA in the long run."

The hunter got up and walked to his hut. He had to prepare.

The area surrounding the warehouse and adjacent buildings was familiar. While the place had been vacant, he often spent the night there after a hunting expedition. Since the property had been leased again, he stopped by from time to time to observe. They had placed a sign at the entrance that read

TD Nature Film Production.

Oftentimes, a *mzungu* and two or more Congolese security guards were present. On most days, there were only security guards. Then, loud Congolese music played and the men got drunk and enjoyed the company of prostitutes. In essence, it wasn't out of the ordinary. Some nights, muffled concert music could be heard coming from the inside the warehouse, yet there was no way to glimpse the activities inside. Gahiji presumed they were working on films and the music was the background score.

One day, while watching the activity at the warehouse after fishing, a fast boat arrived. A tall, blond, powerfully built *mzungu* off-loaded a slain gazelle, which was grilled on a spit that evening and eaten by the assembled men. Despite the years since his childhood, he recognized the man who had called himself Tom. He had met with his father several times when they were still living near Ruhengeri—and they weren't good memories. The boy had watched the *mzungu* talk down to his father and call him names. At the time, the man worked as an agent for a zoo and came to purchase young gorillas. He now suspected the blond man was in the Congo dealing in protected wildlife and using his company as a cover. The Twa had long ago stopped hunting protected species, thus, Gahiji was immediately alarmed. He was afraid they would once again be accused of poaching and face the familiar consequence and driven from the area.

It was still twilight when the boat carrying three men landed on the sandy shore. They pulled their vessel a bit onto the shallow slope and fastened it with a rope to a shrub's low-hanging branches that almost touched the water. Quietly, they revisited their plan.

Each man was armed with bow and arrows as well as a sharpened *panga*. The night before, the arrowheads had been coated with poison. Gahiji's helpers disappeared into the jungle. He moved almost silently on a direct route to the warehouse. If he found evidence of his friend Isaam's presence, he would take decisive action.

Arriving at the fence, he assessed the area and waited patiently for darkness. At the gate, about a hundred yards away from the warehouse, stood a uniformed Congolese guard with an AK-47 smoking a cigarette. From the warehouse, muffled instrumental music filled the air, disturbed only by the dull hum from a generator in one of the smaller, adjacent buildings. It housed a well and a power station. The warehouse entrance was closed and fitted with a clearly legible sign *Do not disturb*. A window in the other outbuilding was illuminated. Bluish flickering flashes of light told the observer a TV was on in the room. The door opened and a uniformed man stepped outside. Suddenly, the noisy music inside the adjacent building obscured the subdued sound coming from the interior of the warehouse and the dull hum of the generator. After a brief patrol of the grounds, the uniformed man passed near the secretly watching observer as he walked over to the guard at the gate and exchanged a few words. On the way back, he flipped a switch while passing the building housing the generator. Spotlights illuminated the gate and the entrance to the warehouse. After briefly glancing at the surroundings, he entered the adjacent building and closed the door.

The glowing fireball dipped below the horizon. The

heated earth breathed and plunged at the speed of a light bulb fluorescing in the African night. The only sound was cicadas sending their peculiar noise over the mirror-like surface of the lake. Occasionally, a fish snapped at the mosquitoes moving in dizzying circles just above the water surface. The disturbed water created undulating ringlets that soon faded into nothingness.

The guard patrolled the fence line. Every time he took a hit of the cigarette, the brief flare gave away his position.

No one noticed the shadowy figure approaching the warehouse. He carefully climbed onto the gently sloping roof using the crevasses and protrusion in the stone wall. Nestled on the incline, he took a moment and cautiously gazed into the darkness. Once sure he had not attracted attention, he disappeared through a hatch into the loft of the warehouse. Warily, he slid on his stomach towards a hand-wide gap in the floor. Light shined through the opening and illuminated a spot all the way up on the roof's underside. The disturbed dust danced in the light. Placing a piece of cloth in front of his mouth, he quietly approached the gap. Breathless, he watched in disbelief the surreal scene in the hall below him. The man hanging from steel-reinforced wooden scaffolding, he knew well. Behind the spotlight, stood a veiled giant figure fiddling with a device mounted on a tripod. The victim's body was covered with signs of gross abuse. Blood dripped from the steel cuffs restraining the man. Wordlessly, he writhed weakly. When the bound man's head briefly jerked back, Gahiji could tell by the man's wide-open eyes and contorted face that he had already lost his senses.

It was clear to the observer that he had to act. The masked man seemed to be performing the barbaric work alone. Apparently, guards were not allowed to watch.

He decided to free the prisoner from his tormentor. He had to act quickly. At this distance, he could not miss despite the dimly discernible outline. Gahiji targeted the tormentor's neck. When the arrow's line snapped, the man moved and the poisoned arrowhead hit his body below the right clavicle. Puzzled, yet not making any movement that could be construed as a response to pain, he looked at the arrow and grabbed the shaft that broke in his left hand as he tried to remove it. Slowly, he turned his head in the direction the arrow had come from. Suddenly, the tormentor's body convulsed backward as if his spine had shrunk. Erratic and with arms flailing, he fell backward like a felled tree and crashed on the sandy ground with a dull thump, pulling down the tripod along with him. Gahiji felt the amount of poison wasn't sufficient enough to immediately kill a body of such size. However, he knew the man would be unable to control his movements and that he could look forward to a slow death by respiratory arrest. Not a single guard had noticed anything.

Quietly, the observer climbed down the backside of the building. Hidden from the guards, he silently crept through the shadows toward the adjacent building the other guard had entered. A window offered a view of the sparsely furnished interior, which he knew was separated from the front door by a small vestibule. On a small table stood a television turned to one of the countless Congolese musical shows. The already glassy-eyed security guard sat in front of it with his back to the door and took a sip from a bottle of home-brewed *kanyanga*.

The choreography of these musical shows was always similar and unimaginative. Scantily clad young women danced rhythmically and tantalizingly around the singer who continuously replied to their advances with obscene gestures, which in turn compelled the dancers to become even more animated with their erotically suggestive movements.

It was time to act. His two helpers from the village were waiting for the signal. Their task had been clearly laid out; proceed to the front gate and take out the guard. After the observer had given the signal, he patiently waited for the deed to be done. After a couple of minutes, he saw his helpers dragging the body into the jungle.

Quietly, he entered the small vestibule of the building and opened the door to the room where the guard watched TV. The uniform man had no idea he wouldn't live to see the end of the broadcast. The singer in the musical show just grinned lasciviously at the approaching, particularly buxom beauty who was swinging her buttocks provocatively, as the head of the man watching was suddenly firmly pulled back. The short gasp that escaped couldn't prevent the sharp blade of the *panga* from closing in on his throat, and with a quick flick slashing it. Except for a final strangled groan escaping while blood and bubbles spewed forth from his mouth as he slid to the ground, the guard made no sound. The hunter turned off the television and exited the building. With a nod, his two helpers came over and helped him break down the door of the warehouse. After finding the light switch, the rest of the warehouse was cast in light.

Only now that his friend's tormentor was lying on the ground, did the hunter realize it was a *mzungu*. The hunter could tell by the pupillary response and panting breath that the man was still alive and pulled the mask off his face. That man he had also seen before.

The spotlighted prisoner still hanging suspended by chains from the scaffolding didn't utter a sound. The three men freed him from the cuffs and laid him on the sandy ground.

Only now did they inspect the rest of the hall's interior. What they saw exceeded the limits of their imagination. Thoroughly astonishment and horrified, out of sight in a corner, they found a guillotine hidden behind a makeshift bamboo wall, its blade still showing traces of blood. Another corner held a collection of iron weapons, sticks, pliers, hammers, bamboo skewers, as well as nail-studded leather whips. Behind another makeshift partition stood a king size bed, its mattress covered with a plastic tarp. The steel bedframe had firmly welded chains on each post with attached steel cuffs. On the wall was a spigot with a rolled-up hose. Silently and wide-eyed, they looked at the torture devices from the European Middle Ages, all of which were unknown even in this violence-riddled region.

Gahiji was the first to find his composure again.

"We have to dress his wounds. Get Isaam to the village and make sure he's taken care of. Then come back and help me get rid of the bodies."

They ripped a piece of cloth into strips and temporarily wrapped the injured's worst wounds. The two helpers were ready to leave with the injured man when the sound of a fast approaching motorboat came from the direction of the northern bay. Shortly after the boat's engine was cut off, they heard someone calling out a name into the darkness. Gahiji had the foresight to turn off the lights. Each posted themselves near the entrance door of the warehouse. After another call went unanswered, the door of the warehouse was opened and a man entered. The three Twa didn't move. Just before the man flipped the light switch, a stone hit him in the back of the head. The big burly man instantly collapsed forward onto the entrance flagstones. Gahiji recognized the man immediately. He was the blond Belgian. Quickly, they bound the unconscious man's hands and feet with the hemp ropes that hung on a wall. Afterwards, they turned their attention back to their injured friend. His racing pulse and panting breath forced them to hurry.

In their concern for their friend, with whom they had worked for years to improve their agricultural yields, they had carelessly restrained the *mzungu*. They had neglected to search him. Suddenly, the sharp crack of a gun resounded. The man had awakened from unconsciousness and freed himself from his bindings. While still lying on the ground, he fired at one of the two helpers, but only hit the man's lower leg. Gahiji's reacted with lightning speed. With a leap, he kicked the man's arm, pulled the *panga* from its sheath on his belt, and forcefully brought it down across the head of the semi-upright Belgian. Without a sound, the man collapsed back to the ground with a deep gash in his skull. He was killed instantly.

The hunter was breathing heavily. Even at this advanced hour while the temperature outside was tolerable, oppressive humidity prevailed inside the warehouse. Everyone was bathed in sweat. Without further discussion, they wrapped a few more strips of cloth around the bleeding wounds of the injured Twa, who now sat painfully twisted on the step of the landing. Using two of the sturdy bamboo poles from the makeshift partitions and a colorful printed blanket, they made a stretcher to transport Isaam. Gahiji was forced to accompany them. He and the second helper picked up the makeshift stretcher and, together with the limping helper, set out for the village.

Along the way, Gahiji thought about how to proceed next. He wanted to protect the village from being connected to the dead. On the other hand, he wanted Darcy to be found, but it had to be in a location that ensured a closer look into the business of the film company .

The *président* briefly consulted with them and then asked a boy to come over who was commissioned with his own nocturnal mission. Gahiji went to his hut and returned with a bag in which a head-sized object was stowed. He had decided. Darcy was to be found on the mainland. With his helper, they headed back to the warehouse. The distance from the shore at the warehouse to across the lake to the coast of Goma was eighteen miles. Considering his boat's fasted speed was seven knots, they could make the trip with the prevailing weather conditions in two and a half to three hours and be well on their way before daybreak.

Back at the warehouse, they searched the pockets of the dead. The wallets of the *wazungu* contained dollar bills, credit cards, and a few keys. Each also had a cell phone. Gahiji divided the money and gave it to his helpers, but he kept the credit cards, cell phones, and keys. The bodies had to disappear. Near where the slain guard had been hidden, they found a suitable area free of shrubbery. In the wellhouse were several shovels. They started digging. After removing only a few inches of soil, they came across the corpse of a mutilated, half-decompose woman. Her condition left no doubt into whose hands she had fallen. Gahiji was overcome by a renewed sense of urgency. As silently as possible, they enlarged the grave and first placed the two Congolese inside.

They immediately became aware that the *wazungu* weight would create problems. Transporting and off-loading their cargo on the coast would be particularly difficult. Hesitant, the helper looked at the hunter. Gahiji made a quick decision and pointed to the guillotine. Together, they dragged the bodies to the killing machine. Alternating, they placed each leg onto the bottom of the two vertically stacked boards with a semicircular notch that usually was intended for the neck of a delinquent. With a thud, the heavy blade of the guillotine severed each leg above the knee. The giant hit by Gahiji's poisoned arrow still showed eye movement. However, the two pygmy men had seen too much to feel any empathy. Once more, the guillotine's blade did its job. Using his hunting knife, Gahiji removed the arrowhead from the upper body of the *mzungu*. One by one, they dragged the carved up torturer and severed legs of the *wazungu* to the prepared grave. After removing the arrowhead from the body of one of the uniformed men, they buried his body along with the others and covered the ground with dry grass. They wrapped Darcy's torso in the blanket they had previously used as a stretcher and carried him to the hunter's boat. Gahiji made sure Darcy's boat key was in the ignition and ready to head out on the lake. He instructed his helper to steer his own boat around the peninsula and to wait for him there off the coast. He walked back and briefly inspected the office and residential quarters. In one room, he found a box of syringes and a bottle of colorless liquid. With multiple strokes of his *panga*, he destroyed the contents. In the wellhouse, he found and kept an ax. A short time later, both boats met at the prearranged location. Steadily, they plowed across the waters of Lake Kivu, heading straight for the northern coastline. They had long since left the small island of Idjwi behind. In the distance loomed the shadowy Mount Nyiragongo, whose bubbling crater flashed at short intervals in the gray haze at the summit.

Gahiji indicated to his helper to stop the boat. He pulled Darcy's motorboat alongside. After the engines were shut down, the boats rocked with the gentle swells of the lake. The last digits of the GPS digital display on Darcy's boat wavered on their last position, 1.792283° latitude, and 29.195700° longitude. They had arrived in the area of the so-called *main basin* in the northern part of Lake of Kivu. There, the lake's maximum depth reached sixteen hundred feet. With the ax, the hunter hacked a hole in the motorboat's hull and jumped to his boat. With faint gurgling, the boat sank taking with it the bagged possessions of the slain.

Four hours had passed by the time they approached the coast. They switched off the boat's motor and paddled the rest of the way. The boat glided silently towards the towering craggy volcanic-dominated dark coast that they knew well from their numerous trips to Goma. It didn't take long to find the spot the Twa had chosen to discard the corpse. They needed to be cautious because the border guards were stationed not too far away and the moon was almost full. Slowly, the boat slid into the little cove. Here, erosion had left a beach of black sand. To avoid unwanted noise, they quietly entered the shallow water and pulled the bow of the boat onto a piece of land. Soundlessly yet quickly, they off-loaded the torso of the dead man. Gahiji reached into his bag and pulled out a mask. He placed it on the disfigured face and secured it with hemp rope. After blurring their footprints, they paddled the boat into deeper water. After a few hundred yards, Gahiji started the outboard motor and steered the boat into the night. Exhausted, his helper lay down and drifted immediately off to sleep.

> The puff adder flicked its tongue as it slithered through the opened window. On the mahogany floor, it briefly coiled and raised its head to orient itself, then slithered towards the bedframe. With a piercing scream, the man awakened from his dream. The *gardien* at the entrance abruptly sat up and intuitively closed his hand around his gun, but soon leaned back. He knew the recurring ritual. The light in the room went

on and he could see the man through the window pick up a book from the shelf.

19

Théo called early in the morning. Ever since their investigation had escalated, they all arrived at the office by six-thirty. This gave everyone time to catch up on reports and check e-mails. Bosco explained to Théo the new situation and the possible involvement of Marie Kamanda in the case.

"It seems we have underestimated the scale of this case," Théo noted dryly. "Joseph and I will pick you up by boat in Kibuye. He suggests we wear something durable. We may have to cut a path through the jungle. I'm sure you still have your old ranger gear. We'll probably have to spend the night too."

Bosco tried to detect sarcasm in Théo's voice because he wasn't sure whether his friend was joking. He doubted he would still fit in his uniform from the eighties, although it would be more than appropriate for this excursion.

In no way am I up for that, pal.

"At what time should we be on Idjwi?"

"Joseph says the *mwami* referred him to the Prrésident of the Twa settlement, but he won't be available until this afternoon. I guess it might get late. I think we should meet in Kibuye at three o'clock, that way we'll arrive on Idjwi around five-thirty."

Bosco regarded his watch and nodded in agreement. "I'll be there, see you later."

Théo and Joseph meet Bosco in Kibuye almost at the same time and headed for Idjwi. The magnetic compass read 300° north-west.

The village Ota Benga had given as his place of residence was located on the east coast in the north.

After a short walk, they reached the settlement. The *président* was already waiting for them. He sat on his stool and wore his fur hat. Joseph briefly introduced himself and Bosco and laid out his concerns in Lingála.

"There is no Ota Benga here," the *président* announced firmly. "Are you trying to blame us for something again?" It seemed he had said all he was going to say.

"I was afraid he would react along those lines," Bosco muttered under his breath.

Joseph was aware authorities had little say in rural areas. Nevertheless, he tried sounding official. "Listen here, this is a police investigation. We are going to take a look around."

The *président* made a dismissive gesture. "Do what you must, but you won't find an Ota Benga here. And, if you don't mind, leave our chickens in peace."

The three police officers refrained from commenting. Unsure as to how to go about uncovering the man they were looking for, they decided to tour the village. Although the inhabitants had retreated to their simple huts, the three men sensed they were being watched.

"I'm not sure if we'll make any progress here," Théo said.

"Neither do I. It's not like we can turn the village upside down," Bosco replied. A man whom they asked if he knew Ota Benga initially seemed somewhat amused, but then reassured them he didn't know anyone by that name.

Without a clue to pursue, they walked back to the Chief's hut to ask more questions. The *président* was a bit more accommodating than before but continued to insist that no one in his community was called Ota Benga.

"Let the fishermen go out this evening, then tomorrow morning we'll see. So, now you are my guests," he said, concluding the discussion in a conciliatory tone.

Bosco could barely conceal his displeasure, but heeding Joseph's advice, he finally agreed. "Okay, but tomorrow morning we must talk to all the young men."

A woman came and asked them to follow. A hut had already been prepared for the visitors. A little later, three women arrived carrying two jugs of water and a bowl with a simple meal of fish and rice. Coming from the direction of the shore, they heard the peculiar singsong of the *sambaza* fishermen.

They woke early the next morning and first had water with banana for breakfast before discussing how to continue their search.

"I have no desire to be strung along by the *président*. Perhaps we should start by inspecting the boats before we deal with the men," Bosco suggested. Joseph and Théo had no ideas of their own and agreed. On the beach, the boats lay side by side, moored on the shore. Many boats were equipped with an outrigger and attached net. Under the wary gaze of two fishermen repairing their nets, they examined the boats. Théo removed his shoes and rolled up his trouser legs to look at the stern of a boat lying in the water. It had an outboard motor, but no outrigger. Apparently, it hadn't been out on the lake last night. Bosco and Joseph had already continued to the next boat when they heard Théo call.

"I've found something. Have a look." Théo met them waving a small plastic bag triumphantly. It contained a few tufts of blond hair. The hair roots bore traces of dried blood. "We should look for a fisherman with blond hair or one that had a guest with blond hair on board."

"Where did you find it?" Bosco inquired.

"Wedged in a splintered piece of wood on the bottom." He pointed to the relevant boat.

Joseph didn't hesitate. Determined not to be brushed off, he ran over to the two fishermen. "Who was the last one to take that boat out on the lake?"

The two men stared sheepishly at the ground.

"I expect you to answer, if not, I will take you with me to Goma. You can sit in jail until you're ready to talk. So, what will it be?"

One of them pointed a finger toward the village, fear written on his face. "Gahiji!"

"Is that his name?" The fisherman nodded silently. Joseph pointed a finger at the person he was speaking with. "You, come along and show us his hut. Come on now, get going!" They headed back to the village.

Gahiji saw them from afar walking purposefully toward his hut. He had no idea how they succeeded in finding him, but he didn't intend to ask them. It was time he disappeared. His meager belongings were quickly bundled. After grabbing his bow and arrows and his panga, he crept through the bushes to his boat at the lake. By the time the policemen entered the nearly empty hut, the hunter was already out on the open lake. The men looked around. A few pieces of wood smoldered in a cooking area.

Bosco frowned. "Damn it, I feel like a complete amateur. Let's hurry to the beach!"

They stormed out of the hut and rudely jostled their leader aside. They were out of breath when they reached the shore. On the horizon, they could make out a dark spot moving quickly in a southeasterly direction.

"I don't think my boat can catch him. It barely runs at eight knots."

"We'll follow him anyway," Bosco said decisively.

"He's trying to get to the mainland." Joseph motioned towards his boat moored a considerable distance away. "Let's go!" Bosco and Théo followed.

Ariane and Fabien reached the border crossing to Bukavu and drove directly to the house of the Congolese. The little house seemed deserted. Fabien tried the front gate and found it unlocked. No one answered his calls, so they entered and walked up to the front door of the little house. The knock on the front door also went unanswered, although it was locked. As on their first visit, they walked around the side of the house and entered the backyard. Ariane called the woman's names several times. When they reached the patio, her hunch was confirmed. The old woman Marie Kamanda had called aunt was lying dead in her own dried blood. They had cleanly slit her throat. Insects were already feasting on the gaping wound. She had laid there for some time.

"I was afraid of that. We must notify Bosco and Joseph at once," Ariane said urgently while painfully maintaining her composure.

20

Joseph steered the boat in the direction the Twa had gone.

Théo consulted the map. "Where does he intend to go?" For a moment, each was lost in thought. Théo interrupted the brooding silence.

"What do you think? Is he heading for the Congo? He could make shore in Bukavu."

Joseph briefly turned around and shook his head. "That's too risky. He'll try to avoid any populated areas."

Bosco consulted the map again. "The nearest accessible land is in Rwanda and it corresponds with his heading. Remember, we know our man is an *impunyu*. We should assume he's trying to escape into the Nyungwe Forest. There, he can find shelter in the numerous settlements of forest dwellers. The rainforest is his home. I know the area. It'll be hard to catch him."

The Nyungwe Forest was a vast cloud forest in southern Rwanda. It was home to many species of primates, particularly chimpanzees, but also birds, snakes, lizards, and many small animals. The Rukarara River originates in the Nyungwe Forest and meets up with the largest river in Rwanda, the Nyabarongo, and together they empty into Lake Victoria. According to local folklore, as well as German Africa researcher Richardt Kandt, that was where the White Nile originated. The Englishmen Burton and Speke, and then Baker, Livingstone and Stanley, had unsuccessfully made numerous expeditions to find the river. The Nyungwe Forest was bisected by a highway between Butare and Cyangugu. The northern part had already been developed for tourism, but rainforest dominated the southern area all the way to Burundi.

Bosco pointed to a bay along the rugged Rwandan shoreline. "He could've made shore here in Rwesero. This spot is near the Nyungwe Forest and it wouldn't take long to escape. As long as he hasn't crossed the highway, we still have a chance of catching him. Keep an eye out for his boat."

"Why wouldn't he go ashore at the end of the bay? He would save himself quite a bit of walking," Théo interjected.

"Perhaps, we'll see, but I don't believe that. There are too many tea plantations. I'm sure he's avoiding being seen by any farmers."

"Hm, I guess one of us should follow him while the others try to cut him off."

"Sounds good, Théo. I'm sure you already have an idea who should be on his heels."

Théo smiled. "Well, you naturally have first dibs, but you're a prosecutor now. With such a dignified position, you shouldn't be scampering through the jungle. So, it'll be me."

Bosco grinned. "Nice touch, referring to it as a dignified position. I wouldn't have thought of it. Anyway, I agree with you."

Amused, Joseph listened to the sparring match between two friends.

"Great suggestion. Théo, let him know you're onto him, otherwise he might hide and wait for nightfall. I'll drop Bosco off at the end of the bay. How will you get him to cooperate? You have no weapon. And, I only have my service weapon with me."

"Give it to Théo, I'll be fine," Bosco replied unselfishly.

After his confrontation with Mayeye, he had decided to disregard the rule about no weapons and instead brought his pistol along. This didn't escape Joseph's attention, but he acted as if he was unaware.

Théo took the pistol and a fully loaded extra magazine. "Where should we meet up? It's not like the area has cell service." He held up his cell phone. "Like here, for example, we have no coverage. And, I'm sure the same rings true in the Nyungwe Forest."

Bosco consulted the map and pointed to a spot. "We'll meet here! I will commandeer a vehicle from a farmer and try to reach the highway between Butare and Cyangugu as quickly as possible. He definitely must avoid the Kamiranzovu Swamp. If I'm correct, he'll try to cross the highway to the east of it. That's where I might be able to cut him off, providing you haven't gotten a hold of him yet."

"Joseph, head to Bukavu and alert our colleagues. Fabien and Ariane are at Marie Kamanda's home. Tell them to ask the authorities in Cyangugu and Butare to send officers to patrol the highway until they meet somewhere in the middle."

Joseph nodded. They'd already been more than three hours on the water and had gone quite a distance into the elongated bay. Using Joseph's on board binoculars to search Rwanda's shoreline, Théo soon discovered the Twa's poorly hidden fishing vessel.

"It looks like you were right. There's the boat."

Joseph steered the watercraft towards a flat rock.

"Watch out for the Twa's poisoned arrows."

"I certainly will. I'm hoping I can convince him to turn himself in."

"I wouldn't bet on it."

Théo hopped off the boat and waved briefly before disappearing into the jungle. As a former ranger, he was a proficient tracker and it didn't take long for him find the trail. He knew Joseph's warning was justified. The Twa's poisoned arrows and trap-setting ability required him to be extremely vigilant. The quarry had made little effort to hide his tracks. Effortlessly, he followed broken branches and fresh footprints in the soft ground.

In the meantime, Bosco had been dropped off at the end of the bay. His target was the house on a small hill above the spot where he landed. Joseph was already on his way to Bukavu.

A Toyota pickup truck stood in front of the house. The owner, a tea farmer, came immediately outside with a worried look on his face when he saw the stranger. After a brief discussion, the farmer agreed to drive Bosco to the national highway connecting Butare and Cyangugu. When they were on their way, he checked his cell phone for new messages. Apparently, Ariane had repeatedly called and left a text message to call her back straightaway. She answered on the first ring.

"Bosco, finally," was her first comment. "The situation is as I had suspected. I think Marie Kamanda and her son are in the hands of kidnappers. We found her aunt at the house on the back patio with her throat cut."

Bosco was at odds with himself and for the second time, he had underestimated the danger.

Could we have prevented this murder?

After a brief moment of silence, he replied objectively, "Please hand the case over to Joseph."

"Where is he?"

"He should arrive soon in Bukavu on his boat. We are trying to catch a man who is a strong suspect in Darcy's murder. So, I need you guys."

"What do you need?"

"Tell Fabien to ask our colleagues in Cyangugu and Butare set up a tight surveillance network on the Nyungwe section of highway. Once taken care of, I want you to head to Butare. You can find me on the eastern side of the Kamiranzovu Swamp."

Ariane consulted her map.

"And who will take care of Marie Kamanda?"

"We'll deal with her later, along with Joseph. Please let him do the initial investigation. He knows what needs to be done."

"But..."

"No buts, I already know what you want to say. It is possible she has also been abducted and taken to Rwanda. However, our first priority is to detain our fleeing suspect. If it is as we believe, then she is safe as long as she doesn't have her passport. In order to receive any inheritance, she has to appear in Switzerland in person. And, Alphonse and Jean-Baptiste are keeping an eye on the Belgian embassy in Kigali."

"I object, Mr. Prosecutor, the situation has changed. As it stands, we cannot arrest her if the boy is being held captive somewhere else."

Bosco had to admit she was right.

"Okay, then bring Alphonse and Jean-Baptiste up to date on the situation. Tell them to covertly surveil Marie Kamanda and her companions if they show up."

"Okay, we'll get things rolling and once Joseph arrives we'll head over to meet you." Ariane snappishly ended the conversation in an icy voice.

Bosco breathed deep after he hung up and added, "I really should tell her to lay off the goat meat."

Some villages still prohibited women from eating goat meat. They believed a woman would assume the characteristics of the animal, such as a bleating voice and stubborn behavior.

He asked the tea farmer to drop him off at the prearranged location. Slowly, he patrolled the road and kept a sharp eye on the rainforest. Traffic was almost nonexistent.

Meanwhile, Théo had entered the Nyungwe Forest and slowed his pace in the rough terrain. His quarry still made no effort to conceal his tracks. Either he was unaware he was being followed or perhaps he didn't care. A concert of thousands of bird voices sounded from the dense tree canopy. He was constantly accompanied by chimpanzees that watched him silently. So as not to attract their greatest enemy, the leopards, chimpanzees only alerted fellow primates to the presence of an intruder if they were unaware.

The Twa remained undiscovered and continued purposefully towards his goal, the southern region of the Nyungwe Forest. By that time, Théo was no longer completely convinced he could catch up to the Twa and hoped Bosco was successful in getting the highway monitored. To make matters worse, the tracks became more obscure and Théo lost precious time picking them back up. Despite his good physical health, his strength began to wane. Abruptly, his path ended at a narrow deep chasm.

This part of the Nyungwe Forest frequently received visiting tourists, so the forest administration was kind enough to install climbing aids and walkways made of tree logs in extremely difficult terrain. Théo looked around and followed the edge of the chasm. The Twa had to have overcome the impediment. Regardless, he didn't want to admit he had lost his prey. At one point, he discovered a spot where the musty ground had been disturbed. He looked down and saw two tree trunks lying one above the other.

Damn it, he's way ahead of me.

Searching, his intense gaze screened the dense bushes on the other side of the chasm. Motionless, his quarry leaned against a tree. Apparently he had been watching him for a while. The distance was too great for an accurately placed gunshot. Nevertheless, Théo drew the pistol and aimed at the man.

"You, over there at the tree, surrender or I will shoot!"

The Twa merely waved at him and disappeared into the thicket. Théo groped for his cell phone in his jacket pocket to check for a signal. As expected, no signal. Frustrated, he shot a single round into the air and set out on the treacherous path across the chasm.

The man was startled. Were they there? He

listened for a brief moment in the dark. As if in a trance, he felt his way into the room with the bookshelf. When the lights came on, the *gardien* briefly glanced up with half-opened eyes, then turned away, and drifted back to sleep.

21

After Joseph received word from Ariane, he immediately rushed to the home of Marie Kamanda and kicked the investigation into high gear.

"We're glad you're here," Ariane said when he arrived.

Joseph briefly shook hands with the two police officers and then devoted his attention to the dead woman. "I'm getting a little tired of this case. What's your opinion?"

"We are convinced Marie Kamanda and her son have been abducted by criminals," Fabien replied.

"Yes, Bosco informed me she was seen with a couple of dubious characters. And, if she went along voluntarily to get her hands on Darcy's money then there was no reason to kill this woman."

Ariane bit back the remark that was on the tip of her tongue. *Like anyone here cares whether there were reasons to kill someone?*

"So, we're sure she's in danger. Can you take care of this? Bosco needs us in the Nyungwe Forest. They are still pursuing the Twa."

Joseph nodded. "Okay, we'll look into this case."

Ariane and Fabien said goodbye and drove to the border towards Cyangugu.

It was obvious the key to solving this crime wouldn't be found in Bukavu. Therefore, Joseph decided to leave the gathering of evidence in the hands of the local authority so he could return to Goma. After he brought his colleagues from Bukavu up to date, he topped off the boat's tank and made sure the spare canister was full. He asked one of the officials from

Bukavu to drive him and his boat to Goma. He lay down on the back seat of the boat and caught some much-needed sleep.

A shot broke the tranquil sounds of the rainforest. From the slightly elevated road, Bosco could see a startled flock of birds rise to the skies, fleeing the brief echo.

Théo must be nearby. He might need help. I should go see if he needs help.

Bosco drew and cocked his gun. After a hundred yards, he reached a small clearing surrounded by tall trees. Once, it had been part of the swamp, but now it was overgrown with tall grass.

Out of nowhere, an arrow hit him and pierced his thigh. The sharp pain almost knocked him unconscious. Bosco collapsed. Like a phantom, the hunter abruptly rose out of the tall grass. Holding a bow, he slowly walked over to the policeman.

"Drop your weapon!"

Lying there barely able to prop himself up on his left elbow, Bosco slowly dropped his other hand with the gun and pushed it aside.

"You should turn yourself in!" Bosco suggested to the man.

The man used a foot to kick the gun away and then leaned over his prey.

"Your colleague suggested the same, but I don't think it is such a good idea."

The leg ached and Bosco groaned.

"I'm sorry, but you left me no other choice."

Bosco tried again. "Turn yourself in and I guarantee you'll be treated fairly."

"That may be, but I'm just not eager to experience the comfort of one of your prison cells."

His hair was long and a few strands covered his pocked black face, making him look much older. The Twa lowered his bow and for a moment didn't say a word. Bosco tried in vain to see the murderer.

"Why are you doing all this?" he asked in Kinyarwanda, the language the man had used.

"Both *wazungu* deserved to die a thousand times. Why do you care so much about those lowlifes when the entire region sinks into bloodlust?"

Bosco couldn't think of an answer and squirmed in pain.

"Don't worry, the arrowhead wasn't poisoned. Otherwise, you'd already be on the way to see your ancestors. The wound will eventually heal."

The hunter suddenly grabbed the shaft of the arrow and gently pulled it out of the wound. A brief, sharp pain shot through Bosco's body. The wound bled profusely. The Twa pulled out a rolled banana leaf from a small bag hanging around his neck. Inside was an herbal mush the hunter applied to the wound. Then, he laid the leaf on the wound and fastened it in place with banana fibers.

Gradually, the sharp pain in his thigh gave way to a dull throb.

"Where's my colleague, the one pursuing you? Is he hurt?"

"No, don't worry, he'll be here soon. I merely slowed him down a little. He's quite fast on foot and almost caught up with me."

"What about Isaam? Doesn't he work in your village?" Bosco blurted out.

The Twa remained silent for a moment.

"We were able to free him and gave first aid, but we were too late."

"Too late for what?"

"He's dead. There was nothing we could do to save Isaam."

"Did you find him in the mining company warehouse?"

"Yes, that's where the *mzungu* drugged and subsequently tortured him. Even though I put an end to his torture, it was too late. The village has buried him."

"Why did you kill Darcy?"

"He organized all of those senseless murders. He surprised us as we were carrying Isaam away and shot one of my men."

"So you cut off his and the giant's legs? Why?"

The hunter wouldn't answer.

"Why the legs?" Bosco persisted.

"The men were too tall."

"Too tall for what?"

"They were too heavy for us to carry, so we had to eliminate some weight. There was a guillotine in the warehouse and I'm sure that madman used it."

So, that's where the traces of molten lead came from.

"The two *wazungu* will not end up in pygmy heaven," he added without pity. Bosco wasn't in the mood to laugh and the Twa didn't expect it.

"Who set the buildings on fire?"

"It wasn't us! Perhaps you should ask the men at SÉCOMA."

"Did you know Darcy and the other man previously?"

"Yes, I knew the giant from watching the warehouse. I knew Darcy from way back."

"Where was that?"

"Back in Mukingo. It's where I come from. He had been blackmailing my father. We were involved in illegal activities."

Bosco sighed. Mukingo was a village at the foot of Mount Karisimbi, which, during his time as a ranger, was exclusively inhabited by incorrigible, poaching Twa who had made his life quite difficult back then. The memories came painfully flooding back and the mystery of Dian Fossey's murder pressed its way to the forefront.

"Your father?"

"Yes, back then he was doing business with Darcy."

"What kind of business?"

"Animals."

"Gorillas?"

"Of course, when there was an order."

"We found a *sumu* in Darcy's apartment. Did you leave that message?"

"Yes, we warned him because his men on Idjwi started exploiting us."

"A *sumu* just like that one, also a wooden puff adder, was found in front of Dian Fossey's hut. Did you have anything to do with that?"

"Darcy knew the symbolism of a *sumu*, especially a puff adder. Yes, the same puff adder was used to scare the American woman. She created problems for us and we wanted her out of the way."

"She was murdered by a *panga* in the same manner as Darcy. Was it intentional?"

"No, that was purely coincidental. The two killings

happened for different reasons."

"Let me get this straight. You placed the *sumu* as a warning outside the American's hut and when she ignored it, you killed her. Is that the short version?"

"Yes, we hated her and she hated us. She was a witch and responsible for us being driven out of Virunga National Park. Ever since 1977, when poachers killed her favorite gorilla Digit, she became increasingly more paranoid and unpredictable. She treated any person who didn't agree with her with utter contempt, even her own co-workers."

Bosco refrained from commenting.

"You should know this. You were there."

"What? Do you know me?"

"Of course, Bosco Kabeera, ranger and tracker. We knew all the American's staff and the forest administration. However, I didn't expect one of you to be behind me."

"Let's get back to Dian Fossey. How exactly were you involved in her murder?"

"My father had been beaten and humiliated by her. When he did not stop hunting, the American woman had me kidnapped as a child," the Twa said, without answering the actual question.

You could have reported her. She did not have many friends at the time," Bosco replied half-heartedly. Even he couldn't believe what he just said.

For the first time, the hunter actually seemed to smile.

"You must be joking, Kabeera. A Twa walking into a police station and reporting the Mother Teresa of the gorillas. Considering the situation back then, what do you think it would have accomplished? I'll give you the answer you don't want to admit: They would have imprisoned the Twa."

Bosco didn't respond. What could he say? The Twa was absolutely correct. Due to her popularity throughout the world, the American had been almost untouchable. Even the government left her alone, even if a few civil servants had wanted to get rid of her, albeit for various reasons. Instead, Bosco asked, "Okay, but still, how was Darcy involved in her murder?"

"Darcy wanted to get rid of Dian Fossey as well. She hindered his business dealings ever since she managed to establish the protected habitat."

"When Darcy's body was found, his face was covered with a mask. The mask of an executioner. I take it that was also your idea?"

"Yes, the mask belonged to my grandfather. He lived at the court of the *mwami*, Mutara III, the ruler of the Tutsi in Rwanda. He was responsible for carrying out the executions of those sentenced to death. He wore the mask."

"Excuse me, your grandfather was an executioner?"

"Yes, back then that task was only performed by Twa. He was also a member of the secret society of Twa, *Ota Benga*, just as my father and I were later on. I placed the mask on the Belgian's head hoping someone would recognize its symbolism because Darcy was an executioner as well."

"Who's Ota Benga? That was the name the boy gave who discovered Darcy's corpse near the border crossing. What's the purpose of your secret society? Moreover, what havoc did Darcy and the other *wazungu* cause on Idjwi? Why are there some many dead bodies?"

Bosco didn't have to think about what he needed to ask, the questions simply spilled out of him.

"Since you have so many questions, Kabeera, I might as well satisfy your curiosity. The secret society's purpose is to prevent the Twa extinction. Unfortunately, we only have meager resources at our disposal, but we try to defend ourselves anyway. The secret society was named after the man, Ota Benga. He was a Twa who survived the massacres by Leopold II's henchmen and a missionary had him deported to the United States. They locked him up in a monkey cage and put him on public display. Eventually, he decided to end his inhumane existence and shot himself."

Bosco didn't attempt to hide his shock. After a minute of silence, the Twa continued.

"Darcy had an ample selection of human material to use for his business. Nobody cared if someone went missing in the eastern Congo. But, all of his subjects were black, men and women alike."

"What business was Darcy in?"

Gahiji remained silent and looked at Bosco as if he didn't understand.

At once, Bosco was aware of the absurd situation. He had hunted a killer, was now injured lying on the ground before him, and interrogating him. Although he was unable to arrest him, the man answered his questions willingly, almost as if he was unburdening himself.

Suddenly, the Twa reached into his jacket pocket and surprised Bosco by handing him a small digital camera wrapped in cloth.

"Look at the photos and film footage. There isn't much there, but once you take a look I'm sure you will be the wiser for it," he said almost cheerfully, and then added, "Don't show the pictures to anyone easily disturbed."

Bosco was confused. This man was a mystery and at the moment he felt inferior not only physically. As was second nature to him, he secured the camera in one of the plastic evidence bags he always carried in his pocket. It was time he finally discovered the rest.

"So, who killed Dian Fossey?"

The question came unexpectedly. The hunter remained silent for a moment and simply stared at Bosco. He seemed to wrestle with himself but decided to respond.

"It was my father."

"Why, because she had you kidnapped?"

"No, it was Darcy who pressured him. However, it made it easier to convince my father that the woman had to go. Not to mention Darcy was running out of patience."

"Why?"

"At first, they waited for the American's visa to expire. Then, in order to force her to make a decision, they placed a *sumu* in front of her hut door. But, she was a stubborn woman and simply ignored the warning."

"That doesn't explain why Darcy was so eager to have Dian Fossey killed."

"The Belgian was afraid he might get arrested. The American woman had a list of poachers' names and their clients that she wanted to hand over to the police. Darcy wanted that list in his possession."

"Did your father find it?"

"No, he only found his *sumu*, the one used to warn her. Later on, that ritual object came into my possession. It is the one we used to warn Darcy and his film crew."

"Hm, I see. I recall she somehow always managed to get her visa extended at the embassy."

"Yes, but I'm sure there was bribery involved. She wasn't particularly picky in her methods."

"One more question. The investigation showed that Dian Fossey was murdered with her own *panga*. I guess your father was unarmed when he went to her hut. Did he actually intend to kill her?"

"He was misinformed. The American woman wasn't supposed to be in her hut. My father wanted to put poison in her drinking flask. However, she was there and woke up when he entered the hut. She fought like a wild animal and my father was afraid she would get the upper hand. He successfully grabbed the *panga* from the wall and used it to defend himself. In the end, he managed to hit her with a fatal blow."

"And who was responsible for killing Digit and the other gorillas?"

"I don't know. Although a few in the village were eager to show her who was king of the jungle. It's kind of ironic; in the end, her unrelenting vendetta against poachers caused the deaths of the gorillas she meant to protect."

Bosco remained silent and the Twa continued. "My father has passed away. If nothing is done about it, one day there will be more gorillas living than Twa. Are we supposed to accept that? What is the idea of wildlife conservation? We understand it's important to preserve certain species of wildlife. But, we are and have always been part of this natural environment. We belong in the rainforest. We live off it and it provides the medicine we require. Now, it has turned into an attraction for tourists who visit our villages and we dance around. Ridiculous. This will not guarantee our survival."

The Twa paused in his narrative. It seemed as if the Twa enjoyed having a representative of the state in a position where he was forced to listen to his point of view, which literally assaulted his ears.

"Recently, we had a group of tourists in our village. Usually, I don't get involved because I can't do anything about it. However, when I witnessed the villagers being questioned and the tourists taking notes, I became curious. So, I asked one of the strangers what they were inquiring about. Apparently, they were interested in which plants we used and for what medicinal purposes. They were biochemists from Germany. It was clear what was happening. First, they steal our knowledge and then they drive us out of our rainforest."

"You are well informed. How do you know all this?"

"In 1985, my parents decided to disappear from Mukingo and placed me in a mission where I received an education."

The hunter was tense, his heavy breathing impossible to miss.

"Give us back the rainforest. Nowadays, it's us who need a nature reserve. We no longer hunt protected species. You have nothing to fear from us."

Bosco refrained from replying to his appeal. "One more question. Why did you discard the dead body on the Rwandan side?"

"We do not trust the Congolese authorities. They probably would have covered up the crime and disposed of the corpse, providing SÉCOMA didn't do it first."

The wound made itself felt again.

"I guess that's a compliment for us," Bosco blurted out. "I'm still curious whether you know Thomas Mayeye."

"Who doesn't know that gangster?"

"Was he in any way involved with the dead bodies at the warehouse?"

"His men from SÉCOMA were guarding the place. But, I never saw him step foot on Idjwi."

"Why did you appear to find the dead man? He would have been discovered eventually."

"It's almost rainy season and we were worried the corpse might get washed downstream or covered by water. We instructed one of our boys to go and report that he had found a dead man on shore."

"Ota Benga!"

"Obviously that's not his real name. Please leave him alone, he had nothing to do with it."

"You told me you occasionally went to the warehouse to observe. Nothing caught your attention? Where you able to hear what the men talked about?"

"As I said, I didn't go often. I noticed the guards enjoyed the company of women and had them brought over. One time, I overheard a conversation Darcy had with the giant. They were talking quite loudly about a man named Hugo. It seemed they were upset with him."

"Hugo? You're sure that's the name you heard?"

"Absolutely! I had the impression this Hugo was important to them. The giant had some reservations about Hugo, but Darcy said he had him under control."

Off in the distance, a barely audible engine noise approached that gradually drowned out the natural noises of the rainforest. Bosco immediately knew he didn't have long to wait for help to arrive. The Twa turned away from the injured man and glanced in the direction the vehicles could be expected to come from. Calmly, he looked at the injured man lying on the ground.

"If you're still interested in the circumstances of the murder of *Nyiramacyibili*, you should search for her notes. Supposedly, they are in an orange folder. You might find Darcy's name on the list, but it's certainly conceivable the Rwandans had a hand in the business as well. I'm sure you won't make new friends once you have the list."

Bosco briefly thought about the consequences of such an undertaking. It would not get off the ground without Mugambages consent.

"Do you have an idea who Hugo is?"

The Twa shrugged.

"I have no idea who he is. I don't even know if the man is a *mzungu* or an African. Many Africans go by the name of Hugo. Presumably, he's business liason. Darcy supposedly had good contacts in Kinshasa."

Bosco wanted to ask more questions since this case was full of mysteries. He also wanted to ask the *impunyu* for more details on Darcy's business transactions, but the Twa abruptly ended their conversation.

"I think it's best if we go our separate ways now. Be happy we had this meeting and leave it at that. You and your men shouldn't try to follow me."

With distinct sarcasm, he added with a smile, "I'll be going now into the heart of darkness."

Without haste, the hunter moved toward the edge of the rainforest. Before he disappeared into the jungle, the hunter turned and briefly locked eyes with his pursuer. For a moment, Bosco stared at the looming green wall of jungle that had swallowed him up. That mysteriously natural impenetrability granted him protection and survival. He was at home there and nobody would be able to follow, let alone find him.

Breathing heavily and under great distress, Bosco managed to stand. He retrieved his gun from the grass and fired off two shots. Shortly thereafter, he heard several cars come to a stop on the roadside. After a short search, his colleagues found him. Ariane and Fabien were accompanied by a few gendarmes from Butare and Cyangugu. Fabien stepped next to Bosco.

"Where is he?"

Bosco raised and nodded his head towards the rainforest.

"Helicopter?"

"Forget it. We have no chance of spotting him. Just get me out of here. Tell one of the men to stay behind with a vehicle."

"Where's Théo?"

"He'll be along shortly. He was following the fugitive, but I was told he lost track of him. Come on, drop me off at the nearest doctor, then you can get in touch with Joseph and together you can coordinate the search for Madame Kamanda and her son."

At Bosco's request, Ariane applied a bandage to the wound without removing the Twa's natural remedy in place.

"He said he would disappear into the heart of darkness and apparently found it amusing. Any idea what he meant by it?"

"Well, it's the title of a book. The English author Joseph Conrad describes the atrocities committed in the Congo during the reign of Leopold II. The main character in his novel is the white ivory hunter Kurtz, who adorns his hut with the skulls of murdered Africans. Each intern in Western media who doesn't actually know where the Congo is, love the quote and repeat it at every opportunity when the need arises to give their readers a thrill and make their neck hairs stand on end. In the early days, it was Dracula, the legend of the blood-sucking vampire from Romania, but nowadays it is "The heart of darkness". Africa is a booming business, especially in Germany. Pictures of its vast savannahs, animals, jungles, tapes of traditional drum playing, and the story with the title "The White Maasai" are hot items. Africa even produces all types of TV shows that offer a little sex and *sumu*. Clinically clean, of course. Africa is the cradle of humanity. White people can feel this too, providing they hear it often enough."

"Oh my goodness," Bosco sighed sarcastically. "Africa really doesn't know how to cultivate its image. In the meantime, no one cares about the harsh reality of what really goes on here."

Thinking about the the white Maasai brought a smile

to his face. The story of the white Maasai had been fully exploited by Kenyans in the tourism business, yet beyond Kenya's borders, the movie was regarded as a joke. Vendors selling souvenirs claimed, with a sly grin, to belong to the same Maasai tribe, offered their services quite successfully, especially to female tourists.

Using Fabien as a crutch, Bosco limped to one of the cars and was driven to the hospital in Butare. The doctor assured him he was in good hands and that everything would be fine. Since there was no indication of fever and the flesh around the wound didn't look infected, the doctor saw no reason to keep him in the hospital. Back in Kigali, Bosco placed himself in the custody of Chantal. At first, she wouldn't stop nagging him, but eventually she quieted down and let him sleep in peace.

22

Joseph went home after his late night ride to get a few hours of sleep but soon got up to go to the office.

I have to put an end to it, but how? So far, there is no evidence. Are they acting on their own behalf or someone else? Where are the woman and the boy?

Determined, he picked up the phone.

"Brigadier, drive over to TD Nature Film Production and bring the Belgian, Piquard to me. If he refuses, arrest him."

"What about the other one?"

"You mean Dallaway, the fine upstanding British citizen, the beacon of *hope and glory*? No, leave him be. He's either drinking or rolling around in the sack with a whore, if he's still able to roll that is."

The Brigadier wasn't sure how to react to his commander's sarcasm, so he decided to answer formally, befitting an officer of his rank.

"Yes Sir, commander."

With a somber face, Piquard entered Joseph's office accompanied by his escort. At first, the Brigadier had asked Piquard nicely to come to the station to answer a few questions, but when the man tried to avoid it by giving him all kinds of excuses, he finally threatened to arrest him. The Belgian had already experienced the comfort of holding cells in countries with a similar stance on human rights. Therefore, he preferred to go along willingly and save himself another traumatic experience.

"Why have you summoned for me, commander? What are you accusing me of? As a Belgian citizen, I have the right to a lawyer as well as consular service," he immediately blurted out, full of bravado, as he stepped into Joseph's office.

"Slow down, Monsieur Piquard. Concerning a lawyer or consulate assistance, we shall see how eager they will be to stand by your side when all is said and done. The Rwandans have been kind enough to ask the authorities for you and your colleagues' illustrious resumes, which we have copies of. I must say, all of you have, or rather had, impressive careers. However, as far as I know, you haven't been accused of anything here yet. Granted, you've been instructed not leave the city, but that is merely for your own safety. Right now, all I want is to speak with you. Please, Monsieur Piquard, take a seat." Joseph pointed to the empty chair facing him.

Piquard briefly pressed his lips together. His already grumpy expression hardened. His crafty eyes, which resembled a ferret, clearly betrayed his distrust and vigilance.

"Get to the point. What is it you want to chat about? Am I suspected of killing Darcy?" he asked after sitting down.

"Of course not, the investigation into Darcy's murder is nearing its completion. However, some strange events have happened recently and you may be in a position to help me. For example, somebody broke into MONUC's laboratory as well as kidnapped a Congolese woman and her son in Bukavu."

He failed to mention the murder of the old lady and the events that occurred on Idjwi.

"And, I'm supposed to have been involved? You just said it yourself, I'm not allowed to leave Goma city limits. And, I actually didn't step one foot out of the city."

"No, you misunderstood, I'm not accusing you. It's simply that both incidents are connected to each other and, in my opinion, there are only a few candidates who, firstly, have a motive and, secondly, are also in a position to carry out such crimes."

"I'm sorry, I'm lost. I still don't understand what you're getting at."

"Let me explain it to you. Concerning the motive, you and your partners, let's say, come to mind. And, for carrying it out, SÉCOMA comes to mind, which, to my knowledge, you still have good relations with. The Captain did not waste much time after Mayeye's death taking over the business."

"What do you mean good relations? As before, they're still employed to guard our property."

"Matengo has requested the property rights be transferred to SÉCOMA."

"Yes, we were already informed to pay the rent to him from now on."

"But here, such transfers of property, as well as other favors, usually require a good argument. The authorities have also awarded Mayeye's private fortress to Matengo."

Joseph had no doubt Piquard could see what he meant by *a good argument* in regard to those incidences and he was curious to see how he would react.

Piquard's eyebrows rose in surprise. He wasn't sure whether he had understood correctly. In general, the commander was considered incorruptible.

After a brief hesitation, he answered evasively, "Yes, I'm sure there are ways to persuade the authorities.

But, I suppose you didn't invite me here to talk about Matengo's business dealings."

"On the contrary, I'm interested in your dealings with Matengo."

"I have nothing to say."

Piquard crossed his arms in front of his chest and tried to adopt a relaxed posture. To Joseph, it seemed the right moment to start applying pressure.

"During the abduction of the Congolese, an elderly lady's throat was cut."

Piquard sat up briefly. Visibly shocked, his eyes widened briefly. But, he regained his composure quickly. Speaking with an exaggerated indifference, he tried to act as if this was news to him.

"Don't tell me, now you are accusing me of being involved in that as well? What would make you think that? I had nothing to do with it."

Joseph knew what he needed to get out of him. He was convinced Piquard was aware of the abduction, but not the murder of the old woman.

"Monsieur Piquard, I should warn you now, if I find out you were involved in this it will have serious consequences for you."

The man in question maintained his composure and stared at the policeman defiantly. "Are we done here?"

"Yes, you may return to your apartment. Make sure to keep yourself available and remember you are not to leave the city limits. For the time being, I will hang on to your passport."

Since Prince saw the two men in the Coco Jambo Club, he was unable to find peace. He still couldn't believe it had taken him so long to cross paths with

Matengo. He was obsessed with only one thought; punish the murderer who killed his family. The meager savings he had allowed him to cancel all jobs. He began studying the gangster's routine. Continually using different locations, he parked his car near the plain SÉCOMA building. The small building next to it housed a generator. The main building had an extensive basement. For security reasons, these windows were barred so they could be left open for ventilation. The house itself was not fenced, but two guards armed with AK-47s stood guard at the entrance. For the most part, Matengo never left the office until late in the evening and drove straight home. He lived on the top floor of a half-empty office building that was also guarded by his men. Prince only went to sleep once the lights there went out.

One evening, he watched a black SUV pull up to the SÉCOMA building and an African woman and a little boy exited the vehicle. Shortly afterwards, a faint light came from one of the basement windows on the opposite side of the building from where the guards were stationed. Prince assumed they were the family of one of the employees.

Like in many African countries, most of the population's daily routine was to somehow make ends meet, which was the same for the people living in the Congo. Any problems white foreigners considered to be insurmountable, Africans solved with inexhaustible creativity and imagination. Some people in the Congo strictly adhere to Mobutu's fabricated Article 15, who at the end of his reign told his followers to simply take whatever they needed. Although Prince could have been accused at times of transporting questionable cargo, which he never wanted to know the contents of, he could honestly say he had never resorted to Article 15. Part of his survival strategy was to stay well informed of any militias' intention to obtain control of the provincial capital. Therefore, he made it a habit of listening to the Radio Okapi program on the drive home. The stationed was controlled by the UN and, in general, regarded as being reliable. This time, when he turned on the radio a little late, the newscast had already begun."...body of a murdered woman who lived with her niece was discovered in Bukavu. The owner of the house, Marie Kamanda, as well as her five-year-old son Maurice, are missing. The police are currently investigating."

It was followed by a description of the missing persons. Prince was abruptly aware he was in possession of some dangerous knowledge. Unable to make a decision, he finally forced himself to collect his thoughts and ignored the rising hostility he felt for the *predator*.

I won't accomplish it alone. I will inform Likongo.

Once Picard returned to his apartment, he grabbed his cell phone and dialed a number. Without announcing himself, he blurted, "Matengo! Likongo interrogated me. He knows. Why did you kill the woman?"

"Unfortunately, it couldn't be helped. She wouldn't listen and started screaming."

"You should be on the lookout. He might cause problems for us."

"Don't worry, I'll take care of him. We still have a

score to settle with him anyway."

"Where are the woman and her boy?"

"Right now, here with us. They are being well looked after."

"What, they're here in Goma? Are you crazy? That's the first place they'll look. It won't take Likongo long to find you."

"They'll be gone soon."

"And then? It's not like she can pick up her passport."

"Correct, at least not in Kigali. But, there are other options here in the Congo."

"What are you up to?"

"Don't worry, leave it to me."

Piquard thought for a moment. The situation seemed to be getting more complicated by the minute and his confidence in Matengo waned.

"I guess I have no other choice."

"No, you do not. I'll keep in touch."

Not waiting for an answer, Matengo hung up.

That son of a bitch Matengo is deceiving himself. Things are getting out of hand.

When it came to Piquard's business dealings, he made sure he was protected from all sides. He knew it was time to disappear. For just such an emergency, he had reported his passport stolen some time ago and had requested a new one. Granted, the new passport had no visa entry, but once he was at the border, it would only pose a slight problem.

Prince drove to Joseph's office and walked in through the already open door. A man in uniform lay on the floor. He had a gunshot wound to the head and was dead. It was one of Likongo's guards. A table was overturned and papers lay scattered on the floor. His attempt to reach the commander on his cell phone was unsuccessful. He had to act, but now he would have to do it alone. He didn't know what he could do for the commander, but at least he could try to free the woman and her boy.

Should I turn to the Rwandans for help?

Prince rejected the idea. It might be too late by the time he explained the situation to the Rwandans and they arrived. As it was, they had no official authority. Instead, he went to his tiny apartment where he picked up a few tools, including a heavy-duty bolt cutter and an instrument that resembled a drawing compass. One leg was equipped with a suction cup and the other with a diamond-cutting wheel.

His skills as a craftsman were well known. Anytime someone lost their house keys, he was asked to open the door. This would be his first uninvited intrusion. He retrieved an impeccably clean, well-oiled 9mm Makarov pistol from its hiding place. During the attack on Mayeye's fortress, he had removed the pistol from one of the slain SÉCOMA men. Ammunition was easy to get in Goma. It was made of lead and therefore easy to manufacture. Moreover, he had his ever-present knife.

The side of the SÉCOMA building he needed to get to lay in complete darkness at night. He knew the guards only patrolled around the building twice at night, so he waited until one of the guards had finished his patrol. He cautiously approached the faintly illuminated window and cut the lock on the iron bars with his heavy-duty bolt cutter. After easily removing the grid, he climbed into the opening and replaced the grid. The curtains were drawn except for a slight gap that allowed him to see clearly inside the room. Apparently, it was a holding cell for people. On the wall opposite the observer, an iron rod was attached. In front of it, the woman and her son sat on stools. Their wrists were secured with wide plastic cable ties and fastened to the rod with a piece of rope. He carefully removed the grid again and set his glass-cutting instrument on the windowpane. The woman and boy looked up in surprise when a circular piece of glass fell into the room. Through the hole, he unlocked the window and pushed the curtain aside. In a previously invisible corner, a man sat with his wrists bound. It was Joseph. He was unhurt except for a bump on the head. Prince quickly climbed through the open window and used his knife to free the bound captives. The entire time, no one made a sound except for the woman, who spoke softly in a soothing voice to her son. He looked a little afraid but eventually quieted. One after the other, the four escaped the holding cell. Without attracting attention, they reached the vehicle Prince had parked in a dark corner. Joseph asked Prince for his cell phone and told him to drive to the nearest hotel. It was already around midnight and it took a moment for his call to be answered.

"Joseph, do you ever sleep?" Théo joked but knew at this late hour it meant business. "I take it you encountered problems?"

"You could say that. It's time to take down SÉCOMA. They captured me and locked me up with Marie Kamanda and her son. Prince came and freed us. Come and take these two to Rwanda. I've lots to do right now and don't have time to look after them."

"Anything else we can help you with?"

"Thanks, I appreciate it, but we have to take care of it ourselves. I'll leave word with the border guards. Get in touch with Bosco and give him an update."

He gave Théo the hotel name where he wanted the two taken. It was located near Grande Barrière.

"Okay, I'm leaving as soon as I hang up. Take care of yourselves."

Joseph made a brief call to the border station. Next, he called one of his officers. With short, precise orders, he commanded him to mobilize all men who weren't already on duty.

"Take fifty fully-armed men and surround the SÉCOMA building. They should surrender unconditionally, otherwise storm the building. However, I doubt it will go that far. Then take control of the building. Send your deputy with the rest of the men to the building where Matengo has his private residence. I will meet them there. The men should remain concealed until I get there."

Joseph called the owner of the hotel, who was a confidant and was told Marie Kamanda and her son had arrived safely and were being well-taken care of. Joseph said goodbye and told Prince to drive to Matengo's private residence. At that hour, the streets were deserted. Twenty armed men waited a short distance from Matengo's apartment for his arrival. The lead officer briefly saluted.

"I just received a call informing me that all SÉCOMA men inside the building surrendered. One of the men on guard was shot dead when he aimed his weapon. We suspect they had enough time to warn Matengo." He pointed up at Matengo's dark apartment windows. "But, there haven't been any signs of movement yet."

"We should definitely proceed under the assumption that he's awake. If he expects we're coming, he'd leave the lights off."

Joseph ordered one police officer to guard the side entrance. Ten men positioned themselves in front of the building. He disappeared with the rest of his people into the stairwell.

Meanwhile, Prince had parked his vehicle at a distance and watched the action. The streets were still deserted.

All men looked up expectantly, waiting for the lights to come on in Matengo's apartment windows when Joseph and his men storm the room. No one noticed the side entrance door open. The guard heard a noise, but before he could turn around, he was shot from behind. Prince immediately grabbed his Makarov as the fleeing shadow ran directly towards him from the side entrance while firing an AK-47 at the men covering the front of the building. The men took cover and returned fire, but failed to hit their target. The killer still did not see Prince. As Matengo tried to run pass the vehicle, Prince quickly opened the door. With full force, the fugitive hit his head on the door. Matengo reeled back dazed and collapsed to the ground. As he fell, he tried to bring his Kalashnikov into a firing position. Prince already had his gun aimed at his head.

"*Predator*, greetings from PKB!"

No matter how incredible it seemed, within a

fraction of a second, all the memories from his inglorious past came rushing back into Matengo's mind before the young Congolese pulled the trigger. The last image Matengo saw in his life was the end of a barrel and a brief, brilliant flash of light. A soft-core projectile has a devastating effect. Matengo's lifeless body fell onto back onto to the ground from his semi-erect position, the face a shredded mess. The flowing blood formed a pool around his head, before slowly morphing into a dendritic pattern in the joints of the paved road.

Prince regarded the dead man. His tension dissipated slowly, without satisfaction.

23

The CID welcomed the news of Marie Kamanda and her son's liberation. Joseph reached Bosco still at home. He was alone, sitting at the dining table, Chantal and the children absent.

"Marie Kamanda and her son have been found and freed. Matengo was holding them and caught me."

"Congratulations. And who, may I ask, came to your rescue?"

"Prince. I had no idea he had a score to settle with him. Lucky for us he had been watching him."

"And Matengo?"

"He's dead. Shot while trying to escape." Joseph didn't mention that Prince was the shooter and Bosco thankfully didn't ask for details.

"I'm glad you are okay. I have a few issues here that need clarification. I hope you will not hold it against me, but if you don't involve me for a while in your neck of the jungle, you won't hurt my feelings. I have to admit it is quieter here."

Bosco heard a brief snort.

"I know what you mean. Trust me, I'm also tired of dealing with it every single day. But, this is Africa. Anyway, I hope we see each other again."

"Yes, I hope so too."

The case was solved. Nevertheless, it bothered Bosco. There were still too many unanswered questions. Granted, they had identified Darcy's murderer, albeit, they didn't have him in custody. It was doubtful they would catch him. Deep down, he felt sympathy for the Twa. Naturally, as a policeman, he couldn't admit that. Repeatedly, he replayed the odd conversation they had in the clearing in his head. A man named Hugo was Darcy's business contact. It had to be the same Hugo whose encrypted phone number was stored in Darcy's cell phone. Only now did he remember the small digital camera in his pocket. He fished the evidence bag out of his jacket and pulled out the camera. It was a Canon Powershot S70, not a professional camera, but it was compact and powerful with a video function for recording short films. The Twa had warned him about the content. Bosco had neither the desire nor reason to continue investigating the case. After initially hesitating, he changed his mind and decided to present the contents to his colleagues at the next meeting. Although his wound ached a bit, he was fit enough to perform his duty. Alphonse had offered to pick him up. A short time later, they were in the CID.

Everyone assembled around the big oval table in the conference room. There was coffee and tea in thermoses. In the middle of the table was a platter of mango-filled pasties. Alphonse's wife enjoyed baking these beignets and knew her husband's colleagues couldn't get enough of them. Bosco poured himself a cup of coffee and took a test sip. The aroma was familiar. A few days ago, he was briefly in the department pantry and found a bag with the logo of Mugambages plantation. Someone had good connections. This kind of quality was not commercially available in Rwanda.

Jean-Baptiste hooked up a projector to a laptop and inserted the camera's memory card. Once he turned on the projector, the first five photos displayed were of the *Hun* cheerfully grinning, surrounded by guards.

Then a video began playing. The focus was at first a bit blurry. It showed a weakly lit naked body. An African male with his arms and legs spread far apart. Suddenly, a beam of light was directed at the body and the camera zoomed in and focused on the man. The audience remained breathless. The beignets were forgotten. A closer shot showed the man's arms and legs being pulled by steel chains in four directions, his head immobilized. Clumps of blood could be seen beneath the steel cuffs. The camera focused on the face of the victim and remained there for a moment. Bathed in sweat mixed with blood, his lips split open, swollen and bleeding, he stared directly into the camera despite the bright light in his eyes. Everybody recognized him immediately. It was Isaam, the long-lost staff member of the Belgian NGO.

A depressed atmosphere dominated the room. Spellbound, they stared at the video. To Ariane, it seemed as if were looking at the human figure Michelangelo had drawn his famous pentagram around. The lens zoomed out again and the camera's angle changed slightly. A huge man wearing a mask and leather clothing entered the picture. It was the same clothing the dead Krauskopf wore on Idjwi. The tattoos on the upper arms eliminated any further doubt. It was him, the *Hun*. The angle of the camera returned to its original setting and the torturer struck the bound man with a whip studded with steel barbs. The five detectives struggled with the visuals. Alphonse wiped tears from his eyes. Suddenly, after the camera was redirected back to the victim, the image jerked around in an uncontrolled manner and came to rest on the ceiling. This was followed by blurred motion before the video stopped.

"Oh my God," Ariane gasped, "those monsters produced *snuff movies*."

Puzzled, everyone looked at their German colleague.

"Those films show people actually being tortured to death. I cannot believe it. They used the de facto anomie prevailing in the Congo in order to engage in their perverse business."

"What kind of person would even want to see such a thing?" Bosco asked baffled.

"There are some sick people in those industrialized countries if they need something like that to get sexually stimulated. They are willing to pay a great deal of money for such a film."

"That would explain those large remittances on Darcy's list," Jean-Baptiste said in a trembling voice.

"Yes," Ariane replied, "most likely. And Mayeye must have been in on it and received a cut."

As everyone silently came to terms with all the images they had seen, Bosco spoke again.

"So, we're looking at the revenge killing of two murderers who brutally tortured their victims to death and filmed it to get rich."

"Correct! And the fugitive Twa uncovered their activities and put them permanently out of business," Fabien said concluding the summation.

The dark dismal atmosphere still hung in the room. Bosco roused his colleagues out of their state of shock. "I want to find out how these *snuff movies* reach the perverse audience."Alphonse regained his composure. "He must have had help. You know, with distribution and so on."

It became clear their investigation wasn't over yet. The images they had seen couldn't be banished as long as the case wasn't properly solved.

"Jean-Baptiste, please check Darcy's computer again. Considering the cheap production, these films shouldn't require much storage space."

"I don't think he'll find anything," Ariane interjected. "We know this from investigating child pornography. Such creations, like online banking, require HTTPS-transfer protocols."

"And what does that mean?"

Jean-Baptiste explained. "It stands for *Hyper Text Transfer Protocol Secure*. This allows data to be safely transferred and stored on inaccessible servers. TD Nature Film Production's website is based on such protocol. It begs the question, why do they need such protocol because I cannot imagine the distribution of their nature films taking place via their website."

"But perhaps for those *snuff movies*. Let's suppose that's the case, can we trace them back to the clients?"

"Not necessarily. They use programs to hide their IP addresses. Nowadays, you can even a hire one of many service providers that guarantee anonymity. If that's the case, we don't stand a chance."

"Okay, Jean-Baptiste, let's leave it at that for now. We have to report this case to INTERPOL. I'm sure they have more options in Lyon. But please take another look at the list of encrypted phone numbers. During my encounter with the elusive Twa, he referred to someone named Hugo that had contact with Darcy. I'm sure the Hugo on our list is the man he was referring to. We have to find out who that man is. Please try again to decrypt the stored number in

Darcy's cell phone that is under the name of Hugo."

Jean-Baptiste nodded unenthusiastically. He had already made numerous attempts at deciphering the encoded numbers and each time he had failed.

"Alphonse, Fabien, you two are in charge of writing up a preliminary summary. I have to convince *PG* not to close this case."

He kept the real reason he wanted to speak with *PG* to himself. He was the only person who could give him access to the orange folder with the list *Nyiramacyibili* had made. However, he was afraid *PG* might think he had lost his mind, which is why he had purposely left out part of his conversation with the Twa when he had told his colleagues about the encounter. Depending on Mugambage's reaction, he didn't need his colleagues mocking him as well.

"Ariane, please get in touch with whoever is in charge at the NGO, what's his name, Marchal or something. Let him know about the death of his staff member. We will also notify him in writing."

Everyone was quietly conversing as they left the conference room. Ariane went straight to her office. On the table lay copies of all her colleagues' reports. It didn't take long to find Marchal's cell number on one of the pages. She was about to dial the number when she inadvertently glanced at Jean-Baptiste's report on the list of coded phone numbers from Darcy's cell phone directory. With her heart racing, she hung up the phone. Marchal's number, 07667900050, except for the last two digits, was identical to the one listed under the name Hugo. If Jean-Baptiste assumed correctly, then decoding either required the last two digits to be divided by two or the number 25 was subtracted. So, providing it was Marchal's number, then he knew Darcy and had some kind of business or relationship with him. If he did know Darcy, he at least owed an explanation as to why he pretended he did not. Why the name Hugo? Perhaps she should just call the number and ask for Hugo. It would be risky. He could simply tell her she had a wrong number, regardless if it was true or not. Then he would be warned. She decided to first research Marchal's personal details. Perhaps he had another name. He must have a resident permit. The CID had via the authorities' intranet, access to the data at the Rwanda Directorate General for Immigration and Emigration. Although a search for any middle name or nickname didn't reveal anything promising, his short biography was interesting reading. Marchal had retained a business visa since the early eighties. However, the type of business wasn't specified. Ariane thought about Darcy's biography. She searched for Bosco and found him back in his office. He was contemplating the best way to convince *PG* of the need to research a case from the distant past. If he didn't present it just right, he might end up spending his remaining years on the force as a desk jockey in order to learn humility. That certainly wasn't an alluring prospect. Nevertheless, Bosco knew as long as he presented a good argument, *PG* would keep an open mind even if they proved to be unfounded in hindsight. His concern was the prosecutor general could be afraid of being pushed to reopen the entire Dian Fossey case and deny his request.

Ariane's new insight was encouraging.

"At least we know he was in Rwanda at the time. But, perhaps it's merely coincidence since the presence of Belgians here at the time was not uncommon."

Bosco thought it was appropriate to let Ariane in on his plan. She knew almost from the beginning of the investigation about the association he had made between Darcy's murder and the circumstances leading up to the death of Dian Fossey. And, she knew about the existence of the orange folder.

"I want to talk *PG* into allowing me to look at Dian Fossey's case file. What do you think?"

She didn't hesitate in her reply. "You have to make sure *PG* understands that the key to solving our case lies in Dian Fossey's case file."

"Well, Jean-Bosco, you have indicated that there are still questions. What further investigations would you like to pursue? As far as I know, the case is solved."

They were sitting at the conference table again. The *General*, obviously in a good mood, served his own coffee while Bosco was still gathering his thoughts.

"By the way, congratulations on a job well-done. That goes for your team as well. Please congratulate them on my behalf. I must say, this case really was beyond my imagination, even if there is no shortage of violent crimes here. So, what's on your mind?"

"Well, Sir," Bosco said hesitatingly. As he explained to the *General* why he wanted Dian Fossey's case file reopened, his initially timid voice found its strength and conviction.

Mugambage's face was unreadable. Bosco couldn't tell if he was in favor of it or not.

"I have to admit, I find your concern somewhat

surprising. That case file has been classified *Top Secret* by the former administration. I myself haven't even laid eyes on it. From what I've heard, the police didn't exactly work the case according to investigative procedures."

"That may be, Sir, but I'm only interested in one name."

"Let me get this straight, if your suspicion is confirmed then these men weren't only responsible for the recent series of murders, but are also responsible for murdering Dian Fossey."

"I presume Darcy instructed the Twa to kill Dian Fossey and that Marchal, whose possible alias is Hugo, may have been connected somehow. I simply want to prove they knew and worked with each other back then. Then I can prove to him that he lied and that he is most likely tied to this case."

The *General* frowned.

"Hm, Jean-Bosco, we don't know who else is on that list. I don't even want to think about it. I understand your reasons, but I admit this undertaking might embarrass me."

Bosco breathed somewhat furtively. At least his concern wasn't immediately cast aside as absurd.

It seemed *PG* was weighing his options carefully, but it didn't take long.

"I have a suggestion, Jean-Bosco. And please don't think I mistrust you, but I've decided to take a look at the case file myself and then I will make my decision whether you can look at it."

It was more than Bosco expected.

"Thank you, Sir!"

PG accompanied him to the door and said goodbye.

Bosco returned to CID headquarters and asked his staff not to disturb him. Restless, he paced back and forth in his office. They were the longest two hours of his entire career. When he stood for a moment at the window watching the traffic on the grounds, he received Mugambages call.

"Jean-Bosco, this list is like *Pandora's Box*. Some of the named Rwandans are either dead or no longer in the country since they are wanted in connection to the genocide. Nevertheless, I've also seen names I wouldn't want anyone else to know about at this point. Therefore, I ask that you understand why I cannot give you the list. But, about your special interest, I would like to inform you that both Marchal and Darcy are on the list and each was quite active back then, as we already know. Both were working as agents for Spanish zoos. At that time, the Spaniards and even the Cologne Zoo in Germany had fewer scruples than other European countries when it came to procuring gorillas. However, I'm asking you not to mention Madame Fossey's connection to this case in your final report. Go ahead and arrest Marchal and make his life a living hell."

The street where Marchal's office was located was quiet. In the driveway stood an all-terrain-vehicle with the logo of the NGO. The four of them, Bosco, Ariane, Fabien, and even Jean-Baptiste, who wanted to come along to do some field work for a change, had arrived together. Fabien disarmed the *gardian* and orde red him to keep quiet. Bosco pressed the doorbell, but no one answered. When no one answered after a second knock, Jean-Baptiste and

Ariane walked around the house to see if anyone was in the garden.

Suddenly, a deafening blast rattled the windowpanes. Fabien and Bosco threw their shoulders full force against the front door, which gave way. With the weapons ready, they stormed the house. Ariane and Jean-Baptiste followed. Marchal sat in an armchair in his study in a pool of his own blood. The wall behind him was spattered with a mixture of blood and grayish brain matter. A double-barrel hunting rifle lay on the floor beside him. He had shot himself in the mouth. The back of his head was literally blown away.

Bosco grabbed his cell phone and informed Natalia. Jean-Baptiste backed discreetly out the door. Fabien began to examine the scene. Ariane took a closer look at the room. One corner featured a large bookcase. The top shelf held a large number of weathered, brownish antique books on manufacturing. Overall, there were forty-eight volumes. One of the books stood out a bit as if it was the last one Marchal had touched. Curious, she removed it. It was a book of poems by Victor Hugo, the great French poet, well-known in Europe for his works such as "Notre Dame de Paris" and "Les Misérables". The collection of poems was titled "La fin de Satan". It was one of the last unfinished works of Victor Hugo.

Leafing through it, she discovered a bookmark in between the pages as well as a pencil-marked paragraph.

> "Ce fut là mon crime. Tout fut dit, et la bouche sublime cria: mauvais! Et Dieu me cracha dans l'abîme.

> Oh! Je l'aime! C'est là l'horreur, c'est là le feu!
> Que vais-je devenir, abîmes; J'aime Dieu!
> Je suis damné!"

Line by line, she translated the poem from *La Fin de Satan:*

> "That was my crime. All was said and the sublime mouth shouted: Horrible! And God spat me into the abyss.
>
> Oh! I love it! There's horror, there's fire!
> What will become of me, abysses; I love god!
> I am damned!"

Hugo! He was an admirer of Victor Hugo. Therefore, his code name was Hugo!

After enjoying a nice dinner together, they sat on the terrace of the Serena Hotel in Gisenyi. It was a lovely evening with a beautiful sunset. The heat gradually succumbed to the refreshing gentle breeze blowing over Lake Kivu. Except for Théo, the *General* had paid out of his own pocket, as he liked to emphasize, a night's stay for all, even Joseph. A nice gesture, although no one assumed the published room rate that would exceed the budget of most invitees, was actually paid to the hotel. Higher administration levels of government departments held regular conferences here.

In the afternoon, many speeches were given. Joseph informed the Rwandans about Piquard's arrest while he was trying to escape on a plane to Kinshasa. They didn't have enough evidence to arrest Dallaway and he was cleared of all charges. After sticking around after dinner for some small talk, *PG* bid farewell. Now, the rest of them relaxed, chatted, and drank a little more than usual.

"Your time here with us is soon ending, Ariane. What plans have you made?" Bosco inquired.

"I'm taking some time off."

"And naturally you will spend it here in Rwanda!" Fabien added leaving no room for discussion.

"Sorry, I have to disappoint you. Joseph invited me to climb Mount Nyiragongo with him. Afterwards, I have an important appointment in Switzerland."

Amused, the Rwandans traded looks between Ariane and Joseph. Both of them tried to avoid looking at each other. However, Ariane couldn't help blushing.

"What, what's everyone staring at?"

Discreetly, she glanced at Joseph. She couldn't tell by his innocent expression how he was taking it. She had to admit, dark skin also had certain advantages and joined her colleagues in liberating laughter.

Epilog

It was a quite mild September in the small town of Bad Säckingen at the foot of the southern Black Forest. The temperature display of the weather station on the high plateau of the spa area hovered around fifteen degrees Celsius. There was a busy bustle in the idyllic spa town.

The establishment of the island-located settlement dated back to holy Fridolin, a monk in the 6th century who built a monastery. The market vendors in the square in front of Fridolinsmünster were taking down their stands and meticulously cleaning the cobblestones of waste. The tourists frequenting the numerous restaurant tables surrounding Munster Square greatly appreciated this deed and regarded it as typical Swabian. Waiters discreetly remarked that they were sitting on the grounds formerly belonging to the Grand Duke of Baden-Württemberg. It must have been scatterbrained politicians who, in 1952 in the Swabian capital of Stuttgart, decided to unify Baden and Württemberg, thus becoming Baden-Württemberg.

In Bad Säckingen Germany is connected via two bridges spanning the sluggish flowing Rhine River, with the Switzerland, the *Schwyz*, as the local jargon made it sound. Back in the '50s, jumping from the hundred ninety meters high bridge into the river and swimming downstream to the nearby island, imaginatively named Fridolin island, was a popular dare amongst pubescent students. Originally, the river's strong current created dangerous vortices in the area underneath the bridge, but the power plant upstream tamed it. The Rhine island, formerly a bird's paradise, was initially put into a miserable state by a clear cut. After symmetrical new planting of poplars, it finally corresponded to the sense of order of the city administration. As the poplars matured, you could only imagine what the pattern original looked like, but a beaver, which must have had its own ideas how the island should look, made use of the undergrowth and nearly returned part of the land back to its original state.

The prevailing Alemannic dialect over time sounded more like Swiss German. Good relations existe between the neighbors. In the fifties and sixties, it was mainly frontier workers who walked or drove the wooden bridge to Switzerland to shop. Meanwhile, the longest roofed wooden bridge in Europe at less than two hundred and four meters in length has been changed to pedestrian only. Vehicles use the bridge further downstream that was built later. In the following years, not only did the exchange rates between the Deutschemark - later the euro - and the Swiss Franc change drastically, but the majority of European and international currencies as well. Then, shopping tourism shifted to Germany and shops in the border region experienced booming business. Pedestrians crossed the wooden bridge, measured at exactly 101.96 meters from the German side, before reaching the border marked by a white stripe on the ground.

Regardless of the shopping traffic, Switzerland remained a tourist destination and passageway to Italy. However, the increase in vehicles available on the market whose occupants were not on vacation had other objectives. These were mostly respectable-looking women and men driving German-made luxury cars. Hiding possible nervousness behind sunglasses, they pulled up to the Swiss border station, lowered the driver's window, and politely answered all the border guards' rather odd questions. Most described themselves as tourists. However, oftentimes their vacation ended in the nearby small Swiss village of Stein, located opposite of Bad Säckingen on the other side of the Rhine. This small town was the headquarters for branches of Swiss banks that, in general, were friendly towards foreign visitors. They offered a wide variety of services and in a back room, *cambi*, they took discreet possession of packages visitors didn't want their country's tax authority to know about. At the time, Germany and the rest of Europe, as well as many countries not in the European Union, were clearly overburdened with the safe handling of larger sums of money. With billions dwindling away, an ever-increasing demand for more revenue was required. Politicians wanting to be re-elected created partially nonsensical projects, whose implementation they offered to fight for. The compensation of these unfortunate developments through creativity in tax policy was less imaginative than the projects, but well tested and proven. Naturally, citizens of those relevant countries embraced this with little enthusiasm. While the majority of the taxpayers had little choice but to abide by the tax increase, the wealthy sought the advice of Swiss banks that had made this the foundation of their business model.

A customer service agent in the Cantonal Bank Stein

AG was about to tally the daily turnover, commonly counting money, when two women walked up to his desk. The regular clientele thought highly of him and regarded the man as a good soul. However, this characterization was rarely known to new bank clients. He had the impression he was standing before an inquisition. Based on years of experience and patterned after traffic lights, he categorized bank clientele. Green represented clients he knew and whose deposits exceeded a certain amount. Regrettably, those clients were immediately referred to the director of the bank, who personally looked after their interests. Yellow was for customers he saw as potential future clients at the bank and where he could earn a modest commission. Red, however, referred to, and here he never erred, people who had become lost and were asking for directions, or people who simply wanted to see a Swiss bank from the inside. In fact, it wasn't unheard for a walk-in to want to entrust him with a packet of only a hundred or perhaps even fifty thousand. He would merely smile indulgently, revealing a series of flawless teeth. Then, he simply accompanied the person to the door, while graciously giving them a few tips on the way out.

The two women who entered the spacious customer service area were about the same size. The blonde-haired woman was a little heavier while the other woman was raven-haired and had silky, light brown skin and an African physiognomy. Both wore casual clothing and were extremely attractive. Although the attire of customers played a role in his color categorization, as he looked at the two women it

slipped his mind. The two women had traveled by train from Brussels to Basel. On arrival at the small train station in Bad Säckingen, the local trumpeter had welcomed them with a refrain from a Victor von Scheffel anthem.

"Godspeed, it would have been so nice,
Godspeed, it should not have happened."

This surprised, in particular, the African woman, who took great delight in it. She had no idea the trumpeter of this small town of Bad Säckingen drove the young generation to despair by reciting the legendary works of he poet. After the overture, the women leisurely strolled through the inner city and then crossed the wooden bridge to Switzerland.

"My name is Ariane Manstein. Perchance, do you speak French?"

Slightly raising his eyebrows yet maintaining an unreadable expression, the bank customer service agent thought it an odd question and immediately registered red.

In accent-free French he replied, "Bien sûr, Madame."

"Great, then would you be so kind and take care of my Congolese friend's request."

In respect to his assessment of the women's financial liquidity, that day the customer service agent of the Canton Bank Stein AG was forced to change his mind at this day.

Addendum

The murder of the often admired yet condemned primatologist Dian Fossey received worldwide attention. Hardly any press outlet failed to report it. The mysterious circumstances of the unsolved crime led to numerous speculations. Apart from press reports and her own work, *Gorillas in the Mist (1983)*, I also consulted the biography written by Farley Mowat, *Woman in the Mists (1987)*, as well as the one by Harold Hayes, *The Dark Romance of Dian Fossey (1990)*. The latter mentioned authors wrote in-depth accounts about the scientist's life, including of her affairs before and during her research activities in the Virunga National Park. Both authors paint a picture of a woman at odds with herself and whose personality rebuffed contact with other people. The only person capable of fairly judging the way she had handled poachers was Rosamond Carr, her closest female friend and at the same time biggest critic. I had the good fortune of getting to know this incredible woman when I was working in Rwanda as a hydrogeologist and visited her several times between 2004 and 2006. Shortly after our last visit, she passed away in September 2006 at the age of ninety-four. Rosamond Carr and her husband came to Africa in the late forties. After their marriage failed, she decided to stay in the country. In Mugongo, at the foot of Mount Karisimbi, she built a plantation for growing chrysanthemums in order to extract pyrethrum, a natural insecticide. She had left the country during the genocide and then returned to Gisenyi where she founded the *imbabazi* Orphanage. Ross, as her children affectionately called her, was not a person who would stab a dead girlfriend in the back. However, during our conversations over tea and biscuits, she repeatedly hinted at, although nicely and which she already captured in her book *Land of a Thousand Hills,* that the humanitarian Dian Fossey and the animal rights activist Dian Fossey were two very different people. The primatologist's brusque and unyielding way once resulted in Rosamond Carr asking her to leave the plantation where she had been a guest many times. Yet over time, the two women warmed up to each other and even became close friends. Rosamond Carr describes Dian Fossey's character as lying somewhere between amiable and hurtful, but she was always determined to stand up for what she believed to be her mission in life, namely, to protect wildlife, especially the gorillas living in the Virunga National Park.

Perhaps she just had the bad luck of not being born a gorilla, as Erich Wiedemann casually remarked in *Der Spiegel* in 1989, or maybe she simply was infatuated with apes, as Helmut Karasek smugly commented in the same article. She saw the people living in the Virunga Mountains as troublemakers who stood in the way of her mission. After some of her gorillas had been slaughtered, she established the *Digit Fund* to finance her own patrol team to destroy traps and hunt poachers. However, it didn't entirely end the poaching. Increasingly, her furious battle, especially against the Twa from the village of Mukingo, which could've been regarded as a campaign of revenge, turned to means that, as Hayes diplomatically expressed, would not be quite politically correct nowadays. There are reports of racist statements to acts of torture performed on poachers. Perhaps, at times, she came across a bit harsh, but it was questionable whether she was racist. Her rule about local employees staying away from the gorillas, so the animals would only interact with and become accustomed to white people, was based on the knowledge that poachers came from the African population. However, her measure had been regarded as having little understanding for local customs. This was unacceptable to the Rwandans. Dian Fossey started, without exception, to distrust everyone. Some of the changing scientific staff attempting to get in touch with the park administration ORTPN were accused of scheming. The American research couple Vedder-Weber, who Dian Fossey had somewhat disrespectfully referred to as the *VW couple*, described the relationship they enjoyed with the primatologist in their book *In the Kingdom of Gorillas* (2001), as almost nonexistent and unconstructive. And, the indecisive attitude of her donors and the bureaucracy of the Rwandan government had to have been demoralizing for the already physically weak chain smoker. When she contracted a bush disease, which according to her, some of her academic staff suffered from, it must have been her main personal problem. In desperation, she threatened to destroy the seven huts in *Karisoke* opposite the park administration, which in a quote of hers she refers to as "scorched earth", thus leaving no doubt about how she intended to accomplish it. In the end, even her trusted doctoral advisor from the University of Cambridge, Robert Hinde, avoided her. And the National Geographic Society, initially one of her main sponsors, also withdrew their financial support. Then she had to pay her employees out of her own pocket. She became extremely bitter once she found out many private sponsors had made contributions, albeit small ones, yet none of them ever reached her. Meanwhile her mentor, Louis Leakey, and the other two *ape ladies*, Jane Goodall and Biruté Galdikas, were well funded. Although the merit of her scientific work was and still is considered controversial, it was, in particular, her colleagues at the University of Cambridge who let her know she was not one of the scientific establishment due to her curriculum vitae as well as her non-academic training as an occupational therapist. The burden of not receiving funds unless scientific results were obtained pressured her to, somewhat grudgingly, start touring the scientific community, during which she encountered more traps and snipers than in the area surrounding her research station. She considered herself a field researcher and did not disguise her contempt for data-obsessed scientists who showed little interest in whether the research subject survived. Those scientists were only interested in one thing, she noted with bitter derision; they only wanted to advance in their scientific field and become silverbacks themselves. Nevertheless, she managed right to the end to discover sympathizers and supporters, including older silverbacks whose chest beating signaled not only scientific interest, but were also heard.

The criminal background story of this book is naturally purely fictitious and draws attention to the neglected minority of Twa. Solving the title will encounter opposition. Yet, I find it strange that, in spite of intensive research, I could neither learn the whereabouts of the wooden puff adder or of the mysterious orange folder with the list of profiteers and animal brokers, both of which are important pieces of evidence. Mowat, who had written about those items, has made no further comments.

However, the general consensus was that the hastily suspected murderers of Dian Fossey, American co-worker Wayne McGuire and tracker Rwelekana, were in fact not the perpetrators. Weber-Vedder explained that pressure by the world press and, in particular, the Americans, urged the investigating authorities to search for a *african solution*. Presumably, Rwelekana was murdered in prison, whereas Wayne McGuire was allowed to leave the country. But later on, in absentia, he was sentenced to death.

Dian Fossey's long-term gorilla research was unprecedented and admirable. Without her commitment as well as her academic staff, it's fair to say the remaining gorilla population would have been decimated. Those who have a chance to observe these gentle giants in their natural environment will most likely be unable to resist their fascinating magnetism. Nevertheless, it is imperative we discover a way so that nature conservation and the protection of minorities can be achieved harmoniously and without working against each other.

Terms and Names

ADFL: Alliance des Forces Démocratiques pour la Libération du Congo Zaire. The Congolese rebel group of Kabila senior.

Bantu: A language group in East Africa. Not, as was originally suspected in the 19th century, a characteristic for racial discrimination.

Banyamulenge: Literal meaning: *Residents of Mulenge*. Mulenge is a town in the eastern Congo in the South Kivu district of Uvira. The Banyamulenge speak a language similar to → Kinyarwanda. They feel they are part of the Tutsi from Rwanda.

Banyaruanda: Literal meaning: *People of Rwanda*. The Tutsi, Hutu, and Twa living in the eastern Congo. Among them are also the →Banyamulenge.

BGR: Institute for Geosciences and Natural Resources, headquartered in Hannover, Lower Saxony.

Bralirwa: Brasserie et Limonaderies du Rwanda. Rwandan brewery in Gisenyi.

C.E.P.G.L.: Communauté Economique de Pays des Grands Lacs. Economic Community of the Great Lakes Countries, i.e., the Democratic Republic of Congo, Rwanda, and Burundi.

CNDP: Congrès National pour la Défense du Peuple. The Congolese rebel movement, founded in 2006, allegedly to protect the Tutsi population of the Congo.

DRC: Democratic Republic of Congo

FDLR: Forces démocratiques de Liberation du Rwanda. A Hutu extremist group founded in 2000, operating mainly in the region of the Great Lakes in the eastern Congo. Many members were recruited from the fugitive ranks of the former Rwandan armed forces of the Hutu regime as well as the Rwandan murderers of the →interahamwe. The group is charged with war crimes as well as with crimes against humanity.

Gacaca: →Kinyarwanda word for *grass* or *lawn*. The *gacaca*, historically known as village courts on the grass, were re-established after the genocide in order to pass judgment on the high number of offenders of lesser degrees (followers). The legal basis was adopted in 2001 as so-called *gacaca* law. The courts finished their work in 2012 and were disbanded.

GIZ; Deutsche Gesellschaft für Internationale Zusammenarbeit (German Agency for International Cooperation)

Hutu, Tutsi, Twa: The most commonly used short version names in literature to designate the ethnic groups living in Rwanda. They are also referred to, in plural form, as Abahutu, Abatutsi, and Abatwa, and in singular form as Umuhutu, Umututsi and Umutwa. In colonial literature, the ethinc group Tutsi is also referred to as Watusi. The syllable A denotes the article. In Rwanda, making designations in connection with an ethnical distinction demarcation are prohibited. Quote: "All of us are Rwandans". Nevertheless, these terms are still being used. People who encounter a local stranger and who are not familiar with the use of the terms should avoid using them.

Impunyu: Pygmies, hunter-gatherers, who use the rainforest as their living environment.

Initiation: African youths must take part in an initiation before they can enter the community of adults. Although tribes practice this ritual in different ways, all usually require the candidate to prepare for several weeks in solitude, away from the everyday life of the tribe. All initiation rituals have one practice in common as a symbol of entering adulthood, which is to cut-off the foreskin of male adolescents and the clitoris of female adolescents. Western aid organizations are trying to end such archaic practices, which, especially for young women, is quite an ordeal.

Interahamwe: Extremist Hutu militias who were responsible for the excessive murders during the 1994 genocide.

Inzinzi: →Songtitel, Kinyarwanda word for *freedom*.

Kanyanga: An illegally distilled alcoholic brew made

from corn, sugar, and other ingredients.

Kinyarwanda: Common Bantu language of Rwanda's population. Today, in addition to French, English is also an official language. Many Rwandans born and raised abroad don't speak French or Kinyarwanda well. Nowadays, English is strongly encouraged and a compulsory subject in school.

MONUC: Mission de l'Organisation des Nations Unies en République Démocratique du Congo. The armed forces of the UN in the Congo sent to keep the peace from 1999 to 2010. They were replaced by MONUSCO.

MTN: Mobile Telephone Network. A telecommunication company serving several African countries.

Mwami: Titel for kings in countries with Bantu languages like Rwanda

NPPA: National Public Prosecution Agency. The prosecutor general's office.

NGO: Non-Governmental Organization. A term established by the UN to limit government organizations that provide social and environmental assistance programs.

ORTPN: Office Rwandais du Tourisme et des Parcs Nationaux. Office of Tourism and National Parks in Rwanda

PNC: Police Nationale Congolaise. National Police of the →DRC (Congo, Kinshasa). Not to be confused with the Congolese National Police (CNP) of the République du Congo (Congo, Brazzaville).

RCD: Rassemblement Congolais pour la Démocratie. The rebel movement that fought Laurent Kabila. It was mainly made up of Tutsi and Banyamulenge. The group split up later.

Sambaza: Sardine-like fish in Lake Kivu. The boats of fishermen are called sambaza-boats.

Sumu: A charm, black magic. Shortly before Dian Fossey's murder, she had been warned by a sumu, a wooden puff adder, a death curse.

Acknowledgements

For their support in the development of the book, I express my gratitude to Saskia, Christian, Peer and Frank from Hamburg, Michael from Flensburg, Rolf from Oslo, Alexie and Roland from Kigali, Jim from San Francisco as well as Ekkehard of Rotenburg (Wümme), whose right, still fully functional eye, also sped-up the proofreading process.

www.ingramcontent.com/pod-product-compliance
Lightning Source LLC
Chambersburg PA
CBHW071648090426
42738CB00009B/1461